FANNY KEMBLE
AND THE LOVELY LAND

Fanny Kemble

AND

THE LOVELY LAND

CONSTANCE WRIGHT

ILLUSTRATED WITH PHOTOGRAPHS

DODD, MEAD & COMPANY

NEW YORK

For Esther Whitmarsh Phillips
with gratitude and affection

FOREWORD

The impetus for this biographical study of Fanny Kemble originated in a reading of her *Journal of a Residence on a Georgian Plantation*, which has been so ably edited for today's readers by John Anthony Scott. Fanny's relations to the times in which she lived, an era of change comparable to our own, and to the land of her adoption, America, seemed worth investigating. In the process, much unpublished material has been used, but, in spite of diligence, no claim to complete coverage can be made, for Fanny, like all of her pretelephone generation, was a profuse letter writer, and is mentioned in innumerable books of reminiscence. She had, incidentally, the habit—criminal, from the point of view of a biographer—of not fully dating her letters, so that the chronology of certain events must be surmised. Such questions are discussed and a good deal of additional information and reference, irrelevant to the narrative, are contained in the Notes and Comments.

The author is indebted to many friends who have given encouragement and advice while the work was under way and to the following institutions for permission to examine and quote from unpublished letters and memoirs: The Historical Society of Pennsylvania, the Massachusetts Historical Society, the Harvard College Library, the Library of Congress, The Folger Library of Washington, D.C., The Columbia University Library,

The Henry W. and Albert A. Berg Collection of the New York Public Library, Astor, Lenox and Tilden Foundations, The Stockbridge Library and Historical Society, of Stockbridge, Massachusetts, The Lenox Library of Lenox, Massachusetts.

CONTENTS

ix

PART III

ILLUSTRATIONS

"And may God guard thee, o thou lovely land!
Evil, nor danger, nigh thy borders come!
Green towers of freedom may thy hills still stand.
Still be thy valleys peace and virtue's home."

F.K. *Ode on the Berkshire Jubilee Festival*
August 22, 1844

❊ *PART ONE* ❊

CHAPTER I

MY SUBLIME FANNY

IN LATER—perhaps one should say in latest—life, in her seventies and eighties, Fanny Kemble, the much-admired English actress, the *diva* of Shakespearean readings, formed a close friendship with a man who was young enough to be her son, the expatriate American novelist, Henry James. He haunted her fireside in London's Cavendish Square. Together they attended London art exhibits and, occasionally, the theatre.

James was much addicted to the society of elderly ladies, since he feared involvement with those his own age. And Mrs. Kemble was no ordinary old lady. On both sides of the Atlantic she had led a full and, at times, a tempestuous life. She had been married to and divorced by an American husband, Mr. Pierce Butler of Philadelphia, to whom she had borne two children, two daughters. After quitting the stage at a moment when all the world, so to speak, was kneeling at her feet, she returned to it, more than a dozen years later, to achieve an even greater success, first as actress and later as reader of Shakespearean drama.

It was at this point that Henry James became aware of Fanny's existence. A small boy, he was riding with others in a carriage near New York City when a lady, mounted on a spirited horse, was seen chatting with some workmen at the side of the road.

"Why, it's Fanny Kemble!" one of the grown-ups in the carriage said. Later, though still a boy, James was taken to hear Mrs. Kemble read *A Midsummer Night's Dream* and *King Lear*. He was uplifted, as only youth can be uplifted, by the great histrionic voice and its delicate shadings, as it shifted from character to character. During the intermission there was a change of costume —white satin, for comedy; for tragedy, black velvet. In 1873, when he was thirty years old, James was in Rome and was introduced to "the terrific Kemble" by one of her daughters, Mrs. Owen Jones Wister of Germantown, Pennsylvania. A few years later the London intimacy was seeded and ripened rapidly.

"My sublime Fanny—the first woman in London—one of the consolations of my life": it was thus that Henry James mentioned his friend in letters to America. There was much, indeed, to draw the two together. Temperamentally they supplemented one another. James, so cautious in the revelation of his personal affairs, so prone to aesthetic hair-splitting, rejoiced in this impulsive, positive, high-spirited creature, who never hesitated to express emotion, who wept at the theatre without embarrassment, who laughed at a joke, full throated. The creation of Falstaff in her readings of Shakespeare's *Henry IV* was considered one of Mrs. Kemble's major achievements.

"A prouder nature [than hers] never affronted the long humiliation of life," James recorded.[1] His sublime Fanny had "cast off all vulgarities," and under the term vulgarity, which today is a vulgar word, James included such unpleasant characteristics as vanity, self-seeking, and hypocrisy. Fanny had her faults, but they were noble faults. Honesty was carried to excess, and she could be cruelly and wittily outspoken. When someone told her she was a clever woman, she exclaimed, "How dare you call me anything so commonplace!"[2] Of Henry Lewes, George Eliot's lifetime partner, she said, "He looked as if he had been gnawed by rats—and left." She advised an overmature actress not to attempt the part of Juliet, since she was better suited to the rôle of Juliet's antiquated nurse.

When James took her to task for some of her *brusqueries,*
Fanny's reply was a sonnet, addressed to her "friend of many
lonely hours." It acknowledged her shortcomings, without attempting to defend them; it expressed her warmhearted devotion
to anyone who, to some small degree, belonged to her. Beneath
her humor, her exuberance, lay a vein of sad self-questioning.
"She was a moralist out of a theatrical nest," James wrote; he paid
tribute to "the beauty of her deep and serious character." [3]

As novelist and cultural historian, James found Fanny's conversation delectable. It was rich in anecdote that could be turned
to fictional use; it represented an amazing backward look to what
James called "an antediluvian age." When Fanny made her debut
as Juliet at Covent Garden in 1829 her aunt, Mrs. Sarah Siddons,
was seated in a box, and beside her was Sir Thomas Lawrence,
the painter of eighteenth-century beauties. Fanny once had
breakfasted with Sir Walter Scott in Edinburgh; she had sung
duets with Thomas Moore, of sentimental Irish fame. These
names stuck in James's memory, but many, many more appeared
in Fanny's reminiscent writings. In her youth she had published
plays and a travel diary, fit to be mentioned in the same breath
with the *Journal* of Maria Bashkirtseff. During the period when
James saw so much of her, seven books appeared, while Fanny's
eightieth year was marked by the publication of her first novel,
Far Away and Long Ago.

Fanny Kemble wrote, James remarked, "exactly as she talked,
observing, asserting, complaining, confiding, contradicting," but
always "effectively communicating." [4] She had no delusions of
greatness as a writer, but writing satisfied some profound and
pressing spiritual need. She never revised her work, which was
markedly uneven. From a plethora of material, James selected
two of Fanny's books for special mention. One was her *Records
of a Girlhood,* which tells the story of her early years and of the
remarkable theatrical family to which she belonged. It ends with
the unvarnished statement: "On June 7, 1834, I was married in
Philadelphia to Mr. Pierce Butler of that city." The other work

James considered superior and "easily the best of her prose"—for Fanny was also a versifier—deals with a later period and an impending crisis, both in the author's life and that of the United States of North America. It was published in 1863, ten years before Fanny and James were introduced to one another in Rome; its title is *Journal of a Residence on a Georgian Plantation in 1838–1839.*

Eighteen thirty-nine—the year in which old John Quincy Adams presented to the House of Representatives some 350 petitions to do away with slavery; 1838—the year in which an abolition auditorium in Philadelphia was sacked and burned to the ground. This was not exactly an antediluvian age to Henry James, though he had not yet been born when Fanny Kemble Butler, as she then signed her name, spent some winter months on two affiliated Sea Island plantations, manned by more than seven hundred slaves. The Civil War, which put an end to slavery, cut across James's early manhood. He did not enlist, as did his two younger brothers, but the war figures as major catastrophe in some of his early fiction; it was connected in his mind with a personal misfortune, an ailment of which he speaks so mysteriously in his reminiscences that his biographers have interpreted it variously, all the way from mild psychoneurotic shock to actual physical castration.

James was not interested in politics and sociology *per se*, but he recognized Fanny Kemble's *Journal* as "the most valuable account of impressions begotten of that old southern life which we are apt to see today through a haze of Indian summer." [5] The antebellum romanticizers, the magnolia-cum-pillared-portico school of literature had begun to flourish in the final decades of the nineteenth century. As antidote, James offered the testimony of one who, in at least one respect, was well fitted to play the part of observer. A great deal of Fanny Kemble's life was passed in America, but she was not an American. English born and English bred, she did not share the deep-grooved racial attitudes that influenced even those Americans who tried to obliterate the grooves. Fanny's attitude toward her adopted land was as ambivalent as that of the self-exiled Henry James. Both might be said to have loved America, without really liking it. Fanny, James declared, never heard the United States praised without expressing certain reservations; she never heard it abused without voicing her admiration and her faith in its future.

Added to all of this was Fanny's eye for detail, exhibited in her earlier work, and her lifelong habit of frank, vigorous statement, arising from what James termed "her excess of animal spirits." He did not enlarge upon the purely personal significance to his friend of the months spent on the seacoast of Georgia, though this was implicit in her *Journal*. She, too, had received her hurt. The undertone of sadness James's delicate ear had detected in Fanny was due, he thought, to her "unprosperous marriage." The great tempest of her life had created "waves of feeling which refused to be stilled."

CHAPTER II

ENGLISH BORN AND ENGLISH BRED

(1809–1832)

FOR THREE GENERATIONS the Kemble family had loved to act, but hated the theatre. They considered their connection with it undignified.

In France, it had taken a royal decree of 1641 to declare that players were respectable people. In England, on the other hand, the theatres were closed by the Puritans for twenty years; when reopened during the reign of England's Merry Monarch, Charles II, so much bawdy had been imported from France that many decent folk, Samuel Pepys notwithstanding, stayed away. It was not until the latter half of the eighteenth century that a compromise was effected between the morals of the stage and the morals of the rising middle class.

In 1753 Roger Kemble, who had begun life as a hairdresser, married an actress and eventually became the manager of a strolling company. Of the twelve children born of this union, the eight who survived took to the stage, though not all of them with parental approval. When the eldest of the tribe, a girl named Sarah, fell in love with an actor, William Siddons, the banns were forbidden, and she was apprenticed as a lady's maid, a lowly, but worthy, occupation. During her brief sojourn in the servants' hall, Sarah electrified the housekeeper, the butler, and the lower echelons of service, by her recitations of Shakespeare. Eventually she was allowed to marry the man of her choice and adopt his profession. Yet another case of backsliding was that of her brother, John Philip Kemble. He was intended for the Church—Roger Kemble was a Catholic—but after being educated at Wolverhampton and at Douai in France, John decided that the priesthood was not for him. His great success as tragedian, closely linked to that of his sister, whom Gainsborough had portrayed as The Muse of Tragedy, opened the way for younger Kembles, male and female, to follow their natural bent.

By 1809, the year in which Fanny (Frances Anne) Kemble was born, on November 27, the social status of the family had risen considerably. Her father, Charles Kemble, eleventh child of Roger Kemble, was handsome and debonair, a good, if not a brilliant, all-around actor. He, like his brother John, had been educated for the priesthood, but had managed to escape the tonsure. The houses of rich merchants and of the Whig aristocracy, most of whom subscribed, at least in theory, to democratic principles, were open to this mannerly and cultivated man. There was no thought of Frances Anne being "placed" as a lady's maid. She was sent instead to as good institutions of female learning as were available, first in England, and later in France. The final polish to her education was given by a majestic lady who had had the honor of numbering among her pupils Miss Mary Russell Mitford, the novelist, and Lady Caroline Lamb, Lord Byron's mistress.

There was much love in the Kemble home, but also a good reason for sending Fanny away to school. She was a difficult child to manage, overactive, willful, and cheerfully incorrigible, the sort of child who could be shut up in a closet to meditate upon her sins and come out smiling, unrepentant. The proprietress of the first school Fanny attended in France was informed by an alarmed neighbor that a little girl was capering about on the roof of the house. "Ah, ce ne peut être que ce diable de

Kemble," the lady groaned.[1] ("It can only be that little devil of a Kemble!")

Fanny herself thought she had inherited what she called her "excitability," and Henry James her "animal spirits," from her mother, Marie Thérèse De Camp, who, born in Switzerland, had come to England from the Continent as member of a child troupe of actors. Little Marie Thérèse danced and sang and was chief breadwinner for her family while her father, a French revolutionary officer, was dying of poverty and tuberculosis. A good *comédienne*, the author of farces and adaptations from the French, Mrs. Charles Kemble was a great help to her husband in his profession, though seriously overshadowed by the fame of the family into which she had married. Her undoubted love for her children, her daughter reports, was most frequently shown in faultfinding. Fanny could not practice for her singing lessons within earshot of her mother; screams from the next room would warn her of the slightest deviation from pitch. "I hate a fool," was such a frequent maternal comment that it became a byword in the household.

Mother and daughter, indeed, were too much alike to get on well together, though there was great mutual admiration and a sharing of certain fundamental tastes. Both Fanny and Marie Thérèse liked to fish, an unusual feminine proclivity; they preferred the country to the town, fresh air and vigorous outdoor exercise to parlor pastimes. From her even-tempered and indulgent father Fanny felt she had heired a sense of order and moderation which served to counterbalance her emotional instabilities.

When, aged sixteen, Fanny returned to England from her boarding school in Paris, she realized that she must not be a burden on her parents. Though the family was living in a pleasant little cottage at Weybridge, a three hours' drive from London, the financial situation of the Kembles was deplorable. In 1820, John Philip Kemble, who for many years had been Manager of Covent Garden, retired to a life of leisure in Switzerland, after having handed over his shares in the theatre and ultimately its control to his brother Charles. Charles had small talent for business and much to contend with, a muddle of legal and financial problems. His sister Siddons was superannuated and no longer available as star attraction. Public support for serious drama had declined. To lure an audience into the vast auditorium of Covent Garden a diversified entertainment was offered. One of the Shakespearean tragedies, or one of the fustian melodramas of the day, would be followed by a farce, by dancing, by singing, or even by an animal-taming act that had been borrowed from the circus.

Young Miss Fanny Kemble looked down her nose at this sort of thing. She thought that the stage was "a disgusting travesty." She saw how worried and overworked her father was. Her elder brother John was at Cambridge—a heavy expense; her younger brother Henry and her sister Adelaide had still to find their places in the world. Fanny was well read in French and English literature. For a short time she had ambitions of becoming a professional writer and could see herself living, perhaps in Italy, on proceeds from her pen. During a happy year she spent in Edinburgh with Mrs. Henry Siddons, a daughter-in-law of the Tragic Muse, Fanny wrote poems, tried her hand at translation, and began work on a Shakespearean play with a French background, *Francis I*. Her father thought so well of it that a production was contemplated, though not immediately achieved.

Playwriting, however, was an uncertain way of earning a livelihood at a time when theatrical runs were short and repertoire the rule. When the *ne plus ultra* came—her father arrested for debt, her mother in tears, and the walls of Covent Garden pasted over by bills of creditors—Fanny offered to become a governess. There was only one other way out of which she knew; as last resort, she might become an actress.

This idea had also occurred to her parents and had been discussed before Fanny went to Edinburgh. She was not surprised, therefore, by a suggestion that she should memorize certain key passages from *Romeo and Juliet* and recite them to her father and mother. Their reaction was noncommittal. "All very well, my love," they said. Fanny retired to weep on the stairway leading to her bedroom.

The next day, however, Charles Kemble took his daughter down to the theatre to see if her voice was big enough to reach its remotest recess. Fanny passed this test, and preparations for her debut began at once. Only three weeks later, on the evening of October 5, 1829, the debutante was dressed as Juliet in a costume having a long white satin train. When her cue was spoken, when her nurse called out "What, Juliet!" Fanny was literally pushed out upon the stage. At first she could hardly speak above a whisper, but soon she had warmed to her part. The house was full; all were curious to see the latest Kemble; applause rolled back across the footlights in opulent waves.

"Well, my dear, they can't say we have brought you out to exhibit your beauty," Fanny's mother said.[2]

Fanny had given promise of being a very pretty girl, but in her teens she had contracted a case of smallpox, which muddied her complexion and coarsened the outline of her features. She was rather short, her build was substantial, and her hands and feet were not sufficiently dainty to conform to the fashion of the day. Like many other successful actresses, however, Fanny could give the illusion of loveliness, of fragility, and even, if necessary, of heroic stature. At first she appeared most frequently as Juliet, but other roles soon were added to her repertoire, those of Ophelia, Portia, Beatrice, Queen Catherine, and finally, of Lady Macbeth. Of the many contemporary plays in which Fanny appeared, the most popular was *The Hunchback*, by James Sheridan Knowles. She also had the satisfaction of appearing in her own play, *Francis I*, and immediately began to write another, *The Star of Seville*, which was based on a drama of Lope de Vega.

Fanny was applauded, though with certain reservations, by the older generation of playgoers, who remembered Aunt Sarah Siddons in her prime; she was adored by younger folk. At Cambridge, brother John had a number of friends who later distinguished themselves. One of them, William Makepeace Thackeray, in speaking subsequently of the past to Fanny, said, "We were all in love with you." [3] The walls of many a scholastic habitation were decorated with Fanny's picture, after a drawing by Sir William Lawrence, who attended all her performances and gave her much valuable advice. Souvenir portraits were also reproduced on teacups, scarves, and handkerchiefs.

A less self-critical consciousness than Fanny's might have been thrown off balance by so much praise and so sudden a rise to eminence. From being a nobody, in the social sense of the term, Fanny had become a featured, a much-sought-after, guest. She was invited to fashionable London balls—she loved to dance—and to magnificent country houses. Formerly she had been dependent on the meager pin money her father could provide, but now the Star of Covent Garden was earning thirty guineas a week. From the royalties she received on the publication of her play, Fanny was able to buy an army commission for her brother Henry, who was handsome, amiable, and unlike the rest of his family, indolent. For herself the youthful plutocrat bought a much-needed trousseau and a saddle horse; she invested in a course of riding lessons and soon became a daring and accomplished rider.

Always, however, in the back of Fanny's mind was that early formed conception of the stage as a disgusting travesty. She recognized, as did a minority of her audience, her lack of training and her dependence on the inspiration of the moment. "Magnificent, my dear," her mother would exclaim, or else, "My dear, you were not fit to be seen!" To maintain a professional, high level of performance, night after night, was impossible, for acting seemed to Fanny neither a serious nor a "useful" occupation. She would rather cobble shoes, she said. She feared the erosion of her own personality, "her real self," by the counterfeit personalities she imposed upon it. There was also the danger of becoming addicted to the theatre and the effect of its constant stimulation on her nerves.

One evening, at Covent Garden, the curtain went down on a shriek from Mrs. Beverly, the heroine of *The Gamester*, who was kneeling by the dead body of her husband. This was all very well, but unrehearsed—and Fanny kept on shrieking. Her father had to lift her in his arms and carry her away to her dressing room. To guard against similar outbreaks, Fanny had imposed upon herself a well-scheduled, humdrum home life. On the morning of her debut, for example, she practiced the piano, just as usual, and read several chapters of an edifying book, the subject of which was "scriptural character."

After her first phenomenal and resounding London success, Fanny went on tour with her father. They played in Bath, Manchester, Liverpool, Birmingham, and Edinburgh. In Dublin, a phalanx of enthusiastic Irishmen followed the actress's carriage back to her hotel from the theatre. As she set her foot to earth they fell on their knees before her.

For the next two years a program of London season and provincial travel was vigorously pursued. Covent Garden had been rescued from death and destruction, but its health was still precarious. When Fanny did not play, attendance was unsatisfactory, and even when she did, during the seasons of 1831 and 1832, there was a marked falling off. For the past twelve months the public had found an emotional outlet in politics. There was more drama than the stage could offer in the House of Commons and the House of Lords, where a reform of Parliament to meet the needs of an industrialized society was being violently debated. To do away with "pocket" and "rotten" burroughs, to extend the franchise and modify the techniques of voting was the aim of the Whig party leaders, many of whom Fanny had met or caught a glimpse of in the great London houses to which she was invited.

Even the Kemble family, though professionally preoccupied, could not escape this universal topic for discussion. Fanny declared herself to be on the side of the Tories, but one suspects that this may have been only for the sake of argument, possibly with her brother John and his confreres, who had been Apostles of Utilitarianism at Cambridge and would have liked to do away with titles of nobility, the Established Church, and even with the army and the navy. Fanny thought John's political outlook "frenzied," but her own was consonant with the times in which she lived. She had an abiding faith in Britain's middle class, but was well aware of her plebian ancestry; she honored the memory of her grandparents, particularly of her two grandmothers, one of whom had been an itinerant actress and the other a Swiss peasant girl. Fanny herself had a facility for rapport with the underprivileged. In Edinburgh she made friends with some of the sturdy fishwives, who, basket on back, hawked their wares about the streets; she had seen their squalid dwellings. "I am humanity proud," Fanny declared after a visit to the Thames tunnel, which was under construction. When she rode on the first train that ran between Liverpool and Manchester, a publicity run, Fanny's admiration went, not to her distinguished fellow passengers, but to the engineers and workmen who had created this marvel of transportation.

When, in the autumn of 1831, a second Reform Bill, passed by the Commons, was tossed out of the House of Lords, riots erupted in Bristol and other industrial centers. The workers were under the impression, which Fanny, for one, had seen to be false, that they, rather than their employers, would benefit by the Bill. Windows were broken, statues of the Duke of Wellington, symbol of reaction and hero of a bygone age, were pelted with mud. Eventually King William IV was persuaded that the country was on the verge of civil war and was urged to create enough new peers to pass a third bill. He did not do so, but brought pressure to bear upon reactionaries to abstain from voting. In June of 1832 the Bill was passed; it was followed by similar measures in Scotland and Ireland. Promoters of reform in various fields were waiting in the wings, eager to press their claims. One group, which wished to do away with slavery in the British colonies, was about to launch a vigorous campaign of speechmaking and placarding of London.

No relief to theatrical stagnation, however, was in sight. Covent Garden was involved in six simultaneous law suits. A petition to the Lord Chancellor had been tabled during the parliamentary crisis. As if this were not enough, misfortunes of a private nature had descended on the Kemble family. John, Fanny's brilliant, but erratic, brother had left Cambridge without taking a degree and had gone off to fight for democracy in Spain, a fiasco from which he returned unharmed, but for months no one had known his whereabouts, or whether he was alive or dead. During Christmas week of 1831 Charles Kemble lay dangerously ill with pneumonia. He was hardly well enough to go back to his work at the theatre when a cholera epidemic crossed to England from the Continent. Large assemblages of humanity, such as those housed at Covent Garden, were considered dangerous.

Charles had hoped that, even if the theatre crashed, he would be able to save enough money to remove his family to the south of France where living was cheap. He tried to economize, but had little talent for cheese paring and was particularly extravagant in the matter of stage costume. With a sigh, Charles spoke of going to act in America, where one of his sisters, Elizabeth Kemble Whitlock, had spent two years and had appeared before President Washington as Lady Teazle in *The School for Scandal*.

Aunt Whitlock, now in her sixties, was a comic character in the estimation of her niece. She was a clumsy, "unfinished" Mrs. Siddons. She wore a wig, which was often askew, and made frequent use of such inelegant expressions as "I declare to God," or "I wish I may die." The thought of following in Aunt Whitlock's footsteps did not appeal to Fanny. She could not refuse when her hard-pressed father proposed that she should go with him, chaperoned by her Aunt Adelaide De Camp, her mother's sister—but, "Go to America," Fanny cried, "How terrible! That dreadful place!" [4]

CHAPTER III

THAT DREADFUL PLACE

(1832)

IN THE OPINION of many British intellectuals, America was not a dreadful place. The editors of *The Edinburgh Review,* for example, had declared it to be the land of the future, "emphatically the New World." Early travelers had gone there, starry eyed, to view the workings of republican democracy. Of late, a more critical breed had crossed the ocean, notebooks in hand, and an avalanche of *Views of* . . . and *Travels in* . . . the United States was about to descend upon the reading public. Early in 1832, the year in which Fanny Kemble first glimpsed the American scene as she sailed into the harbor of New York, a book was published, more widely read, more hotly commented upon by friend and foe, by Whig and Tory, than all the rest.

It was a good thing, Fanny told a correspondent in England, that she had avoided reading Mrs. Trollope's *Domestic Manners of the Americans.* The subject was always cropping up in conversation, and when asked for an opinion, she could truthfully say she knew nothing of the lady or her obnoxious book. Some of Fanny's first impressions, however, coincided with those of America's most strident critic to date. It had been a traumatic experience for Mrs. Trollope to enter an American milliner's shop and have someone introduce her to the milliner. Fanny, being, as she later said, an "English republican," also noted the lack of class distinction in the New World, but without a sense of outrage. Intrusions upon privacy, mosquitoes, heat, and public dining-rooms where one was forced to masticate, cheek by jowl, with total strangers, were much more trying. Friendliness amounted almost to a vice. The Kembles had brought many letters of introduction with them, and shortly after their arrival on September 4, 1832, they were invited to dine with Mr. Philip Hone, former mayor of New York, a retired commission merchant, whose house, facing City Hall Park, was a meeting place for artists and writers of the conservative stripe.

Fanny thought the dinner badly served—there were no finger bowls—and the guests, particularly the female guests, so dull that she did not exert herself. To her host she seemed odd and not particularly attractive until he saw her act a few nights later at the Park Theatre. "I have never witnessed an audience so moved, astonished, and delighted," Hone recorded in his *Diary*. "The expression of her wonderful face would have been a rich treat if her tongue had uttered no sound . . . The curtain fell amid deafening shouts and plaudits." [1] The more Hone saw of Fanny during her stay in New York, the more delighted he was with her. He took her riding in the family barouche with his daughters; he arranged a picnic expedition to view the city from the heights of Hoboken. Puzzled at first by Fanny's nonchalance, Hone soon discovered that she had "a rare talent for conversation."

After three weeks in New York, the Kembles moved on to Philadelphia and eventually to Baltimore and Washington, where they made the acquaintance of President Jackson, Daniel Webster, Henry Clay, and other notables. Boston was reached in early spring. All along the way, the shouts and plaudits had continued. As in England, Fanny was almost universally admired, but her chief appeal was to the young, many of whom had never before seen a performance on the stage. In New York City, a

Quaker parent discovered his teenage son softly ascending the stairs, late one night, carrying his shoes in his hand.

"Where has thee been, son?"

"To the theatre, father."

(A pause of unspoken consternation.)

"Is this the first time thee has gone?"

"No, father, the thirty-seventh."

A still younger boy, an embryo poet, took the ferry from Brooklyn and later wove some of the impressions he received at the Park into his *Leaves of Grass*. When Kemble fever broke out in Cambridge, Massachusetts, Harvard undergraduates sold their overcoats or pawned their watches to buy tickets. Among those who walked seven miles to the theatre and back and waited at the stage door to cheer the leading lady were two law students who, like Fanny, were in their early twenties, Wendell Phillips and Charles Sumner. Both had been urged to view the Kemble offerings by their favorite professor, Judge Joseph Story, of the Supreme Court.

"Judge Story," Wendell Phillips had said, "you come from Puritan ancestors. How do you reconcile all this theatre going with their principles?"

"I do not try to reconcile it," Story replied. "I only thank God I am alive in the same era with such a woman." [2]

To equate theatre going with sin seemed to Fanny a curious provincialism. She did not realize that qualms of conscience came close to frustrating one of the warmest and most significant friendships of her entire life.

While she was in New York for a repeat run at the Park Theatre, Fanny was visited by Miss Catharine Maria Sedgwick, a writer whose novels, dealing with the American scene, past and present, had been published in England and also translated into French, German, Italian, and Swedish. Miss Sedgwick, after seeing Fanny as Juliet, noted in her journal that: "When Nature masters her she is sublime. Her face not beautiful, but the flexible minister of her soul. She has genius, the highest gift to mortals." [3]

Fanny, off stage, was equally bewitching, "an enchantress"—but in the dubious sense of the term. "I have to check my interest in her by remembering she is an actress," Miss Sedgwick told her sister.[4] The novelist was unpleasantly surprised by Fanny's play, *Francis I*, which was given a single performance at the Park. Its tone was much too "mannish." No woman should have attempted such a theme, since, in the character of Françoise, the King's mistress, "the deepest humiliation of the female sex" was personified.

To see a young woman, however, who was so unspoiled, so honest, and so perceptive, though "living in a cloud of incense," was exhilarating. Catharine Sedgwick was forty-four years old; she felt her youth renewed by contact with the Enchantress, and her ancestral principles, like those of Judge Joseph Story, soon evaporated. Fanny, for her part, craved some sort of intellectual companionship other than that of her chaperone, Aunt Adelaide De Camp, to whom she was deeply devoted, but whom she had known since early childhood. Cherished comrades had been left behind in England; to one of them, an Anglo-Irishwoman, Harriet St. Ledger, Fanny wrote on an average of once a week. She also kept in constant touch with an Irish lady of letters, Mrs. Anna Brownell Jameson, whose latest book, *Characteristics of Woman*, had been dedicated to Fanny and illustrated by sketches of her in various Shakespearean rôles.

Feeling an instinctive kinship with the very articulate and very ingratiating authoress who called upon her in New York, Fanny took the first step toward intimacy: she gave Catharine a sheaf of manuscript poems to read. At later tête-a-têtes, she vented her dissatisfaction with the theatre and spoke of the difficulties of being a woman in a man-oriented world.

This was a subject of real concern to Catharine Sedgwick, who, it was said, had refused innumerable offers of marriage because she could not subordinate her life to that of a husband, however worthy he might be. Through her novels and the many short stories and articles she contributed to magazines, runs a thread of prim, but persistent, feminism. It was based upon a religious concept, for Catharine might never have become a novelist if she had not been converted from Calvinism to Unitarianism. Her first attempt at fiction, *A New England Tale*, was intended merely as a Sunday-school tract. It ridiculed the believers in original sin and predestination; it exalted those who had faith in human perfectability.

The most distinguished proponent of these ideas in America was the man whom Ralph Waldo Emerson had called "the Bishop of the New," the Reverend Dr. William Ellery Channing, whose Boston church was thronged and who was much in demand as guest preacher. Channing was an old friend of the Sedgwick family. When he came to New York in May of 1833, Catharine offered to take Fanny to call upon him.

A meeting with Dr. Channing, Fanny thought, would be much more interesting to her than her meeting with the President of the United States. She had "a natural turn for religion," [5] something which she had discovered for herself. Though her father had been educated at a Catholic seminary, he had defected from the Church of Rome, and except for a few childish prayers and a little Bible reading, there had been no talk of religion in the Kemble household. Fanny herself had decided to become a communicant of a Swiss congregation, whose chapel in London her mother attended from time to time. Thereafter the youthful proselyte practiced a few personal austerities: she gave up going to parties on Sunday and no longer read the naughty poems of Lord Byron, a volume of which she used to hide under the mattress of her bed at boarding school.

Unitarianism, though nothing new, had recrudesced recently in England, and the published works of William Ellery Channing were well known. Fanny had been introduced to them by her friend, Harriet St. Ledger; she had urged another friend, who spoke of human nature as "vile," to read Channing's *Essay on Milton*. The Church of England preachers who set themselves up as adversaries to the American orator Fanny dismissed as dull and "puny."

It was something of a disappointment to find that Channing himself was puny, though only in a physical sense. He was a sickly little man; his face and form were undistinguished, and the voice in which the oft-quoted sermons were delivered was feeble. Though Channing disclaimed all knowledge of the theatre, he made some comments which an actress and a devotee of Shakespeare could not accept. Where would you find a modern Juliet, he asked? Where, indeed! Later, for Fanny visited him again in Boston and elsewhere and heard him preach whenever possible, a closer bond, a closer conformation of opinion was established.

It so happened that Fanny came under the influence of Channing at a turning point of his career. He had declared that if Calvinism were true, life would not be worth living; he had not shrunk from the implications of his theology. If man was not vile and not damned to all eternity by divine whim, then he was capable of constant improvement and of building a better world. "Whatever is just, whatever is humane, whatever is true in the golden light of the future, must prevail," [6] such was the basis of his faith. Channing had given his support to prison reform, educational reform, and the cause of international peace. Shortly before his meeting with Fanny, the Doctor took his invalid wife to spend a winter on the Island of Santa Cruz. His birthplace was Newport, Rhode Island, a former port of entry for the slave trade, and as a young man Channing had spent some time in Virginia, but never before his visit to the West Indies had he seen slavery in the raw.

Slavery destroys the soul; slavery condemns a large portion of the human race to an animal existence, Channing told his Boston congregation. He started to write an essay on the evils of slavery that he intended to take the form of an open letter to the South; he laid it aside because a rival voice had been raised.

On January 1, 1831, the first issue of William Lloyd Garrison's *Liberator* appeared. Its charter subscribers were, for the most part, free men of color in Boston, New York, or Philadel-

phia, but Channing's name was also on the list. He could endorse
the call for emancipation, but was shocked by the violence of the
language used by Garrison, who, like himself, was an avowed
pacifist. Channing would have told Southerners that slavery was
their misfortune, not their crime, while Garrison thundered forth,
"On this subject I do not wish to think, or speak, or write with
moderation . . . I will not equivocate—I will not excuse—I will
not retreat a single inch—and I *will be heard*."

Neither Garrison nor Channing approved the colonization
scheme of early reformers who would have returned the blacks
to Africa and thus got rid of them. The opposing agitators, the
self-styled abolitionists, were, at this primordial stage of their
development, so uncouth that a reasonable man, however just,
however humane, hesitated to join their ranks. Those who were
not black—a despised minority—were young. The males, to draw
a hairy line between themselves and the members of the older
generation, wore beards. The females, eschewing the ringlets of
their mothers and their maiden aunts, wore their hair parted in
the middle and smoothly plastered down upon their brows. Fantastic dress and eccentricity were common. There was "Father
Lamson," who masqueraded as Father Time, carried a scythe, and
went to jail because he refused to shave; there was Miss Abby
Folsom who, in the interest of free speech, irrespective of sex,
held the floor at meetings so tenaciously that she had to be carried from the room.

Channing was not present when, on a snowy winter's day, and
in a shabby little schoolhouse on "Nigger Hill" in Boston, the
first society, aimed at abolition, "if necessary gradual, but in-
stantly begun," was formed. Channing must have been aware,
however, of a drop in temperature in his Federal Street Church
when he spoke his mind on slavery. His congregation represented
the élite of Boston. These solidly substantial folk believed in
progress and might go along with their pastor's ideas on disarma-
ment and the betterment of schools and prisons, but to demand
an immediate end to the system of forced labor, so deeply en-

trenched in the South, was quite a different matter—at best, utopian; at worst, maliciously destructive, since much of Boston's prosperity depended on its Southern trade. It was difficult enough to maintain a balance of good will between the two regions, as witnessed by the recent uproar evoked by the Protective Tariff Act of 1832 and the earlier, so-called, Tariff of Abominations.

Even a visiting Britisher, such as Fanny Kemble, had felt the effect of this latest outbreak of sectional discord. She and her father had intended to include Charleston, South Carolina, in their tour, but were told in Philadelphia that South Carolina might secede from the Union, fiery state's righters having recently passed an antitariff Ordinance of Nullification. President Jackson had asked the Congress for military power to enforce federal law, and the Kembles, whose theatrical endeavors in Britain had been so severely damaged by politics, crossed Charleston off their list.

In Philadelphia, and before she had met Miss Sedgwick or Dr. Channing, Fanny heard talk of slavery, the substance of which she entered in her diary. She was told by a member of the local Unitarian Church that one could be fined or imprisoned in the South for teaching a slave to read or write. So great was the fear of insurrection that the blacks were kept in brutal ignorance and were often cruelly treated. "Oh! What a breaking asunder of manacles there will be some of these fine days," Fanny predicted, "what a fearful rising of the black flood!" She foresaw "a fierce and horrible retaliation . . . for wrongs so long endured—so wickedly inflicted." [7]

Fanny, or her informant, was thinking in terms of the Nat Turner insurrection of 1831, in which fifty-four whites were massacred, or the far more massive outbreak in Jamaica, involving twenty thousand blacks and damage to property of a million pounds. The Jamaican troubles were caused by a misapprehension: the slaves thought that freedom had already been granted to them by the reformed British Parliament and was being withheld from them by the local representatives of the master race.

Their rebellion was savagely suppressed, but could not long delay the British Emancipation Act, which was promulgated while Fanny was delighting her Boston audiences in the early summer of 1833.

Fanny's disapproval of slavery, however, was purely conventional, a by-product of the climate of opinion in which she had matured. Except for an Indian pundit she had met in a London drawing room, Fanny had never seen a human being whose skin was darker than her own until she took ship for America. The vessel's steward was black. He was so obliging and served the Kembles so well that Fanny's Aunt Adelaide De Camp on one occasion poured him out a glass of wine and asked him to drink their healths.

"Ah, I can see by that, that you are not an American," said the captain of the ship.[8]

Fanny's unusually mild riposte was that perhaps it was just as well she was not an American. Her reaction to racism and slavery had not yet, but would soon, acquire an inner motivation. In the short time she had been in America, abolitionism had gained momentum. It was no longer the exclusive property of eccentrics and tender-minded idealists. Thousands of antislavery societies had mushroomed throughout the North, and a fair proportion of their membership was feminine. As a woman, Fanny presently found herself engaged in a desperate struggle to maintain her identity as an independent and magnanimous human being.

CHAPTER IV

A RACE WITH ATALANTA

(October 1832–June 7, 1834)

"I DO NOT THINK," Fanny wrote to her friend Harriet St. Ledger, "that during my father's life I shall ever leave the stage: it is very selfish to feel regret at this, I know, but it sometimes seems to me rather dreary to look along my future years and think that they will be devoted to labor I dislike and despise." [1]

Fanny's love for and loyalty to her father was all the more pronounced because her mother's prickly personality had led to constant bickering; to act with him, however, was subtly disturbing. Charles Kemble had the reputation of giving a first-class performance in secondary rôles; his Mercutio was considered by many, and by Miss Catharine Sedgwick, for one, as "a masterpiece." When he took the lead, when he had to portray the suffering which dramatic heroes are created to endure, Fanny felt uncomfortable. "It agonizes me to see his sham agony," she wrote. Not long after the Kembles' American debut, Charles, aged fifty-six, was forced to appear as Romeo to his daughter's Juliet.

To find a satisfactory leading man for Fanny had always been a problem. In England there had been a succession of Romeos, and the only one Fanny had ever really liked was a woman, a Miss Ellen Tree, who was tall enough and broad shouldered enough to look the part; she even offered to pick up the dead body of Juliet and carry it down to the footlights, a bit of stage business that had become traditional in the death-chamber scene. This show of strength Fanny had refused. "I would kick and scream if you tried it," she said.

Fanny did not attempt to hide her scorn and distaste for an unfortunate actor, a Mr. Keppel, who joined the company in New York. He was always forgetting his lines and always hiding his confusion by falling down on his knees before her. "Oh, do get away from me!" Fanny would remark fiercely, *sotto voce*. "Mr. Keppel, you are hurting me dreadfully," she muttered during one of their stage embraces.[2]

Fanny did not like being pulled about by strange men and was only mildly sorry for Mr. Keppel when he was given the sack and her father took over. She had described her friend Harriet, who was lithe and slender and who wore mannish boots and mannish clothes, as Atalanta, the Greek huntress who ran races with her suitors and had them put to death when she outdistanced them. There was a good deal of Atalanta in herself, she recognized. "I do not think I am fit to marry," she had once affirmed, "to make an obedient wife or affectionate mother. My imagination is paramount with me. . . . I think I should be unhappy, and the cause of unhappiness in others." [3]

Though just before leaving England Fanny had been the victim of what she termed an "ephemeral love affair," her manner to the crowds of young men who clustered about her at evening parties in America was distant, not to say hostile. Mr. Philip Hone, during the dinner party he gave for the Kembles in New York, noted Fanny's preference for older, married, men; he did not think her behavior was calculated to make her a "favorite with the beaux."

And yet, how could this fail to be the case when so many beaux sold their overcoats and pawned their watches merely to see Fanny from the farther side of the footlights? One day in Philadelphia Fanny came downstairs for tea and found a young man who had been introduced to the Kembles by an English friend chatting with her father. The young man's name was Pierce Butler. He was a year younger than Fanny, rather good-looking—he wore sideburns—rather dandified in his dress. He was not very tall. Fanny's diary description of him was ironic: "a pretty spoken, a genteel youth." He was said to have a great fortune, she added, and in consequence, might consider himself a great man—in spite of his inches.

Young Mr. Butler stayed for tea. He asked Fanny to go riding with him, and Fanny's appetite for riding was insatiable. She would like to die of a broken neck as she was swept off her horse at full gallop, she said. It gave her a sense of power to feel that she could dominate the beast that carried her. In New York, the horses had failed to measure up to the high standards of a British equestrienne, but in Philadelphia, due to the assiduity of Mr. Pierce Butler, Fanny was well mounted. Whenever she visited the riding school, Butler was there. He was also at the theatre every night she played and at nearly every dance or dinner she ornamented by her presence. Though nominally a lawyer, the young man did not seem to be overburdened by his professional duties. "I wonder what he will do for an interest when we are gone?" Fanny queried.[4]

When the Kembles left Philadelphia, Butler followed them to New York and later to Boston. He could play the flute so well that he was always sure of finding a chair in the orchestra pit of the theatre, close to the stage. A horseback approach to Fanny was even more effective. Every afternoon a clutch of onlookers would gather outside the Tremont Hotel in Boston to see Miss Kemble emerge, wearing a stylish habit, a bright red hunting cap set on her thick, dark curls. To complete the picture, a fashionably dressed young man would be waiting for her and would lift her to the saddle.

The countryside about Boston, with its neat white cottages and blossoming apple orchards, reminded Fanny of England. She and Pierce followed winding lanes; they galloped along the seabeach at Nahant. Their favorite destination, however, was Mount Auburn, which was still a stretch of woodland, though in process of conversion to a cemetery. There the riders would dismount and find a shady seat beneath the trees. Spring was merging into summer. In one of the facile, and sometimes felicitous, poems she composed, Fanny set her first tender feeling for her future husband at some time "twixt the late violet and the earliest rose."

Pierce Butler's first proposal of marriage must have been of similar date, for on June 24 Fanny informed her British friends that "though England will always be home to my heart, it may be that this country will become my abiding place." [5] She considered America "marvelous"—"unparalleled, under every aspect." This did not mean that her mind was irrevocably made up. Fanny had still a feeling that to put a ring upon her finger was of evil omen—and there was still the duty which she owed to her father, who, without her help, might have to abandon his American enterprise. Fanny would have been unbelievably dull not to realize which of the two Kembles the public favored.

After almost ten months of hard labor, a well-earned holiday was planned, a trip to Canada, where a few performances would be given, and with a stopover at Niagara Falls en route. Fanny, who was fascinated, and all but frenzied, by the sight of rushing water, was eager to see the falls. So also, it seemed, was Mr. Pierce Butler.

The first halt of the party, after leaving New York, was at West Point. Thither the Kembles were accompanied by Catharine Sedgwick, who was on her way to spend the summer at the home of her brother Charles in Lenox, Massachusetts. Catharine had heard a great deal about Pierce Butler and was curious to meet him. She was impressed by his good manners and his stylish wardrobe, the chief feature of which was a pair of plaid trousers. Butler seemed to be long on common sense, but short on sensibility; his intellectual inferiority to Fanny was evident. Catharine also sensed that there was tension between these two dissimilar beings. The young man undertook to row the ladies to Indian Spring and midway became so exhausted that he would have turned back, whereupon Fanny put him to shame by taking over the oars and completing the journey. Arrived at the spring, she took off her shoes and stockings, dabbled her feet in the water, and the ends of her hair, which she had let down to hang upon her shoulders. Butler, though unaware of Freudian symbolism, remonstrated with her for her unconventional behavior. That evening he turned sulky because there were two Canadians at the inn who claimed the Kembles as compatriots. After dinner the American went up to his room, and though Fanny knocked at the door and asked him to come down to play his flute, he refused to do so as long as "those damned Englishmen" were there.

At Albany, Miss Sedgwick left the group, and another traveler joined it on the pressing invitation of Charles Kemble, this time an authentic and fairly famous Englishman, Mr. Edward Tre-lawny, the friend of Byron and Shelley, the devoted comrade who had snatched Shelley's heart from the flames of a funeral pyre on the beach near Spezia. On the voyage out, Fanny had read Trelawny's *Adventures of a Younger Son*, and for her he personified the ideal of romantic masculinity. Trelawny had "the proportions of a giant for strength and agility," she wrote. His face was "as dark as a Moor's, with a strange, wild look about the eyes and forehead and a mark like a scar, on his cheek, his whole appearance giving one an idea of toil, hardship, peril and wild adventure." [6]

Being seventeen years older than Fanny and more or less married, though this fact was not dwelt upon, there was no thought of Trelawny's being a suitor. Fanny found him none the less attractive for that. Throughout the Canadian trip, she listened—presumably with shining eyes—to readings from *Don Quixote*, poetic recitations, and tales of hazardous derring-do in the Near East. With Trelawny's hand restraining her, Fanny peered into the gulf from which rose the spray and thunder of Niagara; she threw herself down upon the ground and cried out in ecstasy, "O, God, O God!"

But it was Pierce Butler's hand that saved Fanny from a dangerous tumble on a woodland path near Trenton Falls. He did not try to compete with Trelawny, nor did he sulk; instead, he managed always to be there when needed in an emergency. At an ill-equipped wayside tavern, forks were lacking, and Butler produced some of sterling silver from his luggage. When the friend of Byron and Shelley said how inferior to their poetry was that of Alfred Tennyson, Butler defended the younger poet, knowing, no doubt, that Tennyson had been a friend of Fanny's brother at Cambridge and that she admired his verse.

Nevertheless, when the greatest emergency of all arose, the spotlight was allowed to play upon Trelawny in Fanny's account of the happening. The travelers were on their way back to New York and had just left a hotel near Rochester when the stagecoach in which they were riding overturned, and all its occupants were spilled out upon the roadway. Fanny and her father fell in a heap and were unhurt, and Butler escaped with a scratched finger. Trelawny, however, was stunned, and the forehead of Fanny's Aunt Adelaide De Camp was deeply gashed. As soon as he had regained consciousness, Trelawny heroically disregarded his own hurt in binding up the wounds of his fellow sufferers.

The capsizing of the coach Fanny considered a mere adventure, the sort of thing a traveler remembers later with glee. It had its tragic aftermath, for Adelaide De Camp had received, in addition to the cut on her forehead, a serious injury to her spine. All through the ensuing theatrical season, she managed to serve as Fanny's companion, confidante, and mistress of the robes, but with growing difficulty. When the company was again in Boston in the early spring of 1834, she took to her bed and died.

This was Fanny's first, and perhaps her most grievous, experience of death. It was all the more poignant because she had known Dall, as the Kemble children called their aunt, so long and had taken her great and beneficent virtues for granted.

Adelaide De Camp, like her sister Marie Thérèse, had been a child actress and had been courted by a young man who had great expectations of wealth, but who jilted her when he discovered that he ran the risk of being disinherited if the marriage took place. Dall's refuge from calamity and a broken heart, as it was then termed, was her sister's home. There she devoted herself to her nephews and nieces as an unpaid governess, ever patient, ever cheerful, a buffer between the vivacities of mother and child. When Fanny took to the stage, Dall took to it also. She had sat out all rehearsals, she had been behind the scenes as dresser at all performances.

What had she ever done, Fanny wondered, what was she ever likely to do, that could compare with the life of her aunt—undoubtedly a happy life? For more than a brief moment, self-abnegation seemed to be the only key to happiness, but to go from Dall's bedside to the theatre, from the spectacle of real suffering to its counterfeit, strengthened Fanny's determination to put an end to her theatrical career. With Dall she had once discussed the possibility of making an easy exit from the theatre by marrying. If you continue to work and remain single, Dall had said, you can keep your independence and enjoy a more distinguished position in society than you are entitled to by birth. The first, if not the second, of these advantages would be lost in marriage.

Here was advice, once highly valued; but now Dall's voice was stilled, and as a result of her aunt's death in April of 1834, Fanny's heart was definitely inclined toward matrimony. She was in need of consolation and found comfort in some beautiful reflections on death and sorrow expressed by Dr. Channing. Pierce Butler, however, could show his sympathy, not only in words, but in many practical ways during Dall's final illness. It was Fanny's wish that her aunt should be buried in Mount Auburn Cemetery, where she and Pierce had first drawn close to one another. After the burial, the fiancés frequently visited the unmarked grave, which had been turfed over and hedged about with sweetbriar.

Charles Kemble deeply and sincerely mourned the sister-in-law to whom he owed so much. For him, Dall's death was a calamity, so also was Fanny's contemplated marriage. Charles's thoughts on the subject are unrecorded, but there is inferential evidence of his having tried to prevent the match. It may well be that Edward Trelawny was urged to take part in the Canadian expedition as a counter attraction to Pierce Butler, to whom Charles's manner was only frigidly polite. Later Fanny declared that her father, using Dall as his mouthpiece, tried to persuade her of Pierce's unworthiness, but she was young then, and stubborn, and in love with love, and would not listen.

Even after the engagement was announced, Charles wanted Fanny to return with him to England and act for another year. Fanny at first consented; she told her transatlantic friends to expect her soon. At the last moment, however, the scheme was abandoned. To return to England might lead to further involvement with Covent Garden, and that was a fate from which Fanny recoiled with all the vigor of a hearty, self-assertive ego. With characteristic generosity, she handed over to her father all the earnings of her American tour, and the wedding, on June 7, 1834, at Christ's Church, Philadelphia, was sandwiched in between a sold-out, farewell performance in that city and a farewell performance in New York.

The marriage got due attention from the press on both sides of the Atlantic. Comment, both public and private, tended to be unfavorable. Catharine Sedgwick reiterated her opinion that Pierce Butler was a gentleman and an amiable young man, but he was no more Fanny's equal than the little lamp which stood upon her writing table was the equal of one of the heavenly bodies. "Poor girl," Catharine wrote, "she makes a dangerous experiment; I have a thousand fears for the result." [7]

Sympathy with the prospective groom was, on the other hand, expressed by a newspaper published in Germantown, Pennsylvania, the town near which, only six miles from Philadelphia, a summer home of the Butler family was located. "He who weds her for an angel," —*The Germantown Telegraph* "opined"— "will discover, ere a fortnight, that she is nothing more nor less than a woman, and perhaps one of the most troublesome kind into the bargain." [8]

CHAPTER V

PHILADELPHIA NABOB

(1766–1834)

THE AUTHOR of the item in *The Germantown Telegraph* was, and must forever remain, anonymous. Undoubtedly a male, for the she-journalist was as yet a rare phenomenon, he may have been young enough to be a rival to Pierce Butler, one of the theatre claque, or even one of the beaux Miss Kemble made so little effort to attract at evening parties. Whatever his age, whatever his station, this consumer of sour grapes, this prophet of marital disaster, expressed a widely held, and yet peculiarly indigenous, attitude toward theatrical folk. A Philadelphia diarist of the day, one Sidney George Fisher, put it blatantly. "I do not like this custom of introducing actors into society," Fisher wrote; and again, "If we must submit to democracy in our government, let us at least keep it away from our social circles." [1] A bachelor of modest means, Fisher was invited to all the best houses and could congratulate himself that not wealth, but birth, gave him the entrée.

Philadelphia was a complex community. Its Quaker matrix had been overlaid by a more worldly sophistication during the federal period. Geographically a Northern city, it was also a gateway to the South. Its lowest social stratum consisted of ten thousand free blacks, most of whom were poor and who had now to compete for low-paid jobs with immigrant Irish. On the summit of the economic ziggurat, flourished a group who were considered nabobs, though the term was not in general use. Like the English nabobs, these individuals, or their ancestors, had made their fortunes under Southern skies; since this was elsewhere, they were often considered to be far richer than they were.

To this category, the Butler family belonged. They were viewed by such an acute social observer as Sidney Fisher with admiration, tinged with envy. In a fine house of Quincy granite at the corner of Chestnut and Eighth streets, Pierce Butler's brother John lived with his beautiful wife Gabriella. One of Pierce's sisters, Mrs. George Cadwalader, had a salon, the walls of which were frescoed and its white-and-gold furniture imported from Europe. Pierce's other sister, the wife of Dr. Alfred Elwyn, was also luxuriously installed on Walnut Street.

These residences were all in that part of town where grandfathers were of great importance. Well housed though the Butlers were, there was no one of the present generation as impressive and as picturesque as the founder of the family and the provider of its present magnificence. Pierce Butler's grandfather was twelve years dead and buried in the graveyard of Christ's Church, the church where Pierce and Fanny had plighted their troth. The old gentleman, however, was still very much alive in the memory of his fellow townsmen, and even more so in the memory of his descendants, on whose destinies his hand had rested heavily.

In the year 1766 a newly arrived British regiment spent a short time in Philadelphia before being transferred to Charleston, South Carolina. One of the officers of the Twenty-second Irish Foot Guards was Major Pierce Butler, just twenty-two years old, of Irish extraction, and third son of Sir Richard Butler, a member of the British Parliament. The youthful Major was paternally related to the Dukes of Ormonde, and on his mother's side of the family, to the Dukes of Northumberland. The impression he made on a contemporary was that of "one of the most elegant men in person and deportment that I ever saw." [2]

A younger son, however—and however elegant—was expected to make his own way in the world. Butler moved in good society and not long after reaching Charleston eloped with one of the richest girls in the colony, Polly Middleton, daughter of Thomas Middleton of Prince William's Parish. The Middleton connection owned vast plantations; they were prominent in politics. In 1773, the year of the Boston Tea Party, Pierce Butler resigned his military commission and threw his lucky coin, his bid for fortune, into the rebel pot. During the Revolutionary War he served as Adjutant General of his state. The invading British were anxious to capture and make an example of him. One night, Butler had to escape from a plantation house in his slippers, not having had time to pull on his boots. When Mrs. Butler asked the British captain of dragoons what they would have done to her husband if they had caught him, he replied, "We would have killed him—even in your arms, madam." [3]

Butler, having successfully turned this and other narrow corners, was elected a few years later to the state legislature, where, in spite of his aristocratic background, he championed poor, back-country whites against his own, the planter, class. This may have been due to an aggressive independence, deeply embedded in his nature, or it may have been merely to garner votes for the governorship, an office to which the Major aspired, but without success. Twice chosen United States Senator, and once appointed to round out an unexpired term, Butler's most significant political assignment was that of South Carolina delegate—there were four of them in all—to the Constitutional Convention of 1787, which met in Philadelphia.

In the building which is now called Independence Hall, and throughout a hot July and August, a document, more solid, more realistic, than the Articles of Confederation, took shape. Its down-to-earth vocabulary contrasts sharply with the exalted utterances of the Declaration. Pierce Butler, conspicuous in gold-laced stock and powdered hair, spoke frequently. The aim of government should be the protection of property, he said, since property supports government, and when the question of proportional representation came up, Butler urged "the justice and necessity" of taking wealth into consideration. The wealth created by a black slave for his master, he pointed out, was equal in value to the wealth created by a man who was both white and free.

Debate on this issue acidulated, but the spirit that brooded over the Constitutional Convention was the spirit of compromise, and no one knew better than Pierce Butler the difficulties of creating a union when the interests of the states differed so widely. In return for considering a nonwhite male as three-fifths of a human being in the census of 1790, a continuance of the slave trade for the next twenty-five years, and a fugitive slave law, of which Pierce Butler was the proponent, the South yielded to the North the right of the federal government to impose tariffs.

These were discussions and determinations that cast long shadows into the future. Soon after sharing in them, Major Butler's energies were deflected from politics. In 1791, Polly Middleton Butler died. During the next few years the Major disposed of his wife's South Carolina inheritance. Great profits were to be realized on the coast of Georgia, where in light, sandy soil, the best cotton in the world, long-staple, Persian cotton could be grown. The Major bought land and created two "plantings," as he termed them, one at Hampton Point on the northern portion of St. Simons Island and another nine miles distant, on Butler Island, which, situated in the estuary of the Altamaha River, was suitable for the growing of rice.

The Major grew rich, or more precisely, richer; for a short time Sea Island cotton was worth half a guinea the pound in Liverpool. A manor house was built at Hampton Point, and at the same time, a mansion of Quincy granite rose at the corner of Chestnut and Eighth streets in Philadelphia, the proceeds from the plantations having been invested in city real estate and in thousands of acres in Pennsylvania and Rhode Island.

After an efficient manager for the Georgia properties had been found, the Major ceased to spend his winters in the South, and during the last seven years of his life, from 1815 to 1822, the islands were unvisited. As director of a Philadelphia bank, the horizon of the nabob's financial ventures had broadened; also, perhaps, the long coastal journey to and from Georgia may have become too much for a man who was in his seventies.

As he grew older, the Major became more cantankerous. He had always been a difficult man to down, a trait that had been noted when he debated points of the Constitution in 1787. A lifelong habit of command in all things, great and small, roused rebellion in the Butler household, which had originally consisted of four daughters and two sons. The elder son, Pierce II, died before reaching maturity; the younger boy, whose name was Thomas and who had been educated in England, angered his father by marrying a French girl and spending much of his time in France. The Major wanted his children and, above all, his grandchildren, his posterity, near at hand, where he could superintend their upbringing and direct their lives.

After Thomas had ignored a deathbed plea to return from Paris, where he was then living, the Major rewrote his will. Only a modest share would go to his son, while the bulk of the estate would remain intact under the trusteeship of the Major's favorite child, his daughter Frances, who had a head apparently for business and to whom he had confided his financial correspondence during his declining days. The ultimate beneficiaries would be the offspring of the only one of the Butler girls to marry, Sarah, the wife of Dr. James Mease. This marriage had also failed to meet with the Major's approval, and a proviso of the will stipulated that, if they wished to inherit, the male members of the family would have to change their names to Butler.

Thus it was that the man whom Fanny Kemble married was known as Pierce Butler Mease until he reached the age of eighteen and could legally omit his surname. During the lifetime of his Aunt Frances, Pierce could look forward to a carefree and more than adequate income. Though nominally a lawyer, he did not need to exert himself in his profession, was free to travel, to lead an active social life, and to play the flute in the musical ensemble which rehearsed regularly in the studio of his kinsman, Thomas Sully, the portrait painter. Pierce's father was still alive, but he had been so browbeaten and ignored by his father-in-law that he played little part in the lives of his children after the death of his wife. It was inevitable, therefore, that Pierce should be judged as a grandson, rather than a son. Sidney Fisher, who did not know him very well at this period, heard that Butler had "a great deal of energy and character" and, as a Democrat and a Martin Van Buren man, was taking an active interest in politics. Of this Pierce's grandfather would have approved, but a more intimate acquaintance, a boyhood friend of Pierce's, saw him as yet another rebel to authority.

Joshua Francis Fisher, a cousin of the diarist, did not keep a day-to-day record, but in later life wrote reminiscences enlivened by many anecdotes illustrating the old Major's imperiousness and his aristocratic presumptions. In court the Major had refused to kiss the Bible and insisted on giving testimony on his honor as a gentleman. Once he threw down his glove on the floor of the Senate Chamber and dared anyone to pick it up. A carriage builder who had sued for nonpayment of his bill was challenged to a duel. These gossiping tales were current in Philadelphia, but to them was added a tale which had originated in South Carolina. Joshua Francis Fisher felt that he could vouch for it, since he, too, had married a Middleton of Charleston. In that family it was said that Polly Middleton Butler's property was entailed and should have gone directly to her children. After battling with the trustees, the Major seized control, and in defiance of the law, sold the plantations. The slaves, whose value might have exceeded that of the land on which they worked, were whisked away to Georgia, with the sheriff and his posse in hot pursuit.

Whether or not this accusation was correct, Joshua Francis was eyewitness to at least one minor demonstration of the Major's pugnacious temperament. As a boy, he went to a school in Arch Street with the brothers Butler. For some crime which he may or may not have committed, John Butler was flogged, in those days a routine method of law enforcement. On the following morning, however, John's grandfather appeared in the schoolroom, sputtering with rage and threatening the teacher with his stick. The Major was old; the teacher was a husky young Quaker, who easily disarmed his adversary and for some time held him a prisoner while he argued with him, pressed against the wall. The final tableau which Fisher retained was of the old man, physically defeated, but still vocally abusive, leaving the scene with his grandsons at his heel.

Would such a man have tolerated one more misalliance in his family? Joshua Francis Fisher later became a very good friend of Fanny Kemble Butler, but in looking back, he was sure that the Major, if he had been alive in 1834, would never have given his blessing to her marriage with his grandson. Fanny was an actress, a descendant, not of British earls, but of strolling players. What was worse, she had brought no dower of land or serfs.

Of land and serfs, Fanny knew nothing. She must have been aware that she was marrying a rich man in 1834, but later declared she had no idea of the source of her husband's wealth. In the Greek legend of Atalanta, the virgin huntress is tricked into matrimony by Hippomenes, who throws down three golden apples which she turns aside to pick up. Such a tactic, to discuss dollars and cents with the romantic and glamorous young woman he was courting, would have seemed inappropriate to Pierce Butler.

Just when the truth was out is uncertain, but it came as a shock. "The family into which I have married are large slaveholders," Fanny wrote to her literary friend, Mrs. Jameson. "Our present and future fortune depend greatly upon plantations in Georgia." [4]

Though the estate was now in the hands of a member of the older generation, Fanny considered slavery "a grievous sin against humanity." She would rather go back to "the toilsome earning of her daily bread in the theatre" than to be supported by it.

Though she had not been so naïve as to expect marriage to be a fairyland, Fanny had looked forward to quiet, stability, and ample time in which to think, to work, and to study. From the first, however, even during the honeymoon, most of which was spent at Newport, in the company of Pierce's brother and his sister-in-law, misunderstandings had arisen.

CHAPTER VI

THE DANGEROUS EXPERIMENT

(June 1834–July 1835)

WHEN, SOME YEARS LATER, Pierce Butler cast a baleful, backward glance upon his married life, he drew up a statement which was intended for the use of his lawyers, but which he later had printed and distributed. Though one sided, it cannot be dismissed altogether as evidence in judging a case of intricate human involvement and of ultimate hostility. In its pages the words slavery and abolitionist occur at times, but the real trouble between himself and Fanny, Pierce asserted, was "the very peculiar ideas of marriage held by Mrs. Butler."

After the honeymoon, the bride and groom returned to Philadelphia. It had been decided, much to Fanny's satisfaction, that they would live in the country, at the family estate near Germantown. Butler Place, as the property was named, had been untenanted for several years. While it was being renovated and refurnished, Pierce and Fanny stayed with her in-laws in the house on Chestnut Street.

With no household cares of her own as yet, Fanny was able to devote herself to a literary undertaking begun at Newport. Months before her marriage, she had contracted with Ealey and Cox of Philadelphia, and Murray of London, for a book about America, cast in the form of a journal and based on the diary she had kept from August 1, 1832 to July 17, 1833, that is to say, from the day she sailed from England to the end of her Canadian tour. The proceeds from the *Journal* Fanny had intended to give to Dall; now that Dall was dead, she would donate them to yet another aunt, Aunt Victoire De Camp, Dall's sister, who was earning a meager living in England as teacher in a boarding school for girls.

The work went rapidly at first, but far from smoothly, for Pierce Butler was given the run of the manuscript. He found much to criticize. Fanny, though she named no names and made liberal use of capital letters, followed by a dash, had been indiscreet. It was easy, for example, to recognize who was the Mr. H—— with whom she had dined in New York soon after her arrival; her description of the dinner party would give great offense to Mr. Philip Hone. Butler himself was often offended by his wife's disparaging comparison of American with British ways; never having been in England, he could not refute what she said—and what she said when he blue-penciled her manuscript, drawing lines through sentences and whole paragraphs, was boisterous. On all but one moot point she refused to yield. Dispute as to what should be taken out and what should go in the *Journal* was enlarged to embrace the whole question of matrimony and the duty that a wife owed her husband.

Pierce's views on this subject were conventional and those of his class and epoch. Since Fanny had been married by an Episcopal, Church of England, service, she had promised to obey her spouse, but the word obey does not appear in the Unitarian ritual, and Fanny now considered herself to be a Unitarian. She had, indeed, been gratified to find that the Butler family attended a Congregational church, the pastor of which, the Reverend William Henry Furness, preached sermons which closely paralleled those of Dr. William Ellery Channing. How unreasonable, therefore, of Pierce to expect that his wife should take seriously a vow uttered as a matter of form! Marriage, Fanny insisted, should be an equal partnership, in which neither party tried to coerce the other. God had granted humankind free will, so why should Pierce try to control her? "Is it because you are better than myself? I am sure you would not say so, whatever I may think. Is it because you are more enlightened, more intellectual? You know that isn't so!"

The idea of his wife's appearing in print was so repugnant to Pierce that he actually went to the Philadelphia publishers with an offer of a substantial bonus if they would break their contract. The offer was refused; the arguments continued, and a climax was reached when, one evening in November, only six months after marriage, Butler came home to his brother's house to find that Fanny was gone. She had packed a valise and had left about six o'clock. A note was prominently displayed, stuck, perhaps, in the corner of the looking glass of the dressing table, or skewered to the traditional pincushion. It enclosed a twenty-dollar bill to settle any small debts incurred; it asked that Fanny's clothes should be delivered to a porter when sent for, and that her "poor little" canary bird should be given to Rosalie, the daughter of the painter, Thomas Sully, the only relative of Pierce's with whom Fanny had become intimate.

Pierce was perturbed. He may also have been humiliated by the thought that now his brother and sister-in-law would realize how unsuccessful he had been in taming a troublesome wife. He did not know where to look for Fanny, and he felt fairly certain that she would return.

Return she did, at ten o'clock. Without a word, Fanny went up to the bedroom she shared with her husband and threw herself, fully clothed, on the bed. Pierce did not speak to her; she slept the sleep of physical and emotional exhaustion. In the morning an awkward reconciliation took place, but Fanny would not say where she had gone the preceding night. It was not until a few days later that she admitted to having wandered about in the dark for hours, hunting for a hotel she thought was either on

Second or Third Street. Her ultimate destination had been England.

That Fanny could leave her husband a farewell twenty-dollar bill and could finance a transatlantic voyage may have been due to an advance payment from her publishers. Having given her father all her professional savings, she was now entirely dependent upon Pierce for money. This was one of the features of the married state which she found irksome—she who had been earning thirty guineas a week before she was twenty. Mere financial subservience, however, and mere differences of opinion on the canons of good taste in memoir writing, could not account for Fanny's unhappiness; the roots of her rebellion ran deep. Over and over she told Pierce what she had told others in the past: she should never have married. Over and over she threatened to go home to her family in England. Pierce thought his wife's extravagant behavior was due to the fact that she was pregnant. After the birth of their child, she would return to normal.

Early in the New Year, the refurbishing of Butler Place had been completed, and there, on May 28, 1835, Fanny gave birth to a daughter, who was christened Sarah, not after Fanny's distinguished Aunt Sarah Siddons, but after Pierce's deceased mother. The baby was, unlike its maternal parent, a blue-eyed blonde. Fanny was at first disappointed in its sex, since "the lot of women is seldom happy." [2] The means by which a human being is brought into the world seemed to her unnecessarily agonizing and debilitating, due, no doubt, to the fact that women in general, and particularly American women, wore tight stays, tight bodices, tight shoes, and took too little exercise.

Fanny tried to keep baby talk out of her letters to Harriet St. Ledger and Anna Jameson, both of whom were childless, but she realized that a new and vast emotional dimension had been added to her life. She luxuriated in the physical comfort of nursing her baby and, in the process, seeing its small, beady eyes fixed on hers. To a young friend who had sought advice in selecting a husband, Fanny wrote that "one finds in maternity a channel for all those feelings which are too often miserably disappointed in the partner of one's inconsiderate choice." [3]

As soon as possible *post partum*, Fanny began to ride horseback again, which gave her, she said, a pleasantly unmarried feeling. The move to the country had bettered her relations with Pierce, though this he later denied. Fanny enjoyed settling her establishment and creating a garden, lawns, and shrubbery. At Butler Place, Major Butler had intended to build a mansion for his son Thomas, a mansion which never materialized. The original house, a farmhouse built in the eighteenth century, but added to from time to time, stood close to the Old York Road. It was surrounded by beautiful trees.

In retrospect, Fanny could laugh at some of the early attempts she made to play Lady Bountiful of the Manor to her rural neighbors. Could she teach their children to read and write, she asked? No, thank you, she was told; the children were being well taught at school. On the first Fourth of July spent at Butler Place, Fanny gave a patriotic, alfresco dinner for the local yeomanry. The bottles of wine and beer she placed on the tables were untouched; all her guests were teetotal Quakers.

But to have a home of her own to which she could invite her friends was, in itself, a substantial blessing. Edward Trelawny, who during the winter had been in Philadelphia, came out to the farm and was entrusted with a brooch, enclosing a lock of baby Sarah's hair, to take back to England and to Fanny's mother. The first overnight visitors at Butler Place were Catharine Sedgwick and her fifteen-year-old niece Kate. Kate the Younger was as enthralled by the Enchantress as was her aunt. Fanny made the occasion a gala, and Pierce was so cordial and so hospitable that he rose considerably in Catharine's estimation.

If there was any friction between host and hostess it was fairly well concealed, though Fanny, in speaking of her *Journal*, which had just been published, said it could hardly be called her own after the severe pruning it had received. Needless to say, Catharine had read the book and thought how delightful and how typical of her friend it was; it showed a hundred facets of genius and "half a hundred little faults." Reviewers who had not yet recovered from the assault and battery on American pride perpetrated by another Fanny, Mrs. Fanny Trollope, were not so kind. Fanny's enthusiasms were ignored and only her quips and her colloquial style were noted. "One of the most deplorable exhibitions of vulgar thinking and vulgar expression ever encountered," *The Atheneaum* fulminated. According to *Niles Register*, "the authoress had unsexed herself." [4]

Fanny was, at the moment, busily reworking the only major portion of the *Journal* she had omitted because of Pierce's insistence. He had persuaded her that if she included a strong antislavery diatribe in her book, the house in which they lived might be burned to the ground; he could point to some recent cases of arson in Philadelphia. Instead of destroying her treatise, however, Fanny saved it for future elaboration. What was her aim? Was it merely a literary exercise, or did she have a particular audience in mind?

To Catharine Sedgwick, Fanny complained of some unsatisfactory talks she had had with Pierce on the ethics of slavery. When she asked him if he thought human bondage could be defended on moral grounds, he replied that he could not, in conscience, say yes; when, however, she pressed him to sever all connections with it, he only smiled and would say no more. He did, at least, convince her that slavery was dying out and would soon disappear; this was a dictum she repeated in several of her letters to England. Once Fanny was told, either by Pierce, or by his brother John, that the Georgian lands were declining in fertility; it might be a good idea to move the plantations again, perhaps to Alabama. Or how would she, Fanny, like to live on the banks of the Mississippi?

The question was asked jocosely, but Fanny's reply was serious; she would like nothing better, she said, than to live among the people by whose toil she was fed. She would like to put her relations with them on a Christian footing. According to a plan she had evolved, freedom would be promised, but not immediately granted. At first no wages would be paid; what the slaves earned would be deposited for them in a bank until they had proved themselves capable of managing their own affairs. "We all have some appointed task," Fanny wrote to Harriet St. Ledger, "[something] beyond the half animal instincts of loving husband, wife, or children . . . How I wish—oh, how I wish—we might make this experiment!" [5]

The use of the plural pronoun, we, indicates some hope of Pierce's cooperation, but his evasive smiles, his silences, were baffling. Fanny needed a more receptive audience and communion with more congenial minds. An opportunity for this occurred when she accepted an invitation for her and her baby to spend several weeks with Catharine Sedgwick at her home in the Berkshires. This was the first of many visits to a region which Fanny found enchanting and spiritually sustaining. She already knew Catharine's niece, Kate, and the brother, Robert, the sister-in-law, Susan, with whom Catharine spent her winters in New York. Others of the clan may have come within her ken during the past three years, for there was much interclan visiting, back and forth. Fanny soon discovered that if one loved a single Sedgwick one must know and love them all.

CHAPTER VII

THE HAPPY VALLEY

(July 1835–November 1836)

IT WAS SAID OF STOCKBRIDGE, Massachusetts, that the local crickets, and even the infant frogs, chirruped, "Sedgwick—Sedgwick—Sedgwick."

In a roomy, comfortable house, built on a plateau above the Housatonic River, Catharine Sedgwick was born, the fifth child of her parents, Judge Theodore and his wife, Pamela Dwight. Of ten little Sedgwicks, seven survived to maturity, a better than average quota.

The Judge was a public man, a friend of George Washington, John Jay, and other leaders of the nation, a member, like Major Pierce Butler, of the Continental Congress. This career entailed long absences from Stockbridge and from the bosom of an adored and adoring family. At a time when the standard pattern of paternity was grim and awe-inspiring, the Judge was lovingly demonstrative. "What did your father bring home to you as a present?" someone asked of little Catharine. "He didn't bring me anything," Catharine replied, "but he called me his dear little lamb and his sweet little bird." [1] Any quarrels, any jealousies that might arise were quelled by a mere knitting of the Judge's brows; the family devotion he engendered was both genuine and fervently, romantically, expressed. Catharine, aged ten, wept herself

sick when her sister Eliza was married and at every other wedding of her kin thereafter.

Three of the Judge's four sons followed their father's footsteps
into the law, but the youngest boy, Charles, was so lovable that
he couldn't be spared for a full-scale course at Harvard. Because
Charles had had less formal education than his brothers, the Judge
left him in his will the Stockbridge house and farm. Income from
the farm was insufficient when Charles married. He took a job as
clerk of the County Court at Lenox, six miles distant, and soon
went there to live—for Catharine a catastrophic move. It was un-
thinkable that any but a Sedgwick should live in the ancestral
homestead, and fortunately the eldest brother, Theodore, second
of the name, was able to take over; Catharine, however yearned
after Charles and his family, in particular Kate, who could only
be seen occasionally, not day by day. Being now a successful
novelist, Catharine was able to build an annex to Charles's house
in Lenox, where she could spend her summers and entertain such
appreciative guests as Fanny Kemble Butler.

Lenox, in Catharine's estimation, was far inferior to Stockbridge, a poor little village, cold and windy, clinging for dear life
to a hillside. With Fanny, it was a case of rapture at first sight.
The wildness of this setting, its lakes and mountains, spoke to her.
When she died, Fanny said, she would like to be buried in the
Lenox Cemetery. If allowed to sleep there, she would not rise to
trouble anyone. "I will only ask to be permitted once in a while
to raise my head and look out upon this glorious scene." [2]

From this glorious scene, Charles Sedgwick had seldom traveled far; he was more truly a citizen of the Berkshires than any of
his brothers and sisters, a wise and gentle humorist, the most
genial of men. Fanny felt drawn to him, and even more closely
to his wife Elizabeth, whom Catharine thought she resembled in
face, if not in temperament. Elizabeth, to educate three daughters and also, perhaps, to swell the family exchequer, maintained
in her home a boarding school for girls, which had grown and
prospered. A descendant of Jonathan Edwards, the missioner to

the Stockbridge Indians, who believed that "sinners were in the hands of an angry God," but also that there was a divine, indwelling light in human kind, Elizabeth encouraged her pupils to express themselves, to let their light shine forth. She wrote schoolroom texts for their use; she discussed ethical problems with them on an adult level. Mrs. Sedgwick's girls were allowed —oh, scandal to the neighborhood!—to wear pants when they scrambled up the steep slopes of Saddle or Monument Mountain.

Fanny also wore pants when she joined in these expeditions, or fished in Lenox Lake. She had taken young Kate Sedgwick to her heart; now she found lifelong friends among Kate's schoolfellows. On later visits, Fanny recited poetry to Elizabeth Sedgwick's pupils, sang ballads, read aloud the plays of Shakespeare, and told ghost stories that sent her listeners shivering home to bed. She taught the girls to shoot with bow and arrow. She gave evening parties at which there was folk dancing and much entertainment in the form of paper games, skits, and recitations furnished by the girls themselves.

Because of Catharine Sedgwick's reputation as an author, intellectuals were drawn to Lenox, and travelers from abroad—Alexis de Tocqueville was one—made it a point of pilgrimage. The family also befriended less famous foreigners who had come to America as political exiles from Italy and Germany. They were employed to teach languages in Elizabeth's school and to give lessons to summer visitors. Prominent among them and particularly admired was an intimate friend and disciple of Dr. Channing, Dr. Carl Follen, a native of Darmstadt, a graduate of the University of Giessen, who had lectured in law at Harvard until he joined the Anti-Slavery Society and fell out of favor with the hierarchy. Having studied theology at Giessen, he was soon ordained a Unitarian minister and, as such, held informal religious and philosophical discussions in the Sedgwicks' living room.

When, on his deathbed, Judge Sedgwick declared his intention of joining the Unitarian Church, first Catharine and then all but one of her sisters and brothers, withdrew from the shadows cast by Calvinism. The Judge had also bequeathed strong antislavery sentiments to his children, sentiments which were fortified by a circumstance of their early years.

The mother of them all, Mrs. Pamela Sedgwick, a patient, uncomplaining soul, was often ill and often astray from reality. During her bouts of mania and depression, the only person who could soothe her was a black woman, Elizabeth Freeman, who could neither read nor write and who had been the slave of a certain Colonel Ashley until Colonel Ashley's wife struck her with a red-hot fire shovel.

In 1781, a famous test case was tried at Great Barrington, in which Judge Sedgwick successfully defended Elizabeth Freeman's right to be free. For the rest of her long life, Mumbet, "our dear Mumbet," as she was called, took Mrs. Sedgwick's place in the household. Many a squalling Sedgwick baby stopped crying when Mumbet entered the room, or even when her foot was heard upon the stair. As the children grew older, she gave sound, high-souled, advice. She was also brave. During Shay's Rebellion the Stockbridge house was threatened by marauders who were met at the door by the ex-slave, armed appropriately with a fire shovel. When they were not looking, Mumbet slipped out to the stable to turn loose in the woods a young horse she was in the habit of riding.

Not long after the death of this remarkable woman, Henry Dwight Sedgwick, second of the Judge's sons, delivered an address to the Stockbridge Lyceum of 1831 on the "Practicability of the Abolition of Slavery." The resolute and "naturally superior" personality of Mumbet was cited to disprove what Henry Dwight termed "the folk lore" of black inferiority; if blacks in the Northern states seemed to be inferior, it was only because they carried such a heavy weight of discrimination, and for this the status of their brethren in the South was responsible.

More recently, Catharine Sedgwick had popularized her brother's thesis. In 1835, the year of Fanny's first total exposure to Sedgwick ideology, an article appeared in *Knickerbocker's*

Magazine, describing the Stockbridge burying ground. About the graves of the Judge and his wife, those of their offspring were arranged in ever-widening circles. Catharine had to admit that, "more to our shame," Mumbet was not among them; she was buried in the section of the cemetery reserved for her race, but a lengthy inscription on her tombstone, composed by Charles Sedgwick, last of her nurslings, told of her virtues and her close connection with the family. It ended with the words: "In every situation of domestic trial, she was the most efficient helper and the tenderest friend. Good mother, farewell!"

No visitor to the valley failed to hear the story of Mumbet; it made a deep impression on one who had preceded Fanny by a few weeks and of whose intellectual eminence Catharine Sedgwick stood in awe. In inviting the English authoress, Miss Harriet Martineau, to Lenox, Catharine made elaborate preparations for her entertainment. All went well until one day the two ladies were walking, arm in arm, by the banks of the Housatonic, and they happened to speak of slavery. Miss Martineau, whose narratives, illustrating political economy from a liberal point of view, had had phenomenal success, abhorred slavery, but had a more dramatic suggestion for doing away with it than had Henry Sedgwick. He had mentioned a possible amendment to the Constitution, which could only be brought about by the consent of all concerned. Miss Martineau said it would be better to dissolve the Union at once than for the Northern states to tolerate such a blot on the escutcheon of democracy. Halting abruptly, Catharine, daughter of an eminent Federalist, withdrew her arm from that of her guest and looked upon her with shocked surprise.

Between Fanny and Miss Martineau there was also a lack of rapport. It was predetermined that they should meet in Philadelphia, where Miss Martineau visited the Reverend William Henry Furness, Pastor of the Unitarian Church; she was also intimate with some friends of Fanny's brother John in England. There was too much of the green room in Fanny, too much of the blue stocking in her fellow countrywoman, for more than a mutual respect for one another's opinions to develop. Communication was also difficult, since Miss Martineau was excruciatingly deaf and had brought with her from England an ear trumpet, through which, Fanny feared, she would collect a good deal of misinformation concerning America.

It was left to a mutual friend, a friend also of Catharine and of all the Sedgwicks, Dr. William Ellery Channing, to crystallize Fanny's ideas on what was rapidly becoming for her an obsessive concern. Not long after her return from the Berkshires, deeply sunburnt by the days she had spent in the open air, Fanny had a visit from the Doctor, who brought with him a copy of his latest publication, that of November 1835, a dissertation with a one word title: *Slavery*.

The essay on slavery, begun when Channing was in Santa Cruz, had been taken reluctantly from the drawer where it had lain for several years, unfinished; the impulse to complete it had been forced upon a man who hated controversy, name-calling, and outrageous talk. Channing was severely criticized by an English clergyman who visited him at his summer home at Newport and told him bluntly that "Unitarians know their duty, but dare not act upon it." Even a member of Channing's conservative Boston congregation, Mrs. Maria Chapman, accused her pastor of lacking "insight, firmness, courage." Finally, after a series of anti-abolition riots in New York and Philadelphia, a former assistant of Channing, the Reverend Samuel May, inquired indignantly, "Why, sir, have you not moved? Why have you not spoken before?"

"Brother May," Channing replied, "I acknowledge the justice of your reproof. I have been silent too long." [3]

While *Slavery* was being written, there was further violence. A meeting of Boston merchants in Faneuil Hall denied the right of free speech to the abolitionists, and on October 21, 1835, a well-dressed mob, a "broadcloth mob," as Harriet Martineau describes it in her *Retrospect of Western Travel*, dragged William Lloyd Garrison at the end of a rope over Boston Common and would have lynched him if he had not been consigned protectively to jail by Boston's mayor.

Channing's essay, given to a world of hubbub, of attack and counter attack, undertook to prove eight propositions, lucidly set forth, the first and most important of which was that a human being could never be considered a piece of property. The black man or woman was a child of God beneath a darker skin. Only slavery prevented the unfolding of the moral and intellectual gifts with which their race had been endowed.

Though both slave and owner were corrupted thereby, the responsibility for doing away with the system rested on the shoulders of the master race, for a slave revolt would only bring useless suffering and further repression. It had been argued that freeing the blacks might foster amalgamation—a horrid word, which had been used to incriminate Miss Harriet Martineau because in one of her novels she had allowed a black man to marry an English girl. Channing showed he was aware of the realities of slavery and sex by asking whether any slaveholder could speak of amalgamation without a blush.

In the seventh section of his work, Channing mentioned the abolitionists; he did not claim the title for himself. Their "strength of principle, their native goodness" was praised, but Channing chided them for their noisy, showy methods. This brought forth a comment in *The Liberator*, that "those who are not with us are against us," and a much more savage assault from the opposing camp. The attorney general of Massachusetts accused Channing of inciting to insurrection. Channing's name was spoken on the floor of the United States Senate, where a South Carolinian declared him to be a more dangerous manipulator of public opinion than Garrison.

This, in a certain sense, was true, for the Doctor's book was read in many a well-upholstered parlor, unsoiled, unstrewn by copies of *The Liberator*. It appealed to reason, and it reasserted the faith that reason would prevail. On the morning of Channing's arrival for his visit at Butler Place, Fanny awoke from a delicious dream of being wafted up to heaven. This was the effect that Channing often had upon his proselytes, the translation to a higher sphere where there was no need for good to compromise with evil. After reading *Slavery*, Fanny dismissed any adverse criticism of it by saying that here was God's truth, and that truth would triumph over wrong.

When a few weeks later Miss Frances Butler died, Fanny made no pretense of personal sorrow. Pierce's aunt, the guardian of the family gold hoard, had lived in great retirement and was rarely seen. When she was first seriously ill Pierce spent nine days in Philadelphia, and during this time his brother John, who had retained the surname Mease, changed it to Butler so that he, too, could inherit. It would be necessary for the brothers to go to Georgia in the autumn to inspect their property and to confer with its manager of thirty-four years standing, a Mr. Roswell King, who had been named co-trustee with Miss Butler in the old Major's will. Since the Major's death, King, though nominally in charge, had handed over his duties at the plantation to his son, Roswell junior.

Fanny was desperately eager to accompany her husband and her brother-in-law. Having denounced slavery in the abstract, she was anxious to see its actual workings. It was a very real disappointment to be told how crude the island accommodations now were after so many years of absentee ownership; they were much too rough for a lady and her baby daughter.

"You do not know how profoundly this subject [of slavery] interests me," Fanny wrote. "We dispose of the physical, mental, and moral condition of some hundreds of our fellow creatures . . . In every point of view, I feel we ought to embrace the cause of these poor people. . . . They will be free assuredly, and that before many years. Why not make friends of them instead of deadly enemies? Why not give them at once the wages of their labor? . . . Oh, how I wish I was a man! How I wish I owned these slaves!" [4]

CHAPTER VIII

AN APPOINTED TASK

(November 1836–December 1838)

SINCE PIERCE BUTLER'S TRIP to Georgia would take him away
from Philadelphia for at least four months, Fanny was privileged
to spend the winter with her family in England. She, Sarah, and
Sarah's Irish Catholic nurse, Margery O'Brien, sailed in November of 1836.

The autumn crossing was ferociously stormy, but at its end
lay London, "more rich, more beautiful than ever," and relatives
and friends, unseen for four long years. The Kemble family was
no longer housed beneath a single roof. Fanny's brother John,
after flirting with two professions, the Law and the Church, had
made an auspicious start as a linguistic scholar; he had published
a first translation of the Anglo-Saxon poem of *Beowulf* and was
married to a German girl, Natalia Wendt, the daughter of his
professor at the University of Göttingen. Brother Henry was
with his regiment in Ireland; only Adelaide, youngest of the
brood and now twenty-two years old, was left at home with her
parents. Fanny arrived just in time to be present at her father's
farewell performance on the stage, which was no more final,
incidentally, than many another theatrical farewell. Again all
hopes for the future were centered on a budding talent in the
younger generation. Adelaide had a mellifluous, high soprano

voice and none of Fanny's difficulties in staying on pitch. She was about to make her operatic debut on the Continent, with Covent Garden as her ultimate goal.

Fanny had expected to go back to America in March, but Pierce proposed coming to fetch her, and his coming was put off from month to month. After the quiet life she had been leading at Butler Place, a London season seemed "riotous." The season of 1837 was climaxed by the death in June of William IV, the last to reign of the unlamented sons of George III. Fanny was present when Victoria, aged eighteen, but touchingly self-possessed, opened Parliament with a beautifully enunciated greeting to "my Lords and gentlemen."

The little Queen's preference for lords and gentlemen of the Whig persuasion went without saying, and at Holland House, the pleasure dome of Whiggery, presided over by a lady who managed to be outrageously rude to practically everyone, Fanny made some new acquaintances and met a few old friends. One of the latter sort was Sydney Smith, a clergyman more famous for his wit than for conventional piety. In an article in *The Edinburgh Review*, Smith had inquired, in substance, "Who ever reads an American book, or goes to an American play?" In somewhat the same vein, he pretended to believe it impossible that such "a pleasing and intelligent young lady" as Fanny Kemble should have married an American. "Now do, my dear child, be persuaded to give up this extraordinary delusion," he said.

Fanny pointed first to the ring on her left hand and then to her baby as proof positive of matrimony, but for once she did not undertake to defend her adopted country, or, more specifically, her husband. She and all others present were convulsed with laughter at Smith's sly joke at American expense.

To become better oriented to the land which was now her home, was, however, Fanny's aim. She often paused in the midst of some hectic enjoyment to think of the quiet Pennsylvania farm and of the duties to which she and Pierce were pledged in the United States. The length of her stay distressed her. Pierce had an annoying habit of procrastination, but in this instance, a good excuse for his delay. He had been appointed delegate to a state Constitutional Convention, in tribute, possibly, to his grandfather; the convention had been scheduled for May and was later postponed until the following November. When Fanny went to Liverpool in August to meet his incoming ship, she knew that her husband's first experience of England would be brief. A farewell, bon voyage note from Sydney Smith urged her to be "courageous and of good cheer," as if she were returning to a penal colony.

During the dismal westward voyage most of Fanny's time was spent in bed. She was again pregnant and profoundly depressed. Marriage posed an insoluble problem, she wrote soon after her landing in New York; a woman should be her husband's best and dearest friend, but friendship could only exist between equals, and equality in marriage seemed to be impossible.

Throughout the bustling Constitutional Convention, Fanny was impressed by the intelligence and commonsense of the delegates, most of whom were uneducated men, and yet, having been homesick for America in London, she now felt homesick for England. She feared that Butler Place, where she had "no intimates, no society, no intellectual intercourse," [1] might prove all too lonely. As it turned out, most of the winter was spent in Philadelphia, for Pierce fell ill with pains in his chest, bouts of fever, and night sweats. Again his relations with Fanny were exacerbated by a literary project.

While she was in England, Fanny had begun to write yet another play. Unlike *Francis I* and *The Star of Seville*, it had a contemporary theme. Charles Kemble one evening brought home from a dinner party gossip of a tempest in the top teapot of society. Henry William, nineteenth Baron de Ros, had been caught cheating at cards. Proof was irrefutable. A mock epitaph for the Baron's tomb had been composed: "Here lies Henry, twenty-sixth Baron de Ros (sic) in joyful expectation of the Last Trump." The anecdote was so suggestive that Fanny went at once to her desk and at a single sitting wrote the crucial third act of *An English Tragedy*, a tragedy which had a strongly ironic flavor. The antihero of her drama is a reprobate, who has seduced the wife of his best friend. His fellow aristocrats can forgive him this pecadillo, but not his winning at dice with loaded ivories.

Fanny tried to finish her play while she was staying in Philadelphia, but could not get on with it. Once more Pierce Butler had read what his wife had written and thought it indelicate. *An English Tragedy*, he said, should never appear in print or on the stage.

Pierce might have saved his breath. The play, when completed, was sent off to London, to William Charles Macready, who was now the manager of Covent Garden. Fanny had overcome her writing block at the Lenox Inn, where she spent a refreshing six weeks when the autumn foliage was at its best. Earlier, on May 28, 1838, the third birthday of her daughter Sarah, Fanny had "perpetrated," as she phrased it, a second daughter, who was to be her namesake. Pierce was well enough to take his entire family to Rockaway to escape the summer heat, but not well enough to go on with them to the Berkshires. After seeing her husband settled in New York under the care of a physician, Fanny took the Hudson River steamboat on her way to Albany.

At the Inn, Fanny found two charming sisters, relatives of the Sedgwicks, Mary and Frances Appleton, whom she had first met while on her honeymoon at Newport. With them and with Kate Sedgwick, she rode for many miles a day on horseback. A letter that went to Mrs. Jameson was buoyant. "We laugh and we talk, sing, play, walk, run, scramble and saunter—and amuse ourselves extremely!" [2]

Catharine Sedgwick was also writing to Mrs. Jameson, who had come to America while Fanny was abroad, armed with an introduction to the Sedgwicks. Fanny's baby Fan was too small to be of much interest as yet, Catharine wrote, but she was delighted with little Sarah, who was so unlike her mother in appearance, but seemed to have inherited her mother's restless intelligence. Sally was a babbler; her most frequent remarks were "Why?" and "What for?" Catharine was also enthusiastic on the score of Fanny's *English Tragedy;* she thought that "an angel might have written it." [3]

During Mrs. Jameson's visit to Lenox the preceding summer, she and Catharine had had many discussions of the Fanny problem, more specifically, the problem of Fanny's marriage. Mrs. Jameson could speak of such matters from personal experience, marital troubles having brought her across the ocean. For ten years she had been the wife of a man who did not want to live with her, who had been a colonial judge, first in Dominica and currently in Canada. After a fruitless attempt at reconciliation in Toronto, Mrs. Jameson went back to Britain, but did not allow her friendship with Catharine to die. In the letters that went back and forth, Fanny's name constantly appeared. "Heaven may solve the problem we could not," Catharine [4] had written when she first heard of Pierce's illness, his pains in the chest and fever.

It was unlike Catharine Sedgwick to express, even by implication, a death wish, but she had always been dubious of Fanny's chances of happiness and was even more so after something which happened at the very end of her friend's stay.

Pierce Butler's health had improved under the care of his New York doctor. Though his symptoms might have suggested tuberculosis or heart trouble, he had been told that he was suffering from rheumatism and was advised to spend the winter in the South. Since his brother John could not go with him, Pierce had decided to take Fanny and the children to Georgia. When he came up to the mountains in October and made his announcement, Fanny was exhilarated; this was the very thing for which she had asked two years earlier and had been denied.

The last evening in Lenox was spent, as always, with the Sedgwicks, and in speaking of the plantations, Pierce said, for the first time in Fanny's hearing, that he thought it was right to own slaves.

Fanny rounded upon him, her eyes "fairly glowing" with indignation. "By what right?" she demanded.[5]

Pierce was silent for a few moments; Catharine noted how pale he looked. At length he said that his authority was the Bible.

"I don't admit it," Fanny cried. "I have a higher authority against it."

Before Fanny could denounce the infallibility of Holy Writ, Pierce had turned to Catharine. To her, he said that the idea of slavery being an evil was something altogether new.

So also was the idea of popular government, Catharine reminded him; so, also, was representation of the people and democracy in general.

There the dispute ended, or there, at least, ended the account which Catharine sent to Mrs. Jameson. The problem had become acute. Catharine wondered if there was enough mutual love and respect between husband and wife to ride out the oncoming storm. "I tremble," she concluded, in somewhat larger letters than usual, "for this winter's experiment."

That there should have been talk of slavery in the Sedgwick household was not unusual. Recent events had kept the topic uppermost.

While the Butlers were at Rockaway, Freedom Hall, an auditorium built by abolitionists in Philadelphia, was reduced to a heap of charred rubble. There had been other outrages throughout the winter, the most sinister of which was the death of Elijah Lovejoy, in defense of his printing press at Alton, Illinois. A tumultuous meeting followed, held in Faneuil Hall and chaired by Dr. Channing, to protest the murder. Channing's latest controversial publication was an open letter to Henry Clay, urging him to block the admission of Texas to the Union. The admission would entail not only an enlargement of slave territory, but also the adoption of an imperialist foreign policy. If the Lone Star

Republic were annexed, Channing prophesied, the United States would "enter on a career of encroachment, war and crime . . . The seizure of Texas will not stand alone. It will darken our future history."

With Catharine, but more particularly with Catharine's sister-in-law Elizabeth, Fanny had argued various points, and to Elizabeth, before that final evening in Lenox, she confided what her next writing venture would be, a study of slavery on her husband's plantations. They were superior plantations, she had been led to believe. Pierce had told her how well they had been run in the days of his grandfather and how kindly the slaves had always been treated, even when under the unsupervised management of an overseer. A literary model for Fanny's work was at hand, the *Journal of a West Indian Proprietor*, by the English romancer, Matthew Lewis. Once more Fanny would keep a diary, and this she would transform into a series of letters addressed to Elizabeth.

To set the ball rolling after Fanny's departure, Elizabeth sent on to Butler Place a communication she had received from a defender of slavery, who had learned of Fanny's intention. In refuting the arguments of this unknown individual, Fanny showed she had absorbed Channing and Sedgwick doctrine, but could also draw on other sources.

With scorn and anger, Fanny had read the widely circulated *Message* of Governor George McDuffie of South Carolina to the legislature of his state in 1835. The *Message* proved to the Governor's satisfaction, but not to Fanny's, that slavery was consistent with democracy and the will of God. The pampered slave of a kindly master, Fanny conceded, might be happy, but his happiness was inhuman; it was that of a well-fed horse or dog. And there were cruel masters. Fanny had had access, on Chestnut Street, no doubt, to Southern newspapers; she had seen advertisements of slave auctions, which divided mother from child, of rewards offered for the return of fugitives, branded on the cheek, or scarred by the whip—"details of misery," she interpolated, "that it would be difficult for imagination to exceed."

Elizabeth's apologist, knowing that Fanny was English, mentioned the "miserable Irish," whose plight was of concern to humanitarians on both sides of the Atlantic. Fanny freely admitted that many an Irishman was "starved, naked and roofless," but at least he could rejoice in the name of freeman and could seek his fortune where he chose, as witnessed by the thousands who every year left their bogside hovels to emigrate to America. In Philadelphia Fanny had seen the bad effect this influx had had upon the condition of Northern blacks which Henry Dwight Sedgwick so deplored.

No more than Dr. Channing, no more than Miss Harriet Martineau, could Fanny be frightened by the bugaboo of amalgamation. She had learned, but not, perhaps, by reading Southern newspapers, of a demimonde of beautiful quadroons in Louisiana, existing for the delectation of Southern gentlemen. As for bonafide marriage between the races, that was a matter of such purely personal preference that she and Elizabeth had not even bothered to discuss it.

To top off her first Letter to Elizabeth, Fanny tried to respond to a transmitted exhortation to visit her husband's plantation with an open mind. "Assuredly," she wrote, "I am going prejudiced against slavery, for I am an Englishwoman, in whom the absence of such a prejudice would be disgraceful. Nevertheless I go prepared to find many mitigations . . . much kindness on the part of masters, much content on the part of slaves." [6]

In other words, Fanny was determined to play fair with Pierce, who, in taking her to Georgia, was playing fair with her, since he knew her opinions so well. The sheer adventure of what lay before her also had its appeal. In going to the islands, Fanny wrote, but not to Elizabeth, she might "die of fever, be shot from behind a tree for abolitionism, or swallowed by an Altamaha alligator." [7]

CHAPTER IX

SOUTHWARD

(December 1838)

AFTER TEDIOUS DELAY, and on Friday morning, December 21, 1838, the Butlers left on a strenuous nine days' journey to the South. The party consisted of Pierce, Fanny, the two children, the children's nurse, Margery O'Brien, and Miss Elizabeth Butler, Pierce's aunt, a twin sister of the recently deceased Miss Frances. While the others went on to Georgia, Miss Butler would visit friends in Charleston.

Hitherto Fanny had traveled only in the more thickly populated areas of the United States; now she was to plunge into the wilderness. Between Philadelphia and the Georgian islands lay massive segments of unfelled forest and undrained swampland. The travelers were to go by land and sea, by steamboat, rail, and horse-drawn coach. After she had reached her destination, Fanny wrote a description of the trip to Harriet St. Ledger, who had recently followed some of the well-worn and well-equipped travel routes of Europe. Fanny's travelogue did not suffer from an understatement of the hardships she had encountered. In pioneer America there were no snug inns, no bedside cup of tea, no well-organized means of transportation. All was makeshift, hurry, and confusion. Railroad bridges were in use before the last rivet had been driven. Rails themselves ceased abruptly in the middle of a forest, and the occupants of the cars were turned out into the cold at midnight. For nine days Fanny, a fanatic for personal cleanliness, loudly demanded, and seldom obtained, a clean towel.

Without serious mishap, however, and early on Christmas Day of 1838, the overburdened steamer which the travelers had boarded at Wilmington, North Carolina, bumped against a bar in Charleston harbor. There would be a two-day wait before the next leg of the journey, also by steamer, to Savannah. Fanny had time to see something of the town to which Major Pierce Butler had come in 1766 and where much of his youth was passed. She approved of Charleston's air of picturesque antiquity; it reminded her a little of an English port, of Southampton. The streets and the handsome waterfront promenade were empty at this season. Charleston's aristocrats had gone to celebrate Christmas on their plantations, which could be safely visited in wintertime, when there was no danger of "country fever," a form of malaria, lethal to whites, but to which blacks were immune. Miss Butler was relieved to find that the family she had come to visit had remained unfashionably in town.

Since the best hotel in Charleston had been destroyed by fire the preceding summer, the Pierce Butlers had to patronize a second-class establishment, the proprietor of which was a woman of color, but whose servants were apparently her slaves. At Portsmouth, Virginia, Fanny had had her first contact with specimens of the social class she had come to investigate and had been struck by their dirtiness, their ragged clothing, and a certain lazy recklessness of manner, unbecoming to "rational humanity." When the train from Portsmouth stopped for some time at a way station, the carriages were surrounded by a crowd of curious blacks. Little Sarah Butler, whose healthy appearance and bright pink cheeks had excited admiration throughout the trip, leaned out the window, and an elderly woman, grinning from ear to ear, held up a small, black counterpart and offered the child, her grandchild, as a waiting maid for "Little Missis." Fanny was not amused by the joke. Little Missis was being taught to wait upon herself, she exclaimed indignantly. The rebuke set off a tintinnab-ulation of guffaws and incredulous giggles, and Fanny was glad when the interchange was cut short by the train's sudden, unher-alded departure.

In Charleston also there was dark, mysterious laughter and, on Fanny's part, a feeling of repulsion. The entire staff of the second-rate hotel stood grinning in wonderment and delight about the dining table, without the faintest idea of how to serve their guests. When banished from the room they kept poking their heads in at the door to spy and smile upon the visitors. "Their laziness, their filthiness, their inconceivable stupidity, and unconquerable good humor, are enough to drive one stark-staring mad," was Fanny's comment.[1]

Less irritating, but also less reassuring, was another feature of Charleston life, the tolling of bells and the beating of drums at sunset, announcing a curfew. Fear of black insurrection was endemic throughout the South. No Charleston slave was allowed to be abroad after dark without a pass. When Fanny inquired about the function of a large building under construction, she was told it was to be a jail for the fifty or sixty persons who were arrested every night. One of the blessings of slavery which Governor McDuffie had failed to mention in his *Message to the South Carolina Legislature*, Fanny noted, with heavy-handed irony, was the possibility of having one's throat cut while one slept!

Of Savannah, Fanny had little to say in her letter to Harriet, for time was short between the arrival from Charleston and the departure for Darien, the mainland town which served as urban center for certain of the island plantations. The small vessel that bore the travelers down the coast was named the *Ocmulgee*. The exotic Indian name, the low-lying reedy shore, which showed no signs of human habitation, gave Fanny, and also Nurse Mar-gery O'Brien, the feeling that they were approaching the ends of the earth. At the mouth of the Altamaha River two trading vessels were anchored, one flying the harp of Ireland for Margery and the other Fanny's beloved Union Jack. These links with civilization were left behind as the *Ocmulgee* steamed up the river.

The low, irregular roofs of a town appeared above the undergrowth. Fanny was below in the cabin as the vessel's flank grazed the wharf at Darien. As she and Pierce appeared on deck with their children, a shout went up from the black oarsmen of two barges that had drawn alongside: "Oh, Massa! How you do, Massa? Oh, Missis, Oh! lily Missis! Me too glad to see you!" There were shrieks, whoops, whistles, and grunts, sounds so innately African that Fanny could not reproduce them for the eye and ear of Harriet St. Ledger, three thousand miles and more away.

"The strangeness of the whole scene," Fanny wrote, "its wildness . . . the affectionate shouts of welcome of the poor people, who seemed to hail us as descending divinities, affected me so much that I burst into tears and could hardly answer their demonstrations of delight. . . . We were presently transferred into the larger boat, and the smaller one being freighted with our luggage, we pulled off from Darien." [2]

On their way to the Butler plantation, the barges crossed various arms of the river and passed through an artificial canal. As they approached the home shore, the steersman of the barge blew a blast on a huge conch shell. The decks of a small schooner that was lying at the wharf were suddenly thronged with humanity—black, vociferous humanity, leaping up and down, dancing, shouting, laughing, and clapping their hands.

"On our landing from the boat," Fanny continued her narrative, "the crowd thronged about us like a swarm of bees; we were seized, pulled, pushed, carried, dragged, and all but lifted in the air. . . . They seized our clothes, kissed them—then our hands, and almost wrung them off." Fanny was afraid her children might be smothered, but looking back, saw that two white men, the captain of the schooner and the plantation overseer, were making a way for them and Margery O'Brien through the melée. Fortunately there was not far to go. After the door of the house, an overseer's cottage, had been closed in the faces of "our riotous escort," Fanny and Pierce looked at one another and laughed loud and long.

Fanny's laugher was as hysterical as her flurry of tears on the deck of the *Ocmulgee*. The "poor people" had seen Pierce before, but why were they frenzied with joy at sight of her, a stranger? Whether she liked it or not, the role of descending divinity had been forced upon her.

The island on which Fanny, her husband, and her children had landed was Butler Island. In the early days of Butler enterprise it was spoken of merely as "the tide island," for much of its surface lay below the level of the sea. Protected from rise and fall by dykes, the island's rice fields were crisscrossed by irrigation ditches to let in the fresh waters of the Altamaha.

At first this plantation was of minor importance compared to the venture in cotton at Hampton Point on St. Simons, which, throughout its length and breadth, was humanly inhabited when Butler Island was the home of deer and waterfowl, bull snake, and alligator. At Hampton Point, Major Pierce Butler had indulged his passion for building. In addition to the Great House, there were several other houses on the estate, one of which was reserved for guests.

In 1804, an old friend of the Major, Colonel Aaron Burr, who had just shot Alexander Hamilton in a duel and was anxious to withdraw for a time from public view, occupied the guest house. Burr was appreciative of the Major's hospitality, the excellence of his accommodations, and the number of servants assigned to keep him comfortable. Even then, however, the heyday of Hampton Point was on the wane. The chief superiority of Sea Island cotton over the short-staple variety, which could be far more widely grown, lay in the comparative ease of separating seed from fibre. After Eli Whitney's cotton gin had been patented and launched, the value of the Major's phenomenal crop declined.

"Tide Island is too valuable to be trifled with," the Major's overseer wrote to his employer while the plantation's marshes were being cleared and brought under control. Tide Island could be counted on as a steady, if not spectacular, moneymaker.

The overseer, Mr. Roswell King, was a canny New Englander, a native of Windsor, Connecticut, who did not like being "scraped out" of a single penny. He took over the management of the plantations in 1802, and due to rheumatism and old age, resigned his job in 1819 to his son, Roswell junior, who, having been brought up in the South, could be counted on to become a good planter. The planter's most important function was the exercise of absolute authority over some hundreds of human beings. That an ethical problem was involved, King recognized in an aphorism which he included in one of his reports to Philadelphia. "The art of disposing of power with moderation is a great art," he wrote.[3]

While the Major was in personal command of his estate, certain rules were laid down concerning his slaves. They were kept close at home; they were not allowed to visit their kind on neighboring plantations, and a guard against intruders was stationed on the wharves and at the gate of Hampton Point. Only occasionally were the Butler people allowed to visit Darien to sell the products of their leisure; a canoe, or skiff, biggins delved from cypress wood, bags of Spanish moss, which grew luxuriantly on the island trees and which could be used to stuff pillows and mattresses. Because they came in contact so rarely with outsiders, the inhabitants of Hampton Point and Butler Island were almost unintelligible; their speech was a rich, an almost uncontaminated Gullah, with an odd confusion of pronouns, which they may have brought with them from Africa.

Here, as on most plantations in this region, the task system was in force, and the tasks were estimated close to human capacity. At certain seasons the slaves were worked from dawn to dark, encouraged thereto by a black driver, who was armed with a whip. The driver was not allowed to apply more than a dozen lashes to one of his gang in the field, the gangs consisting of women as well as men. Fifty lashes were set as the limit of punishment for more serious crimes, a proviso reminiscent, no doubt, of the army codes which the Major had administered in his youth.

After the Major ceased to visit the plantations, the Kings, father and son, maintained his policy of exclusiveness and of a rigid, but well-regulated, discipline. Roswell junior even went so far as to say in an article published in *The Southern Agriculturist* for November 1828 that "a master or an overseer should be the kind friend and monitor to the slave, not his oppressor." [4] The whip was too much used, he thought, and it was a great mistake to lacerate the victim, particularly if he was young and would have to bear the scars of his rebellion throughout his entire life. Digging stumps, clearing trash, and confinement to the plantation for six months, or a year, were sufficient deterrents.

It might seem as if, in the absence of the owner, or owners, a regime of mild, sweet reason had been instituted, but overseer, as well as slave, could not escape the inexorable necessity of showing a year's end profit, if not by whip, then by guile. The elder King confessed that when his underlings complained of their tasks being too heavy, he would speak them fair, but privately tell the drivers to keep up their pressure.

And the underlings could not be hoodwinked! They had a life, a history of their own, deeply hidden, but for public consumption a mythology which they could share with the master race. For them, the era of the Major's personal supervision had become a Golden Age. Then there was someone who would listen to their complaints. Then there was less to do, and more to eat, even though Roswell King, Jr., had told readers of *The Southern Agriculturist* that he sometimes spent as much as two cents per capita, per day, to add such delicacies as molasses to the diet of the Butler slaves. He was proud to say that none of the pickaninnies on the plantation were so hungry as to be tempted to eat dirt.

The legend of past abundance and of active benevolence was kept alive by certain old people on the estate who had been house servants. They could remember how the Major insisted on their being clean and neatly dressed. The house at Hampton Point was well staffed. It was equipped with a saltwater tank in which fish could be kept alive and swimming until the cook was ready to prepare them for the dining table. Guests came and went. The grove of orange trees, planted between the house and river, bore fruit aplenty and when in bloom, perfumed the air for miles around. Now the Great House was tottering to ruin, and the riverbank had caved in, leaving a wreck of drowned, deracinated trees, their blackened branches swaying beneath a prism of swiftly moving water.

It was against this backdrop of splendid past and dilapidated present that Fanny should have viewed the welcome of her husband's slaves. She diagnosed their delirium of joy at first as merely "a lively sense of benefits to come." This to a certain extent was true. Later, however, Fanny came to see that she and her children represented continuity. For years, the Major had debated with his overseer, who was also his man of business in the South, the possibility of selling the cotton plantation, with or without its serfs. This matter was never discussed, one may be sure, with those it vitally concerned, but a word here or there, the mere lifting of an eyebrow, might have sparked the ever-present fear of dispersal and the end of an imperfect, but familiar, world. The fact that Massa had married and had a wife and children who would carry on after he was gone might save some of Massa's possessions from the hammer stroke of an auctioneer.

CHAPTER X

FOR ELIZABETH

(December 1838–April 1839)

THE SIX-ROOM COTTAGE that sheltered the Butler family during their stay on Tide Island, a jerry-built affair, with its bare, unpainted walls, its sagging doors and window frames, and its detached, dirt-floored kitchen, was the meanest habitation Fanny had ever experienced. When some six weeks later she went to live on St. Simons, the accommodations were a shade less primitive and far less cramped. Fanny's sitting room there was large enough to be described as "barnlike"; it contained a chintz-covered object, resembling a sofa, and a pinewood table, covered with a green baize cloth. At this table Fanny would often sit alone of an evening, making entries in her *Journal*, entries that later would be transformed into the letters to Elizabeth. The only light in the room was from the fireplace and the candles on the table.

While she wrote, Fanny would become aware of the stealthy opening and shutting of the door. One after another, men and women would enter, their bare feet noiseless on the bare floor. They would seat themselves about the fire, squatting down on their hams in a semicircle, "the blaze from the pine logs . . . shining on their sooty limbs and faces, and making them look like a ring of ebony idols, surrounding my domestic hearth." [1]

Having finished her writing, Fanny would close her book and, always brisk in coming to the point, would ask, "Well, what do you want?"

Immediately, as if by clockwork, all the figures would rise at once and say in chorus, "Me come say ha' do, Missis." Without another word, "like a procession of sable dreams," Fanny's visitors would glide from the room.

From the first the master's wife had been the object of quenchless curiosity. Fanny could not walk alone along the dykes of Butler Island, and even when she had a horse to ride on St. Simons, she was followed and spied upon from the bushes. The spies were puzzled by her behavior. Why, when they called her "missis," did she cry, "For God's sake, don't call me that"? What else could they call her? Eventually Fanny had to give up trying to convince her fellow islanders that they were not her property, that they belonged to her husband. She would do what she could for them, she repeated over and over, but in the end she could only be their go-between to higher authority.

Because, on the rice plantation, there was little opportunity for the strenuous exercise that was so important for Fanny's physical and emotional well being, she took to going on the river, and a boy named Jack, who was too frail for hard physical labor, was assigned as her companion. Jack was the son of a former head driver and therefore a member of the island's upper class, if one could call it that. He had the intelligence of a precocious child and showered Fanny not only with requests, but also with questions about the outside world.

One day when Jack had asked Missis to please ask Massa for permission for him and his family to keep a pig, Fanny cut short his interrogation with a question of her own; would he, Jack, like to be free?

A look, which Fanny later described as "an illumination," transformed the boy's face, but it was "only a lightning flash." Jack was confused; he didn't know what to say; he stammered and at last brought out, "Free, Missis! What for me wish to be free? Oh no, Missis, me no wish to be free, if Massa only let we keep pig!" [2]

The subject of pig was safe. It was returned to again and again, and to it was added a pious wish "to work for Missis and Massa until me die."

Fanny despised hypocrisy; she hated flattery and lying, but for a moment she felt she had penetrated the barrier of secrecy which servitude had erected between herself and a fellow mortal. The desire for freedom, though hastily concealed, was there.

Fanny was pained by the constant self-abasement of Jack and his folk, but this too was a form of flattery. If she lifted a log to throw it on the fire, a protest would rise to "let be!" There was "plenty nigger" to stoke the flames. When she turned away in disgust from the offal cleaned out of a large drumfish, the cook assured her that it would be eaten, but it wasn't good enough for white folks, only good enough for nigger. The word nigger was synonymous with slave. It was used as a taunt by the Negroes themselves. How insolent they were to one another! "You nigger—I say, you black nigger, don't you hear me?" they would shout.

Except for an old woman who, in her day, had served the Major and his family and who was known as House Molly, to distinguish her from the many other Mollies on the plantation, Fanny's domestic staff stank abominably. But why shouldn't they stink, she asked herself, considering the conditions under which they lived?

On her first exploration of Butler Island, Fanny inspected the rice mill, the blacksmith's shop, the cooper's shop, all competently manned by blacks, and then went on to view the five settlements or "camps," as they were called. Each consisted of some ten to twenty cabins and a communal kitchen, where grits, the staple item of diet, was cooked in mighty cauldrons. The cabins themselves were flimsy affairs, pinned to the earth by immense chimnies. For their occupants, old and young, ten or more in number, there was but a single room, perhaps twelve-foot square, with adjoining, roughly partitioned cubby holes for sleeping. There was no furniture, except bedsteads, strewn with Spanish moss and covered with filthy blankets. For sewage system, an open ditch, in which the tide rose and fell, ran behind the settlement. On a chilly January morning only a few young children would be crouched about the cabin fire, tending their infant relatives who, at noon, would be carried out to be nursed by their mothers, working in the field.

Fanny, who was nursing her own baby, and who had seen to it that her children had their daily sponge bath, even when en route from Philadelphia, started a "wash baby" campaign. She distributed soap, she scolded, she offered penny bribes. She and Margery O'Brien, who was sometimes mistaken for the real missis, sewed layettes from bolts of flannel, bought in Darien. Though the babies might be swaddled in rags, they all wore caps, which Fanny considered unsanitary; infestation by body lice was common; infestation by flea was universal in the cabins.

The most disheartening discovery of all, however, for one who had had a little, but only a little, contact with the poor and wretched of the earth, lay at the end of Fanny's initial tour of inspection. Just beyond one of the settlements stood the plantation hospital, a whitewashed, two-story building, divided into four large rooms. "But how shall I describe to you the spectacle which was presented to me on entering the first of these?" [3] Fanny inquired rhetorically of Elizabeth. There were six windows in the room, only three of which were glazed and so dirty that they admitted little more light than those that were shuttered against the cold. Some of the inmates, the ones who could crawl, were huddled about the fireplace on low settles. The rest lay on the floor, wrapped in tattered blankets, without bedstead, mattress, or pillow. Since this was a woman's ward, most of the patients were maternity cases, though other varieties of illness were represented. On a later visit, Fanny noted a young girl whose hands and feet were being devoured by some hideous tropical disease, and an epileptic, a huge woman who screamed and thrashed about in convulsions.

Amid the dirt, the noise, and the stench, Fanny stood, tears pouring down her cheeks. She then set vigorously to work, throwing open the windows, building up the fire, and sweeping up as much as possible of the trash that littered the floor. Fanny was somewhat hampered in her efforts by Rose, the plantation midwife, who followed her about and clucked an admonition to "let be."

So this was the way that people lived and died and were born on a plantation that was considered superior for its kindness, its efficiency! Fanny went home to express her indignation to Pierce and to the overseer, who said, somewhat shamefacedly, that when he first came to the estate, less than a year ago, he thought the hospital could be improved. He had received little encouragement, however, from his predecessor in office, Roswell King, Jr.

Fanny may not have read the article which Roswell King, Jr. had written for *The Southern Agriculturist*, but she had heard the former overseer praised extravagantly by all the Butler family, and when he came over from the mainland to visit the plantation, she was much impressed by what he had to say.

"I hate slavery with all my heart," King asserted. "I consider it an absolute curse wherever it exists. It will keep those states where it does exist fifty years behind the others in improvement and prosperity." [4] To say slavery was an evil which could not be cured was, according to King, "all nonsense." As soon as people realized how little their interests were served they would get rid of it. This was sound doctrine *à la* Channing and *à la* Sedgwick; it might even have served as a capsule history of the British Emancipation Act.

Fanny also relished, as confirmation of yet another of the prejudices she had brought with her to the South, King's description of the poor whites of Georgia, the pinelanders, who preferred a life of barbaric sloth and semistarvation to "working like a nigger." Fanny had observed some of this class on her journey from the North; to her they had seemed barely human.

A more subtle corruption of the white race by slavery was even evident in Fanny's small daughter, who was not yet four years old. Little Missis, as Sarah Butler was now addressed, lorded it over a troupe of admiring, servile playmates, who trailed her from morning till night. She had only to express her desire for a swing, and a rope was thrown across the bough of a tree; a dozen pushers stood at attention to send her flying through the air. The sooner Sarah was removed from this atmosphere the better, Fanny thought. She herself felt she would rather die than lead the life of some of the planters' wives she met in Darien, languid, querulous ladies, whose conversation was overloaded with complaints of their black handmaidens and their envy of Mrs. Butler, who had a white nurse for her children.

There was, indeed, only one local family Fanny could admire. The Hampton Point estate was bordered on the west by a plantation that belonged to an elderly Scotchman, an octogenarian, Mr. John Couper, who had come out to America more than sixty years earlier; he had arrived in the islands about the same time as Major Butler, but unlike Major Butler, had never left them in search of greater wealth. The Couper house was neatly kept; there was, nearby, a tidy kitchen garden, in its center a fruit-bearing palm; the grounds were bright with flowers.

Fanny, whose green thumb had itched as soon as she saw the magnificent shrubbery, the bay, the wild myrtle, and the magnolia grandiflora that flourished in the swamps of Butler Island, visited the old gentleman frequently. They talked of horticulture, a field in which Couper rated as an expert, but most frequently their conversation turned on the care and nurture of human beings in this latitude. Mr. Couper, who had known the Major well, confirmed the testimony of House Molly and other ancients: namely, that the old days on the Butler plantation had been better days. From what she saw of the Couper establishment, Fanny judged this to be an example of slavery at its best, centered as it was on a kindly and intelligent man, who stayed at home and attended personally to each detail of management.

The managers of the Butler plantations, she was beginning to realize, had been hard taskmasters. Fanny, so obviously an easy mark, heard tales of cruelty which she knew to be exaggerated, but which she nevertheless passed on to Elizabeth—for who could say that they were groundless? The first time she saw the driver of a field gang, armed with a whip, she snatched it out of his hand. He, seeing the expression of her face, which Catharine Sedgwick had once said was "the flexible minister of her soul," mumbled an excuse; he seldom hit nigger; the whip was only used "for measure," whatever that might mean.

Each day a queue of petitioners waited outside the overseer's cottage to file their complaints with the Missis, and most of the complainers were women. In the good old days, Major Butler had lightened the tasks of mothers-to-be and increased their food allotment; after they had given birth they were allowed five weeks to recover on the rice island, and four in the more bracing climate of St. Simons. These maternity privileges had been curtailed by the Kings. Though the birthrate was high, so also was the rate of infant mortality, and a whole series of gynecological misfortunes—backaches, hemorrhages, prolapses of the uterus—were attributed by Fanny to mothers having been driven out to the fields too soon.

That slavery bore more heavily on women than on men seemed obvious. The lot of a woman in the free world might be unsatisfactory and subservient, but there, at least, society provided her with a natural protector, a husband, a father, or a brother. Here promiscuity was encouraged, and family life was so loose, so almost nonexistent, that the only tenderly protective relationship possible was that between mother and child.

With thoughts, perhaps, of what she had written earlier about amalgamation, Fanny noted that some of the islanders were mulattoes. She remarked a striking resemblance between one of the drivers, Bran, and Roswell King, Jr.; she was told by Pierce that they were probably brothers. There was a boy, Renty, on St. Simons, who knew he was a son of the younger King and traded on his parentage in asking for favors. Fanny could not believe that the white man's sexual advances were always welcome; she added rape to the list of the overseers' misdeeds.

It had always been easy, at times too easy during her stage career, for Fanny to slip into the skin of another human being. As a young girl in England, she had once visited a women's prison, one of a group of respectable ladies whom the Quaker philanthropist, Elizabeth Fry, invited to go with her. On this occasion, Fanny came close to making a spectacle of herself. No sooner had the two groups of females, the fallen and the upright, so to speak, sat down, facing one another, than Fanny was overcome with shame at the distinction. She wanted to go sit among the prostitutes, the shoplifters, and the abortionists. So was it here in this remote spot, though here her place was not among the fallen, but among the oppressed, whose unpleasant characteristics —filthiness, lying, laziness, and stupidity—were due to their oppression.

Never was the sense of identification more keen than on the river. Trips back and forth between the two plantations were made in a thirty-foot-long skiff, named *The Water Lily*. As the black men rowed, they sang. Fanny, herself a ballad singer, attributed some of the tunes she heard to Scotch, or even French, folk song, a dubious derivation; but to her the words were more fascinating than the air. Praises of Fanny's personal charms were extemporized, in particular her "wire waist," since hers was the only corseted figure they had ever seen. The opening words of a tribute to small Sarah Butler ran:

> Little Missis Sally,
> That's a ruling lady! [5]

One day when she was about to go back from the rice island to St. Simons, Fanny hurried back to the house to get a life preserver. The wind was blowing furiously, and the surface of the

Altamaha, turgid at best, had become a sea of foam. There were eight rowers in the boat beside the steersman. No breath was wasted in song, for the labor of rowing was tremendous, particularly at the end of the course, when the wildly racing river poured into an inlet of the ocean. The men were in high spirits, however, and one of them said there was not another planter's lady in all of Georgia who would have made this trip alone with them through the storm. Fanny thought scornfully of the Southern women she had met who seemed to be so afraid of black men, and exhilarated by the sense of danger, she cried out that if anything happened, if the boat should capsize, she would have nine chances for her life instead of one.

The answer came back to her in chorus: "So you would, Missis; true for dat Missis!"

But only rarely was identification joyous. Day after day, Fanny took her complaints and expressed her horror of what she saw to her husband. To Elizabeth, she deplored Pierce's indifference, his blindness. At times she felt sorry for him, for he, too, was a victim of a system for which he was not responsible. She had to reproach herself for "the childish excitability" of her temperament. One moment, Fanny was trembling with rage and vituperation, the next she was completely consoled, enraptured by the beauty of the islands, their flowers, their foliage, their birds, even the pattern of brilliantly colored shells traced upon their sands.

Fanny had expressed the hope that her plantation sojourn would not destroy the respect she should feel for Pierce, but when she heard him refuse to alter the work schedule of some pregnant women, she thought how despicable he looked as he faced the bedraggled, toilworn delegation—cool, well dressed, unmarked by sweat, clean handed. Did he feel no shame for his easy, idle existence at their expense?

A small gesture, or rather, a gesture Pierce failed to make at a moment of high emotion, seemed to Fanny to epitomize his attitude. While the family was still living on Butler Island, a strong, and therefore a very valuable, slave, named Shadrach, developed pneumonia. Though the doctor came over from Darien to see him more than once, Shadrach died after a three-day illness. Cotton cloth for a shroud was supplied by Fanny, and she and Pierce, who had watched beside the dying man, attended the funeral. It was held according to custom, possibly an African custom, at night.

"The coffin," Fanny wrote, "was laid on trestles in front of the cooper's cottage, and a large assemblage of the people had gathered around, many of the men carrying pinewood torches. . . . Presently the whole congregation uplifted their voices in a hymn, the first high, wailing notes of which . . . sent a thrill through all my nerves. When the chant ceased Cooper London began a prayer, and all the people knelt down in the sand, as I did also." [6]

Fanny began "to cry very bitterly" when the black preacher invoked a blessing on master, mistress, and their children; there was need for tears, as well as prayer, she thought. She wept again at the burial ground. It stood close to the river, and the fact that the open grave was found half full of water caused cries of sorrow and lamentation. Cooper London read from the Book of Common Prayer; he was the only slave on the island who could read. As she heard the familiar opening words of the burial service, "I am the resurrection and the life," more august than ever before in this strange, torchlit setting and with the murmur and rustle of the great river for orchestral accompaniment, Fanny sank once more to her knees, as did all the rest—all but one.

Only Pierce remained standing. In a Philadelphia church it was not his custom to kneel, but by refusing to do so here, Fanny felt he had, in the face of death, denied the brotherhood of man.

A gulf had opened between them, and they could only speak, and sometimes shout, to one another across it. To do him justice, Pierce had been more or less ailing all winter, and Fanny's taunts and accusations must have been exhausting. The most violent scene that took place between them was occasioned by Pierce's

offering to give one of his slaves to Roswell King, Jr., who was
collecting a gang for a plantation he had bought in Alabama.
Fanny overheard the black man pleading wildly with his master
not to be sent away to some distant place and not to be separated
from his wife Psyche, who was Margery O'Brien's assistant in
caring for the Butler children. Pierce said nothing to lessen the
man's anguish, and Fanny, who immediately sought out her husband, wept and raved. Again Pierce was silent. That he had
meant to punish her for her hysterical outbreak Fanny realized
when she learned indirectly of the offer to King having been
withdrawn. Pierce had made sure the black family would not be
separated by buying Psyche and her two children, who happened
to belong to the present Butler Island overseer. Difficult though
it was to apologize, Fanny ran to her husband to say she had mis-
judged him.

A time came, however, when there could be no such happy
ending to their encounters. Fanny told one sad tale of suffering
too many and vouched for its truth. Pierce turned upon her an-
grily. "Why do you listen to such stuff?" he shouted. "Why do
you believe such trash? Don't you know the niggers are all
damned liars?" [7] He would hear no further complaints. Fanny
was only doing harm, rousing discontent, encouraging idleness,
for which there would have to be chastisement.

True though this might be, Fanny could not remain silent and
inactive. During her final weeks on St. Simons she considered
herself to be an outlaw. She subverted boys by paying them to
open paths through the woods in their spare time. She held religious services, something which had always been discouraged on
the Butler estate. To an attentive audience, Fanny read from the
Bible, a miscellaneous prayer book, and a copy of *The Imitation
of Christ*, supplied by Margery O'Brien. The Statute Book of
Georgia might forbid it, but Fanny began to teach a youth
named Aleck, a brother of her boy Jack, to read, his fellow student being little Missis Sally, that ruling lady.

Later, in his printed *Statement*, Pierce accuses Fanny of going on a hunger strike and trying to leave the islands alone, thus abandoning husband and children. None of this appears in the letters to Elizabeth; on the contrary, the last letter closes with a comment on the hold that children have upon their mothers, slave or free. Fanny quotes a remark of the hated Roswell King, Jr. In reply to a statement that it was dangerous to take Negro servants north for fear of their being lured away to freedom by an abolitionist, King said: "Oh, stuff and nonsense! I take care, when my wife goes north with the children, to send Lucy with her; her [Lucy's] children are down here, and I defy all the abolitionists in creation to get her to stay North." [8]

To this Fanny added the postscript that Mr. King was a very wise man.

PART TWO

CHAPTER XI

A DISEASED MIND

(April 1839–December 1840)

BEFORE GOING TO GEORGIA and while she was still in Lenox, Fanny received news of her mother's death. The word came, not from her family, but parenthetically in a letter from a friend, for Charles Kemble and Adelaide were far away in Italy, and Marie Thérèse had so cut herself off from those she loved that she was almost completely isolated. That her mother's personality had deteriorated, that, in current parlance, her mind was "diseased," Fanny had realized during her stay in England. She had dreaded going to the lonely cottage in Surrey to say good-bye, fearing an emotional scene that might be too much for her own powers of self-control. It was impossible now for Fanny to grieve for what she had lost; having children of her own, she could only grieve for what might have been.

Her mother's going, however, suggested to Fanny the possibility of a letter making its leisurely way across the Atlantic to tell her that her father, whose health had been none too good, was also dead. She must get to England soon, before it was too late, though there seemed to be little hope of that at present. Pierce's rheumatism had not been cured by his winter in the South, and the doctors had prescribed a visit to the Hot Springs in Virginia. If Fanny went with him, the children would have to be left at home; she disliked life as lived in fashionable hotels and, apparently, was not overurged to travel with her husband. Pierce, as usual, left her in doubt as to his plans. He was often absent from Butler Place that spring. During one of his absences he wrote a letter, of which he apparently kept a copy, to Mrs. Charles Sedgwick; it was dated, "Near Philadelphia, May 31, 1839."

"My dear Mrs. Sedgwick," Pierce wrote, "yourself and your husband are the only persons to whom I dare to speak of my misery.... I have done all that deep love for a wife, the strongest affection for my children, and an earnest desire to secure peace and happiness for myself and them have dictated, but all has failed." [1]

His domestic sorrows, Pierce continued, had been hidden from his brother and sisters, since he was certain they would be prejudiced in his favor. He was writing to Elizabeth and Charles because Fanny had always considered their marriage to be ideal. Their opinions had great weight with her; a word from them might have a magical effect.

Though Pierce was convinced that he and Fanny still loved one another, "only lately has she taken up the idea that she has become indifferent to me; this arose, I think, in Georgia and now has full possession of her mind. With all but me she is rational."

As an example of Fanny's irrationality, Pierce told how only four days earlier, on May 28, the children's joint birthday, Sarah's fourth and Fan's first, was celebrated, as it seemed, to their mother's satisfaction. Two small cousins came out from town for the event, and a happy time was had by all. Immediately after, however, Fanny asked Pierce when the steamer *Great Western* would sail for England. She refused to sleep with him, and demanded a separation in violently abusive terms. "You can never repair the injury you have done me in marrying me," she said. "I will not remain here to be your housekeeper, your child's nurse, or what you make me that is still more degrading and revolting." [2]

A separation seemed to be the only solution, but—"what could I do with two motherless children?" Pierce inquired. Or even with one? Fanny had suggested that if he would not give them both to her, she should take Sarah and leave him baby Fan. They had never, he added in conclusion, quarreled about the children. As a mother, Fanny was above reproach.

On June 6, on a day when the Sedgwicks' house in Lenox was full of company, Pierce's letter reached Elizabeth. She answered it at once, though half a dozen conversations were going on within earshot. Of course, she would write to Fanny, and, she hoped, with good effect. She would also show Pierce's letter to her husband as soon as they had a moment to themselves.

Not even Catharine Sedgwick, who was now in Europe with her ailing brother Robert and his wife, not even Mrs. Jameson, or Harriet St. Ledger, knew more of the Fanny problem than did Elizabeth. She had always counseled patience and an active good will on either side. A year earlier, while visiting Butler Place, Elizabeth remonstrated with Fanny for the cold reception she gave Pierce when he came home, ill, from Philadelphia. Why, her husband Charles would simply *die* if she treated him like that, Elizabeth had said! Fanny's excuse was lame; she was always tongue tied when she felt most deeply, she declared. To Pierce, Elizabeth spoke of Fanny's deceptively chilly manner while he was driving her to town at the end of her visit. She urged him to spend more of his time at home, to which he replied, rather pathetically, that his presence only seemed to make his wife unhappy.

All of this Elizabeth retailed in a long, eloquent plea for sanity, for rationality. She pointed out to Fanny how much she had to be thankful for: prosperity, a husband who loved her, even if he did not always show it, and above all, two beautiful children. Fanny had no right to desert them, since she had "voluntarily put herself in the way of becoming a mother." Suppose she actually went away and took Sarah with her, wouldn't Sarah, who even now was so precocious, soon reproach her for what she had done? Fanny's outlook was morbid. From her mother, whose fate should be a warning to her, she had inherited tendencies which could be combatted and curbed by an effort of the will. "My poor dear Fanny," Elizabeth urged, "my precious, my almost idolized friend, do let me persuade you that your mind is diseased."

The word, diseased, did not occur in the letter Charles Sedgwick wrote to Fanny. He only begged her, "for the sake of all who love and trust you," not to yield to her present impulses, since he was sure they would not last. He seconded Elizabeth's recommendation that Fanny should come to Lenox—"come at once."

Fanny was only too glad to come. As soon as Pierce had left for Virginia she and the children set off for the Berkshires. There, as always, her spirits rose. Elizabeth had reminded her of something her own daughter, Kate the Younger, had said: that she, Fanny, would never be completely happy, no matter what the circumstances were. Fanny had agreed to that, nor did she need to be told of her likeness to her mother. One reason for her disapproval of the theatre was that its excitement might lead to just such a breakdown as Marie Thérèse had suffered.

One evening at the Sedgwicks there was a discussion of hypnotism, animal magnetism, as it was then called. Fanny said that her husband had a magnetic effect upon her, as did others to whom she was devoted. A letter to one of these, Harriet St. Ledger, was almost lighthearted. With one heavy exception, Fanny wrote, she had all she could ask for on this side of the water: "good friends, my precious children, and an easy, cheerful, cultivated society." Fanny, who, while in Lenox, thought nothing of riding seventeen miles a day, also listed among her blessings her "capital" horse, Forrester, who was "a bright bay, tall and large, and built like a hunter. . . . He grins with delight, like a dog, when I talk to him and pat him." [3]

In the autumn, reunited with Pierce, Fanny seemed to at least one superficial observer to be on good terms with her husband.

Joshua Francis Fisher, Pierce's schoolboy comrade, drove out to call at Butler Place, bringing with him his cousin Sidney Fisher, the diarist, who had met Fanny before her marriage and admired her, even though he disapproved of stage folk in the holy of holies of society. The Fishers were charmed with the cordiality of their reception, and an animated debate on the intrinsic qualities of true art took place, Fanny maintaining that art should always be an exact copy of nature.

"She is a very gifted person," Fisher journalized, "and her qualities of heart and character are as excellent as those of her intellect." Pierce, also, was "extremely gentlemanlike in manner, and has, I think, many excellent traits of character; great energy and firmness with good feeling." [4]

Fisher concluded his account with a familiar pronouncement: the Butlers were very rich and lived in handsome style.

But were they as rich as they seemed? The economy of the United States was in recession; Fanny's household budget had been reduced, and she complained to Mrs. Jameson of being short of "pin money." As always, Fanny thought of earning something by publication, possibly of her play, *An English Tragedy*, which had been rejected for Covent Garden by its manager, William Charles Macready. Macready, however, considered the tragedy "one of the most powerful of the modern plays," which had come across his desk. Though full of "poetry and pathos," its subject matter was too painful, too "shocking." The script was now in the hands of Harriet St. Ledger, but Fanny wondered if an American editor might not find it interesting.

Yet another manuscript was at hand, far richer, far more bulky. Ever since her return from Georgia, Fanny had been copying and expanding her diary notes; she had done a great deal of work on the "Letters to Elizabeth" while at Lenox, and one may assume that her friends there had been allowed to look over her shoulder. The question of publication, a mighty question, need not be immediately considered, for Fanny felt her stint was incomplete. Pierce intended to go South again, and Fanny fully expected to go with him. She would take her opus with her; she would gather fresh material.

Soon after the first of November 1839, Butler Place was closed for the winter, and Pierce and his family went to stay for a few weeks in the house on Chestnut Street. The weeks went by; Christmas and New Years came and went. Whether Pierce was actually ill, as he later averred, or whether bad health was merely an excuse for dawdling is uncertain. Fanny became restless. She rode alone on horseback through the poorer sections of the city and along the wharves, in spite of Pierce's telling her this was both risky and unladylike. It was also unladylike for a woman to worry over finances and pursue her husband with questions. Fanny wrote to her father, asking him to let her use the income from the funds she had handed over to him on quitting the stage and which had been deposited in a Philadelphia bank. At present, she remarked, disparagingly, they were all living at John Butler's expense—Pierce had refused to say why.

It was not until after the first of February that the Butler brothers departed for the islands, too late in the season to take womenfolk or children with them. Fanny went back to Butler Place, to more solitary rides on Forrester, and to lonely, uncompanioned evenings after the children had been put to bed. Her heart softened toward Pierce when she heard of his continued sufferings. She had hoped he would be better when "freed from the gloom and disquietude which my thrice unhappy temperament seems to throw over you. . . . Oh, my dearest, what can be done for you?" [5] Fanny suggested a trip to a European spa, and that John Butler would be glad to go abroad with his brother. She did not offer to go herself.

While he was in Georgia, Pierce also heard from Elizabeth Sedgwick. Without showing Pierce's letter to her friend—that would have been a breach of confidence—Elizabeth felt she had convinced Fanny of her husband's concern and of his sincerity. Her present mood of remorse was a healthful sign. To make sure that the cure was permanent, Elizabeth besought both husband and wife "to know each other's hearts completely."

Thus, throughout the winter, there had been constant communication between Lenox and Philadelphia, between Lenox and Butler Place. In this way Fanny learned of a tragic loss to herself and to the antislavery cause. On a night in January of 1840, a Long Island steamboat caught fire; only four of the passengers and crew escaped, and among those who perished was Carl Follen, Dr. Channing's friend and Fanny's, in Channing's estimation "an almost perfect man." A memorial service was planned, but Follen had been so identified with abolitionism that no church in Boston, not even Channing's own, would open its doors. Only after three months had gone by was a service held in an obscure chapel in Marlborough, and by that time Channing's oration, a tribute to his friend, was in print. A copy had been sent to Fanny by one of the Lenox group. She kept it by her for frequent rereading, just as she frequently consulted Follen, in imagination, asking him whether what she had in mind was right or wrong.

Whether it was right or wrong for a beneficent deity to impose suffering on the human race, Channing could not say. His sermon, however, insisted on the necessity for relieving all wretchedness which was due to human frailty. To Carl Follen, the most grievous sight in the world was not "misery in its most agonizing forms, but the sight of man oppressed, trodden down by his brother." To lift him up and make him free was "the grandest work on earth." [6] Channing did not specify that the lifted man should be black, but no one could mistake the connotation.

Meanwhile, in New Haven, Connecticut, some fifty black men were on trial for murder and were in danger of being returned to slavery. Kidnapped, illegally landed, and illegally sold, in Cuba, the human cargo of a Portuguese ship, the *Amistad*, had risen up, seized weapons from their sleeping guards, and killed the captain of the vessel. The steersmen were chained on deck and bidden to head for Africa, but after the sun had gone down they steered in the opposite direction. Eventually the *Amistad* was overhauled by a United States brig and convoyed to the nearest port. The case brought against the mutineers was complicated, involving, as it did, marine law and jurisdictional and extraditional issues. The abolitionists provided able counsel and after an interpreter had been found, gave the story of the Africans some colorful publicity. The decision of the court, however, went against them.

Fanny heard from Elizabeth that the case would be appealed and she handed on this information to Theodore Sedgwick III, who was a lawyer in New York, a son of Theodore II and grandson of Judge Theodore I. He had been active in behalf of the *Amistad* prisoners and had just sent Fanny a review he had written of an antislavery book by William Jay. "Your very name pledges you in some sort to the cause," she told him.[7]

When, in March 1841, the men of the *Amistad* were freed, old John Quincy Adams having argued their case before the Supreme Court, Fanny was unaware of their victory and thought they had been sent back to Havana. Again she had spent a large part of the summer in Lenox, while Pierce was in Virginia. She had shared in the joyful return of the Sedgwick party from Europe, where full use had been made of the many letters of introduction she had supplied. Catharine had not only renewed and fortified her friendship with Mrs. Jameson, she had also met Harriet St. Ledger.

To Harriet, Fanny wrote that the publication of her *Plantation Journal* had been urged. "I have sometimes been haunted with the idea that it is an imperative duty," Fanny wrote, "knowing what I know and having seen what I have seen . . . to show the dangers and the evils of this frightful institution. And the testimony of a planter's wife . . . should carry with it some authority."[8]

On the other hand, being a planter's wife, and having been allowed to visit the islands on sufferance, it would be unfair and also unwise to publish the "Journal" without the consent of the Butler family, an almost impossible proviso. Fanny no longer spoke of slavery to "the people with whom I live," since to do so only ended in passionate appeals on her part, silence or sharp rebuttal on the other. Once more, Fanny begged the question by saying that she might revise and enlarge her impressions if she went South, which again seemed a definite possibility. No book of hers, she was sure, could be of as much practical use to the poor people of the plantations as her residence among them. She did not want anything to interfere with that.

But, according to Fanny, some drastic interference came from John Butler, who said his sister-in-law should never see the islands again; she had had a bad effect upon the slaves; she had disrupted discipline.

Pierce Butler's *Statement* tells a different tale. In November, and after Fanny had communicated with Harriet, a request came for her to contribute something in writing which could be sold at an antislavery fair in Philadelphia. Pierce "represented to her the shameless indelicacy on the part of the abolitionists in attempting to enlist the wife of a slave owner. I told her it would be impossible for her to go south." It might even be unsafe for Pierce to go, unless he went on record with a contrary opinion. This might embarrass him, "since very few could believe that it was out of a husband's power to control his wife."

Fanny, however, sent an autographed contribution of some sort to the Philadelphia fair, and as it turned out, Pierce did not need to vindicate himself in the eyes of the slaveocracy. Hopes of going to England had been deferred when John Kemble wrote that because Adelaide had engagements to sing in Naples, Palermo, Malta, and Constantinople, neither she nor her father would be in England until after Easter, 1841. A later bulletin told of Charles Kemble's return to England and of his serious illness; if Fanny wished to see him again, she must hurry. She, Pierce, and the two children sailed on December 10. That all of them went was made possible through the good offices of "an older member of the Butler family," in all probability Pierce's Aunt Eliza, who had shared the rigors of the Southern journey in 1838 and who may have thought that a complete change of scene might lessen domestic tension for her favorite nephew.

CHAPTER XII

HOUSES IN PICCADILLY

(December 1840–May 1843)

CHARLES KEMBLE was not only alive when the Butlers reached England on December 20, 1840, he was well on the way to recovery. After a short stay at the Clarendon Hotel, Pierce rented a house on Clarges Street. Charles came to recuperate; John and Henry Kemble came to visit. John was living the frugal life of a scholar at Addlestone with his wife Natalia and his two children. He had succeeded his father as official Examiner of Plays and was editor of a liberal, privately supported quarterly, *The British and Foreign Review*. Henry was far less strenuously occupied by his military duties in Ireland—a charming fellow, a splendid horseman; he and Fanny made a dashing pair on London's bridle paths.

When, in May, Adelaide Kemble arrived from Italy, where she had been singing at San Carlo and La Scala, the house on Clarges Street became the center of what Fanny described as "a musical maelstrom." Adelaide seemed almost a stranger. She was handsome in a foreign way; she had even acquired an accent during the years she had spent on the Continent. It was Adelaide's ambition to retire to Italy as soon as she had accumulated a competence; England seemed so cold, its skies so melancholy.

Engagements to sing in London multiplied. Adelaide appeared at Buckingham Palace, at a Polish benefit, arranged by the

Duchess of Sutherland, and at a great fete given by the Duke of Wellington to King Frederick William IV of Prussia. Fellow artists, critics, and promotors found their way to Clarges Street. During one of the many informal musical evenings there Fanny went upstairs to look in at the nursery; she found Sarah wide awake. "Well, how many angels have you got down there, I would like to know?" Sarah asked.[1] Her elder daughter, Fanny informed one of her American friends, was now "a strapping girl, with blue eyes and a billow of light hair, and manners that are like nothing in the world but those of Brinhilda [sic] in the *Nibelungenlied*." [2]

Adelaide's voice was small. Fanny felt it had been strained to include the high notes necessary for such roles as that of Bellini's Norma. She was often moved to tears, however, when she heard her sister sing. They shared a common outlook, but Adelaide was "a thousand times quicker, keener, finer, shrewder, and sweeter than I am." [3] There was no room for jealousy in Fanny's heart, though now she saw herself a secondary object of interest and admiration.

A debut at Covent Garden had been scheduled for November. During the summer Adelaide made a tour of the Rhineland, appearing frequently with a handsome, rising young pianist, Franz Liszt. The Butler family and a group of Kemble friends and admirers followed Adelaide about. To Fanny, the Rhineland seemed far less beautiful than the Hudson, except, perhaps, for its garnish of medieval castles, and they were merely relics of a barbaric past.

Wherever she went Fanny carried with her the image of America; it was always more resplendent when seen from a distance. News from American friends arrived by every packet. In October a letter reached Fanny at her new London address in Harley Street, the purport of which she confided to Pierce. A friend of Dr. Channing and of the Sedgwicks, Mrs. Lydia Maria Child, had asked permission to print part of Fanny's Georgian

Journal in the periodical that she was editing in New York, *The Antislavery Standard*.

Though Fanny and Lydia Maria Child had never met, they were well known to one another by reputation. Rumor of Fanny's experiences in the South had traveled far; letters she had written while in Georgia to the wife of Carl Follen and to Mary Appleton had been read at antislavery meetings in Boston, on the outskirts of which, at Cottage Place in Roxbury, the Childs had made their home before moving to New York. A writer of popular novels, of household manuals and children's books, an editor of the first American children's magazine, Mrs. Child was considered such an important author that she was granted a reading card by the Boston Athenaeum. This was hastily withdrawn when, in 1833, her *Appeal in Favor of that Class of Americans Called Africans* was published. A copy of the *Appeal* was removed from the shelves of the Athenaeum with a pair of fire tongs and was thrown out the window; copies of earlier works, such as *The American Frugal Housewife*, which was in its thirty-third edition, were burned in the South, and Mrs. Child was invited by an outraged Southern lady to visit Atlanta, Georgia, where she could have lodgings in the calaboose "with as much nigger company" as she desired.

Pierce was not only scandalized, he was also alarmed, when Fanny showed him her answer to the request from *The Antislavery Standard*. She could not send her "plantation diary," she had written: if she had felt at liberty to publish that, she would have done so long ago! In its stead, she offered the travel letters she had written on her way to Georgia; they would be of interest to *Standard* readers, since they contained much firsthand observation of slavery.

Having, in honor bound—and in defiance—shown her letter to her husband, Fanny gave it to him to post. Pierce threw it into the back of a drawer; there Fanny found it several weeks later. Her anger blazed. A second letter to Mrs. Child, telling all the circumstances, was written and dispatched. If this were pub-

lished, Pierce could see himself set in the stocks, for every abolitionist and every successful tamer of wives to view. He wrote at
once to Elizabeth Sedgwick, begging her to intervene, to communicate with Mrs. Child, and to expostulate with Fanny. Only
after she had heard from Elizabeth, who advised restraint, did
Fanny consent to break her promise of sending the travel letters.
She bitterly condemned herself and her lack of steadfastness.
"However great your contempt may be for my want of purpose," she told Mrs. Child, "it cannot possibly exceed my own." [4]

Nearly every letter from America told of antislavery activities,
and nearly every letter spoke of homecoming. Having been
abroad for more than a year, Fanny was anxious to return. The
depression of 1837 was unresolved. The Bank of the United
States in Philadelphia, in which Kemble funds had been deposited, had, for a time, closed its doors. Fanny felt Pierce should
attend to his affairs in person, but he was, as ever, uncommuni-
cative in financial affairs and vague in promises of departure.

Pierce had thoroughly enjoyed his stay in England, in particular, his contact with distinguished persons. In March 1842,
the Butlers were invited to spend ten days at Belvoir Castle, the
country seat of the Duke of Rutland, where a military band
marched around the castle every morning to rouse the guests
from sleep and again in the evening to summon them to dinner.
The Duke, and Lady Londonderry, made an arrangement for
Fanny to be presented at Court, in feathers, train, and a full
complement of jewels, hired for the occasion. Pierce was also
presented by Edward Everett, the American minister; greatly to
the disapproval of the children's American nurse, he went down
on one knee to kiss the hand of Queen Victoria.

Fanny did not object to contact with dukes and duchesses, but
she considered their existence an anachronism. In describing her
stay at Belvoir to Theodore Sedgwick, she wrote that aristocrats were "pretty, pleasant, gay, grand, and in some of their

aspects good," but if he wanted to see them as they were now, in all their splendor, he had better hurry.

As a result of her varied excursions into high society, Fanny received a bill from her dressmaker for £97, a sizable sum. Pierce showed no sign of paying it. Fanny determined to settle the account herself. She contributed a review of a book by Victor Hugo to John Kemble's quarterly. Inspired by the performance of the dancer, Fanny Elsler, whom she had seen in Philadelphia, Fanny wrote a ballet, based on the legend of Pocahontas. This she handed over to her father, who, to her sorrow and commiseration, was once more the manager of Covent Garden. Fanny also adapted a melodrama by Dumas, *Mademoiselle de Belle Isle,* for the London stage and was receptive to a suggestion from Charles that she should write an original play of her own, a sequel to *The Stranger,* a drama by August Friedrich Ferdinand von Kotzebue.

Kotzebue's *Stranger,* an early nineteenth-century example of the problem play, had been enormously succesful in England. At its close, an erring wife grovels at the feet of her husband. He raises her in his arms; he embraces her as the curtain falls. Has he really forgiven her? Is it right for him to do so? Fanny pondered these questions. Men, she realized, had always considered faithlessness to the marriage vow as the one unforgivable sin of which a woman was capable. She had to admit that the security of the family and the rights of inheritance and property were involved, but these were questions of social expediency. She could well imagine other, more serious, transgressions.

An idea for continuing the Kotzebue play occurred to Fanny one morning while she was brushing her hair. Yes, the husband, a good man, if there ever was one, might forgive his wife, but it was very unlikely that they would live happily ever after. They had children, whom the woman had abandoned to follow her lover: they, in turn, would come to judge her far more harshly than did their father.

In the heat of inspiration, Fanny looked around for writing

materials and seized on a child's copy book, which belonged to Sarah and which was lying on the dressing table. She began to sketch the outline of her play, but soon desisted. The theme undoubtedly cut too deep. During one of their altercations Pierce had threatened a separation, something which Fanny had suggested in the past, and of which Elizabeth Sedgwick had pointed out the consequences. There was no question of a lover; Fanny had no desires in that direction, but she could not abandon either of her children now: her valkyrie Sarah, her "little white mouse" of a Fan, who, being less robust and less forward than her sister, was equally appealing. Fan and Sarah were the legal property of their father. To be separated from him would mean being separated from them.

Under stress of these considerations, Fanny's state of mind bordered on panic. One evening when Pierce was out—he often went out alone and was sometimes absent for days at a time— Fanny sat, doing worsted work, in a room on the ground floor of the house. Though she wanted to go upstairs, she could not bring herself to do so. "I fancied," she wrote to Harriet, "that every step of the stairs would have morsels of flesh lying on it, and the banisters would be all smeared with blood and hairs. In short, I had a fit of the horrors." [5]

This was no hallucination. Fanny was convinced of the unreality of her vision, but for a few moments she thought of sending for a cab and driving to Covent Garden, where she could sit in Adelaide's dressing room while Adelaide was singing on its stage. Somewhat earlier Adelaide had considered going with the Butlers for a tour of America; now, however, she was engaged to be married to an eligible young man, Edward Sartoris, who was not only well off, but who also made his home in Italy. For her sister to give up her profession for matrimony seemed a sad exchange to Fanny; to her, all marriages were suspect.

Twice, according to Pierce, Fanny tried to break out of the net. In April she left for Liverpool to engage a passage, but he hurried after her, overtook her at Birmingham, and persuaded her to wait until they could all go together. The second "desertion" was in July. Pierce learned from the cabby who had driven Fanny to the railroad station that she had taken a train bound for Southampton. He thought she had gone to her brother John's and again caught up with her. Some money was forthcoming for Fanny to visit friends in Edinburgh, taking Sarah with her, but the amount was so small that she was able to stay for only a very short time. She and Pierce met in Liverpool; once more peace was patched up on the understanding that they would sail in October.

The chore of packing was actually underway, and the Butlers were staying temporarily at the Clarendon Hotel, when, for reasons unspecified, Pierce changed his mind. He took a house in Upper Grosvenor Street, near Hyde Park, near also to the home of Mr. and Mrs. Edward Sartoris. Though she was now married, Adelaide had consented to fill out another season at Covent Garden before migrating to Italy.

Fanny went to stay with her sister. Though she saw her children every day, her meetings with Pierce were rare and perfunctory.

Letters went back and forth. Fanny made a fervent appeal. "Our position is so perilous," she wrote. "I look at our children and tremble lest God should strike them for our sins . . . For God's sake, and for your children's sake, Pierce, my husband, oh, still most tenderly beloved, let us be wise before it is too late." To this Pierce replied: "On my soul and conscience, I have done everything in my power to make you happy . . . I have not succeeded. . . . The fault has been entirely your own. . . . If you will govern your irritable temper, and if you can consent to submit your will to mine, we may be reconciled and happy. I firmly believe that husband and wife cannot live happily together upon any other terms." [6]

The terms were harsh. On the score of temper, Fanny was ever humble; she admitted that to curb her irritability would give her "severe moral labor" until she died, and she could not promise a complete success. As for Pierce's second condition of unquestioning obedience—"I am sorry to say that I cannot entertain this proposition for a moment. I consider it my duty not to submit my conduct to any other human being."

The old, the fundamental, deadlock had been reached. Adelaide attempted to break it by calling upon Pierce in person. She would soon be leaving London, and Fanny must find another abiding place. It was Fanny's suggestion that she should come to live in the Grosvenor Street house, but not as Pierce's wife. She could never look upon him with indifference. She could never forget that he once had been her lover and was the father of her children. "I cannot behold you without emotion," she wrote. "My heart still answers to your voice, my blood in my veins to your footsteps." But the emotion thus magnetically aroused was only anguish, an unendurable pain from which Fanny begged relief. If Pierce would not receive her, perhaps he would give her enough wherewithal to take lodgings in the same house as her father.

This Pierce was loath to do. He had never appealed to Charles Kemble for help, thinking him "a man of mild and gentle disposition and in no way calculated to control the very opposite nature of his daughter." [7] Pierce did not reject either of Fanny's proposals, but had not communicated with her when there came a midnight knock at his door. The servants had all gone to bed. Pierce opened to find Fanny standing on the threshold. With nothing but pride in her pocket, she had come to stay. A maid had to be roused to make up a bed for her.

For weeks thereafter, Mr. and Mrs. Pierce Butler came and went and accepted or refused invitations without consulting one another. Their alienation was widely known, but as long as appearances were maintained, they were considered a single social unit.

Fanny got much advice, some kindly meant, some the reverse. One of her older women friends, Lady Dacre, whom she affectionately addressed as "granny," begged her to be less outspoken in her condemnation of slavery, Fanny having read aloud to her and to members of her family selections from the *Plantation Journal*. A member of the beau monde and its chronicler, a Kemble acquaintance of many years' standing, was less sympathetic. The famous memoirs in diary form of Charles Greville, an unexpurgated version of which did not appear until 1938, contains a caustic comment upon Fanny. Greville notes that in December of 1842 he had seen a good deal lately of Mrs. Butler, who "has discovered that she has married a weak, dawdling, ignorant, violent tempered man, who is utterly unsuited to her, and she to him. . . . With all her prodigious talents, her fine feelings and noble sentiments and lively imagination, she has no tact, no judgment, no discretion. She has acted like a fool." [8]

Fanny's chief foolishness had, according to Greville, consisted in expressing her detestation of slavery, which "laudable though it might be," had given great offense to Pierce, who was a great slave proprietor and who "was ruining himself by his lazy, stupid management of his affairs."

Thus spake the voice of worldly convention. And there were others than Adelaide who tried to remedy the unhappy and unseemly state of affairs in Grosvenor Street. Mary Appleton, who had been in England for some time and who was now married to a Scotchman, Mr. Robert Mackintosh, went to Pierce with an offer from Fanny to obey him in every particular, except in matters of conscience—and the only serious matter of conscience which Fanny could imagine was slavery. Fanny would, presumably, cease to nag her husband on the subject of a return to America.

This particular cause for nagging was removed when in early spring Pierce actually engaged a passage and did not cancel it a few weeks later. At the same time he announced a reduction in their scale of living. Butler Place had been leased and they would live in a boardinghouse in Philadelphia. On hearing this, Sarah wept, and even Fanny, who had led such a peripatetic life, expressed regret for the only home she had ever had in the United States.

Economy would not begin at once, however. To prove that the breach had been healed and that Pierce Butler was once more in control of his wife, two large soirees were given, to which two hundred people were invited. Among those present, in black satin and ringlets, was Miss Hall, the governess, whom Pierce had put in charge of Sarah and Fan and who would go with the family to America.

CHAPTER XIII

ENEMIES AND FRIENDS

(May 1843–February 1844)

FROM HER ENGLISH ASSOCIATES, Fanny had heard words of praise for William Ellery Channing. The latest edition of the Doctor's sermons had been lent her by Charles Greville, who, apparently, was less irritated by Channing's lack of worldly wisdom than by Fanny's.

Although her ship was bound for Boston, Fanny could not look forward to another meeting with her revered friend. Channing had died on October 2, 1842. From Elizabeth Sedgwick had come an account of the Doctor's last visit to Lenox, where he spent a month in the rooms Fanny usually occupied at the Inn. Weekly meetings for religious discussion were held in the Sedgwicks' house, a custom established some years earlier by Carl Follen.

On August 1, the ninth anniversary of the day the British Emancipation Edict became law in the colonies, Channing preached a sermon in the Lenox Church, reminding his listeners of a century-old testimony against slavery, delivered by a Housatonic minister at Great Barrington. In days gone by Channing himself had mulled this matter over with his friend, Henry Dwight Sedgwick, now deceased. Like Henry Dwight, Channing called for an amendment to the Constitution, banning slavery. He had urged the move in a recent pamphlet, *The Duty of the Free States*. If the Southern bloc in Congress would not agree, let them leave the Union, let them go in peace. This was the proposal which had so shocked Catharine Sedgwick when it was first suggested by her English visitor, the redoubtable Miss Harriet Martineau, but which was now acceptable to her and many others.

With the politically minded wing of the abolitionist movement, which had held conventions in upper New York State in the summer of 1840, which had formed a Liberty party, and which had presented a presidential candidate at the last election, Channing had little sympathy. At heart an anarchist, he distrusted all political activity, unless, as in the case of the emancipation edict, it could be accomplished without violence.

Those who heard Channing speak to this effect at Lenox did not realize that this was a swan song. Having been a semi-invalid most of his life, this frail little man might live forever! Two months later, however, the end came tranquilly at Bennington, Vermont. Channing's body was taken to Boston for a crowded memorial service and was buried in Mount Auburn Cemetery.

To Mount Auburn Cemetery Fanny went as soon as she set foot on American soil. When in the area she never failed to visit the grave of her Aunt Adelaide De Camp, the saint she adored and longed to emulate when, as now, she felt that most of her troubles were due to her "undisciplined and imperfect character." [1] Fanny flung herself face down upon the grave.

Dall's loving kindness and self-sacrifice seemed to rise from the ground. There was need of these emanations when, on reaching Philadelphia, Fanny found herself the inhabitant of a boardinghouse. The American boardinghouse was an institution of which she had frequently complained. It lacked privacy; it had no facilities for entertaining friends, except on a very modest scale. To these drawbacks were added, for the dispossessed mistress of Butler Place, no garden to tend, no fields to roam, and no horse to ride; Fanny's gallant Forrester had been sold to a livery stable.

For exercise, Fanny walked the city streets until the summer ripened and the heat from the pavement scorched the soles of her feet. Her children drooped. Pierce at length took notice and removed them all to Yellow Springs, a dilapidated resort in Chester County. There the temperature was that of Philadelphia, but at least there was a clear, cold pool in which one could bathe. When Pierce came out for the following weekend all returned with him to town.

Fanny, at least, could not complain that her friends had deserted her. In Boston she had been met by Elizabeth Sedgwick and by Elizabeth's daughter Kate, newly married to a Boston Lawyer, and a family connection, William Minot. The news of Kate's engagement had sent Catharine Sedgwick to bed for a few days until she could reconcile herself to such a grievous loss. Had she, perhaps, reserved for her beloved niece her own self-imposed role as vestal virgin of the family hearth? In July and August, when, by rights, she should have been in Lenox, Catharine visited Fanny in Philadelphia. While there she wrote two long letters to Anna Jameson.

Anna lived in St. John's Wood, and it is more than probable that she was present at one of the farewell receptions the Butlers gave before leaving London. A fellow guest at these functions was the children's governess, Miss Hall. Because of the independent life that Pierce had led, even before their estrangement, and because of his reluctance to go back to America, Fanny suspected a liaison. To Mrs. Jameson, Miss Hall seemed a likely suspect, and her surmise had been passed on to Catharine.

Catharine, however, thought that Anna was mistaken. Miss Hall was much too drab to be Pierce's mistress: a well-meaning woman, dull and narrow minded, who stood in awe of Fanny's ill-concealed hostility. While Catharine had no doubt of Pierce's being involved with some "licentious woman," and possibly with more than one, she saw Miss Hall as merely his obsequious tool.

The children were kept so busy by their instructress that except for a short walk early in the morning or late in the evening, there was no time when their mother could have them to herself. Once Fanny took Sarah with her to the Unitarian Church, where an antislavery sermon was preached by William Henry Furness. If Pierce got wind of this, Fanny was sure Sarah would be forbidden to go a second time. She would have liked, of course, to take the children to Lenox, but they were whisked away instead to a farm Pierce owned in Chester County. If Fanny went alone to the Berkshires, she must pay for the trip herself.

While in England Fanny had sold a collection of her verse and she had enough in pocket, apparently, for present needs. In September she asked Theodore Sedgwick to see if Harper Brothers would bring out an American edition of her poems. Fanny had come to relie heavily on Theodore for advice in financial and legal matters. She had read one of his speeches that had found its way into print, probably his *Thoughts on the Proposed Annexation of Texas*, which first appeared in the *New York Evening Post*, as one of a series of essays, signed Veto. The long Texas debate had shown signs of coming to a favorable vote, since two Southern senators, Walker of Mississippi and Preston of South Carolina, had providentially discovered that Texas was part of the Louisiana Purchase of 1803. Theodore's reactions were similar to Dr. Channing's, but unlike Dr. Channing, Theodore was politically concerned. He had joined the Whig party in 1836, and though he despised slavery and saw it as a key issue, he could not call himself, strictly speaking, an abolitionist. The admission of Texas he saw as a threat to the Union; it might encourage the Southern states to secede. And there were also international risks involved. How would England view this move toward American aggrandizement?

"I read your speech with great pleasure," Fanny wrote; "it was good in every way . . . I cannot give up my hope and confidence in the institutions of your country. They are the expectation of the world, and if Americans themselves, by word or deed, proclaim their scheme of free government a failure, it seems to me that the future condition of the human race is ominously darkened . . . God bless you and prosper you in every good work." [2]

Fanny also told Theodore that she was not going alone to Lenox, but was taking with her an old friend, Margery O'Brien, the Irish girl who had gone with the Butlers to Georgia as the children's nurse. Not long after that momentous winter, Fanny had had to part with Margery. She had discovered that Sarah, who, like herself, had a turn for religion, had been taught to say *Hail Mary*. Though Fanny had no objection to her daughter's becoming a Catholic later in life, she did not want her to be influenced at such an early age. Servant and mistress, Unitarian and papist had nevertheless kept in touch with one another. While she was abroad Fanny heard of Margery's marriage and of her divorce from a brutal and worthless husband; for this step, she had been disowned by her devoutly orthodox family. Poor and ill, wasted by consumption, Margery might get even more benefit from Lenox than Fanny expected for herself. For both of them, their stay would be short.

On her return from the Happy Valley, Fanny went to Theodore Sedgwick's house in New York and there met the man who had refused to produce her play, *An English Tragedy*.

Throughout most of his theatrical life, the English actor, William Charles Macready, kept a diary, a safety valve by which the steam of his dissatisfactions could escape. Macready was a good hater, and most of his hatreds were due to professional jealousy. As a young man, he had played with Sarah Siddons, and later with Charles Kemble at Covent Garden. Charles, with whom Macready once almost came to blows, was "an old coxcomb." Macready's feelings for Fanny were mixed. He had read her *Journal* of 1835 and thought it "vulgar and trashy." He had, however, turned down her tragedy with regret and when he called upon her later in London was impressed by her "frank and genuine manner." After a long conversation, this hard-to-please commentator wrote that he had rarely exchanged ideas with a person he liked so much. Having heard in England of the Butlers' marital troubles, Macready did not venture to inquire for Pierce when he met Fanny at the Sedgwicks'.

A few days later, however, the actor was invited to dine with both of the Butlers at the Astor House. There were other guests: Mr. William Cullen Bryant, Editor of the *New York Evening Post*, who might be useful at the start of Macready's second tour of the American theatre, and a Harvard professor, Mr. Henry Wadsworth Longfellow and his bride of two months, who had been Fanny's companion so often at Lenox, Fanny Appleton.

Talk at table was animated, and Macready again admired Fanny's conversational brilliance. "Mrs. Butler spoke admirably well," he wrote, "but quite like a man. She is a woman of most extraordinary mind. What she said on most subjects was true—the stern truth, but what in the spirit of charity should not have been said in the presence of one who was obliged to listen to it—alas!" [3]

And the one who, alas, was obliged to listen to it was undoubtedly Pierce Butler, with whom Macready, an aggressively masculine individual, instinctively aligned himself. Macready did not record the subjects discussed. One can only guess what they were—but did Fanny perhaps mention Longfellow's latest book? It had been written during a long voyage home from Europe, a collection of antislavery poems, the last of the series addressed to Dr. Channing, whom Longfellow thought was still alive and still speaking out against:

> The old and chartered lie,
> The feudal curse, whose whips and yokes
> Insult humanity.

It was to be expected that Macready would see the Butlers again in Philadelphia, where he was going to act *Macbeth* at the Walnut Street Theatre with America's latest Queen of the Stage,

Miss Charlotte Cushman. Macready had not yet met Miss Cushman, but Fanny had seen a good deal of her and had applauded and encouraged her during an earlier engagement in Philadelphia. Charlotte had been a pupil of Elizabeth Sedgwick, but before Fanny became intimately acquainted with the school. The latter's sponsorship, however, meant much to a young woman who had had no prestigious family to launch her career and who had worshipped Fanny from the topmost gallery of a New York theatre. A warmhearted, exuberant soul, Charlotte was prone to emotional friendships with those of her own sex. Fanny's response to some of her advances had been tepid, but she was very much touched when, on her return from Lenox, she found her room at the boardinghouse had been decorated with flowers. Since the Cushman repertoire was scheduled to include some of the plays which Fanny herself had made famous, she sent Charlotte a girdle and headdress she had worn as Julia in Sheridan Knowles's play, *The Hunchback.* For eight years now these memorabilia had been packed away in a trunk at Butler Place.

When, late in October, Macready arrived and rehearsals began, he conceded to Charlotte a mind which was sympathetic to his own, though he thought she still had much to learn of her art. He could not help noticing, as others had, a strong facial resemblance to himself. Both Macbeth and his lady in the Walnut Street production had squared jaws and broad and bulging foreheads.

Soon, however, Macready began to carp. Charlotte, a born partisan, had spoken to him indignantly of Pierce Butler's ill treatment of his wife. Having seen what he had seen and heard what he had heard at the Astor House, Macready was sure there were faults on both sides. He was also convinced that in any contest between the sexes the woman should be the peacemaker and the first to yield.

It was not until November 6 that Macready, who wished to avoid involvement, made up his mind to call upon the Butlers. He may have been relieved to find that only Mrs. Butler was at home and that she had a guest who was staying with her, Miss Catharine Sedgwick, the novelist. For a time a three-cornered conversation was pleasantly trivial, but when Macready asked Fanny what she was writing and told her she should be turning out powerful dramas that would have an influence on society, Fanny began to cry.

Macready withdrew at once. He could not realize how cruel, how ironic, his exhortation to write something that would influence society seemed. A week earlier Fanny had notified Pierce of her determination to ask for a legal separation. She had also consulted Theodore Sedgwick, who advised a settlement out of court. He called on Pierce, who happened to be ill in bed, and on November 6, the day of Macready's call, Theodore was writing from New York, accepting in Fanny's name and with her consent, the terms Pierce had laid down. In return for a separate establishment under the same roof as her children, Fanny would promise not to act upon the stage, not to openly advocate the cause of abolition, and not to publish anything of which Pierce disapproved. The sum of twenty-five hundred dollars per annum, about a third of Pierce's current income, would be paid in quarterly installments, Theodore Sedgwick acting as financial intermediary.

But still William Charles Macready, increasingly dour and increasingly splenetic, continued to hear of Fanny's sufferings. Charlotte Cushman told him, for example, of having sent flowers to Fanny on her birthday, November 27. In thanking her, Fanny said this was the only remembrance she had received, and she was only glad that one more miserable year of her life had come to an end.

In asking for a separation, Fanny had accused Pierce of infidelity. She had found two letters addressed to her husband in a feminine hand. It is hard to believe Pierce's statement that the letters were among his papers and had never been opened; he accused Fanny of opening them. The letters were unsigned, but Charlotte Cushman had impulsively offered to get more definite evidence. She had either revealed or intimated her intentions to Macready, who cast her forthwith into outer darkness. Charlotte was "an *intriguante*," he wrote. He feared she might even compromise him, who was "a stranger in a strange land." Macready had no facts to go on, but emphasized his distrust of Charlotte by quoting Tom Brown's well-worn rhyme:

> I do not love thee, Doctor Fell,
> The reason why I cannot tell.[4]

CHAPTER XIV

A POINT OF DEPARTURE

(February 1844–September 1845)

CATHARINE SEDGWICK had written to Anna Jameson that Fanny would put up with her present humiliating situation only as long as she had access to her children. A move to get them back into her own unfettered hands was made when, on February 4, 1844, Theodore Sedgwick, who only three months earlier had advised a settlement out of court, notified Pierce Butler that Fanny would sue him for divorce on grounds of adultery. In his reply, Butler appealed to Theodore's sense of masculine solidarity. "Your own conscience," he wrote, "should teach you that a faithful legal adviser . . . should not lend himself to the angry passions and jealous fancies of an excited woman. . . . Even when the proofs of a husband's infidelity are undeniable, any honest lawyer and true friend would be anxious to soothe the indignant feelings of the injured wife." [1]

A written rejoinder to this reproof was sent back to New York unopened. Pierce now knew that all the Sedgwicks were against him. No less than four of them had visited Philadelphia during the last few months. When Elizabeth Sedgwick refused to eat at his table, saying she resented his treatment of Fanny as a friend, and as a woman, Pierce accused her of treachery. Her mind was diseased, and she must have caught the disease from her "idolized friend." He could not be discouraged, however, since God had given him a strength he had never felt before to do his duty toward Fanny and toward his children.

It was not like Pierce Butler to invoke God as an ally, and his doing so at this time may serve to date his return to the faith of his grandfather, whom Pierce's schoolmate, Joshua Francis Fisher, remembered as taking communion regularly at Christ's Church, Philadelphia. The old Major's eldest daughter, however, was an agnostic. Pierce's mother would not allow her children to read the Bible and only let them go to the Unitarian chapel because "they would hear very little of religion there."

"The Butlers never did have any religion," Pierce's Aunt Eliza said, when she heard of her nephew's having joined the Episcopal Church. "I think he must be crazy."

Be that as it may, Pierce did not allow himself to be intimidated by the threat of a divorce, and only a few weeks after Theodore's announcement he came close to being called into court himself as a correspondent. In March Pierce went on what was represented as a business trip to New York in company with a Mr. and Mrs. Schott and Mrs. Schott's sister, Mrs. Ridgway, who was considered one of the most beautiful ornaments of Philadelphia society. The party put up at the Astor House. On the day of arrival trouble arose in the Schott menage. The wife demanded a separate room from her husband, and the husband accused his wife of improper relations with Mr. Butler. Once, he later affirmed, while he was sick in bed, Mrs. Schott had spent the hours from 10.30 P.M. to 1 A.M. alone with Butler. Only the tears and entreaties of Mrs. Ridgway prevented her brother-in-law from taking immediate action.

Returned to Philadelphia, the foursome dispersed. Mrs. Schott went to the home of her father, Mr. Richard Willing, and preliminaries to a severance of the nuptial bond were set in motion. Schott did not impede them; to be parted from his wife was the greatest blessing which could be bestowed upon him, he thought. He was, however, bound over by the mayor to keep the peace, and in consequence, left Philadelphia for Baltimore. In a letter to his wife, telling her she had "fallen from her original purity and had forfeited all rights to protection," [2] Schott hinted that any blood which might be shed would rest upon her soul. Pierce Butler had also let Mrs. Ridgway know that he expected to be challenged to a duel. He would, of course, accept.

In due time, at Bladensburg, Maryland, the scene of many such affairs, and only five miles from the National Capital, the duel was fought. Schott and Butler were placed back to back by their seconds and were set in motion. At ten paces, they were commanded to wheel and fire. Though this maneuver was repeated, and Schott's seconds protested that he might be handicapped in wheeling by a sore foot, there were no casualties. Later there was talk of a combat between Schott and his ex-brother-in-law, a Willing. Though the affair never took place, a mock account of it was given in verse, concluding with the statement that:

> Between these heroes did ensue
> A duel fierce and hot
> For Schott shot Willing willingly,
> And Willing, he shot Schott.

But the duello as a means of settling quarrels between gentlemen could not be laughed out of existence—not just yet. Fanny considered it as much a token of barbarism as the castles which decorated the hilltops along the Rhine. She was shocked to find this form of premeditated murder condoned in the New World. Just before her arrival in Georgia in 1838 an affair of honor had ended fatally. The original dispute had had merely to do with the boundary line between two estates, but on December 3, 1838, one inhabitant of St. Simons, John Wylly, met his neighbor, Dr. T. Fuller Hazzard, whom he had challenged unsuccessfully to a duel, in a hotel in Brunswick, struck the Doctor with his cane and spat in his face. Hazzard was armed. Though he was tried eventually for manslaughter, the jury failed to convict, and on

Wylly's tombstone the dead man was described as "a victim to his generous courage."

Fanny had heard so much talk of the Wylly-Hazzard killing that, in writing up her diary notes, she may have actually thought it was contemporaneous with her stay on the island, or she may have transposed its date in the manuscript, which was still merely a manuscript and still in her possession in 1844. Any comment on the Schott-Butler duel that happened to reach her ears must have had a familiar ring. Schott, who was inclined to be timorous, was praised for his daring in having challenged Butler. Butler seemed to the circles in which he and the diarist, Sidney Fisher, moved, "to have behaved with great propriety throughout." [3]

Sidney Fisher, as his jottings testify, had valued Fanny for the same reason William Charles Macready valued her: she was a marvelous talker; she had known so many interesting people; she had witnessed so many interesting events. Now, like Macready, Fisher began to hedge. Fanny was still a fascinating companion, but she was too "*prononcée*," she was "the reverse of feminine in her manners and conversation." The two met one day when riding out into the country on horseback. Fanny was mounted on a bright bay horse—and the horse's name was Forrester. He had been bought back from the livery stable, Fanny told Fisher, with some money she had received for a book of poems which had recently been published by Harper & Brothers.

Fisher was himself a versifier. He bought the book, which was available in local bookstores, and thought it was not nearly as good as he had expected it to be. The American edition was dedicated to Catharine Sedgwick. Though there were several sonnets addressed to unnamed ladies, there was only one which could arouse curiosity. It began:

> Lady, whom my beloved loves so well!
> When on his clasping arm thy head reclineth,

That Fanny should refer, with or without poetic license, to her marital troubles seemed to Fisher to be in very bad taste.

Frances Anne Kemble in
early life.

Pierce Butler.

Fanny Kemble as Beatrice. Painting by Thomas Sully, 1833.

Major Pierce Butler, etched by
Albert Rosenthal.

Fort Frederica Association of Sea Island, Georgia

Ruins of the rice mill
on St. Simon's Island.

Liverpool, last of the Butler slaves.

Fort Frederica Association of Sea Island, Georgia

Live oak with Spanish moss on St. Simon's Island.

William Ellery Channing, engraved by J. Horsburgh after S. Gambardella, 1839.

Catharine M. Sedgwick.

Fanny Kemble as Bianca. Painting by Thomas Sully.

Portrait of Fanny Kemble Butler
by Henry Inman.

The Brooklyn Museum, gift of Charles A. Schieren

The Detroit Institute of Arts, gift of Dexter M. Ferry, Jr.

"The Lovely Land." Monument Mountain, Berkshires. From a painting
by Asher B. Durand.

Mrs. Kemble in later life.

The book, to be sure, had been placed in England and sold in America before Fanny's verbal agreement with Pierce, but it, no doubt, strengthened his determination to prevent his wife's appearances in print as well as on the stage. Even Fanny Appleton Longfellow recoiled from Fanny's poems. She thought them "too bitter and morbid for a Christian woman." [5] In Philadelphia, they alienated what little sympathy there was for an ex-actress, who had never completely found her place in the community into which she had married.

To win a suit for adultery, names would have to be named in court and incidents described, though, according to Lawyer Gerhard, the misdemeanor need not be of recent date. An unsuccessful attempt was made by a British attorney to follow Pierce's footsteps in England. Footsteps nearer home might lead to women whom Fanny knew or had rubbed shoulders with in society and whose virtue, like that of Mrs. Schott's, could be successfully vindicated on the field of honor.

Sometime during the late winter or early spring—the date cannot be fixed exactly—Fanny and her advisers became convinced of the impossibility of winning a suit. Fanny asked Charlotte Cushman to abandon her efforts as private detective. She expressed to her overzealous ally her gratitude, but warned her that she might be "the object of malevolence."

Pierce's malevolence was demonstrated when, in May, he announced to Fanny's lawyers the departure of his children for a two months' stay at Newport. On their return, they would live in a house he had just bought. If Fanny wished to live there also, she would have to give up all connection with those "vulgar, pernicious meddlers," the Sedgwicks.

Fanny was appalled. To whom could she turn for advice and help if not to a Sedgwick? Just when she most needed someone to champion her, the Reverend William Henry Furness, Pastor of the Unitarian Church, offered her his services.

Fanny's friendship with Furness and his wife had begun in the summer of 1836 when they came to stay briefly near Butler Place and she brought them gifts of flowers and vegetables and wished that they could stay forever. The growth of the Unitarian Church in Philadelphia was a tribute to Furness's engaging personality. He was as allergic as Dr. Channing to controversy, but, roused by the gutting of Liberty Hall in 1838, he had developed the habit of including an antislavery admonition every Sunday, either in his sermon, or in a prayer. Fanny was gratified to note how few of the congregation had given up their pews in protest.

Though Pierce Butler was no longer a member of his flock, Furness interviewed him and was the bearer of some very bad news to Fanny. If she was to live within sight and sound of her children, a signed agreement would be necessary. It would include all the earlier promises and a complete renunciation of the Sedgwicks; she must not see them, she must not even communicate with them.

Fanny asked for time to consider. Summer, with its unbearable heat, was upon her, and this summer there was more than heat to bear, an epidemic of violence and destructive hate in Philadelphia. Following a convention of the Native American (Know Nothing) party, there was gunfire in Irish ghettoes. While the police stood idly by, Roman Catholic churches and row after row of houses were burned. Fanny was horrified and personally harrowed by an accident to her little Fan, who, just before the children were moved to their new home, fell over the bannisters and broke her arm; she might have broken her neck! The rides on Forrester also came to an end. Fanny's beloved horse slipped in crossing a wet plank, broke a tendon in his leg, and was so badly crippled that he had to be destroyed.

Fanny fled to Lenox and its "perfect atmosphere of love" for consolation, but her friends could only give her love; they were as impotent as she. This was a Jubilee Festival Year for the Berkshires. On August 22, speeches were delivered by Mark Hopkins, the President of Williams College, by Catharine and Theodore Sedgwick, and by Oliver Wendell Holmes. Fanny contributed

an ode in which she laid the blessing of a stranger on the lovely
land and hailed Lenox as the spot where Channing had spoken—

> the last sacred words to freedom given,
> The parting utterance of that holy one.

On her return to Philadelphia, Fanny moved to another boardinghouse so that she could be nearer to the children, but she
rarely laid eyes upon them. Once she met them in the street, and
they passed her without speaking. Fanny ran after them and
seized Sarah by the shoulder. "How can you do this to your
mother?" she cried. Sarah replied that Miss Hall had told them
not to speak, and their father had told them to obey their governess.

In December, impelled by a letter from her sister Adelaide,
urging reconciliation—Pierce's stand, incidentally, had been endorsed by Edward Sartoris and by Charles Greville—Fanny let
Pierce know of her willingness to sign the agreement. This did
not result in an immediate admission to the house, which was
under repair. It was not until March 1845 that Fanny was told
she might move in, and then there began a game of hide and seek
with the children. Miss Hall was given a vacation, and Sarah and
Fan were sent to Pierce's Chester County farm. Fanny followed
them, but she had no sooner arrived than the children were returned to Philadelphia to stay in John Butler's house on Chestnut
Street. Fanny went back to share the new establishment with
workmen and the smell of paint.

Yet even when the children were in residence, Fanny realized
how far they had drifted out of her control. One day Fan was
so fractious that the governess slapped her. Fanny heard the
screams and ran to Pierce to remind him unavailingly that years
ago they had decided never to use corporal punishment in bringing up their children. Again it was Sarah who defied her. When
Fanny protested, Pierce told her, in the child's hearing, that she
had forfeited all right to authority.

A supreme frustration coincided with the girls' birthday on

May 28. As a special treat, they were to go with some friends to Butler Place, but there would be no room in the carriage for their mother. If she wanted to share in the festivities, she would have to hire a conveyance and follow after. It was some consolation to Fanny to have Fan, who had seen the tears in her eyes, offer to ride with her, but long before the birthday, she had decided on her course of action. She would admit defeat and go back to England, as her brother John had advocated. John could not support her, but she felt she could for a time accept the hospitality of her father, to whom she had once given a sizable sum. How eventually she could earn her own living, she did not know, Pierce having laid his interdict on the theatre and on her writing activities.

Fanny wanted her friends in Lenox, in Boston, and in New York to know her intentions and approve them. She was not leaving America for good; she would return as soon as possible. In Lenox, Fanny had made two new friends, who were not Sedgwicks and with whom she could communicate. One was Charles Sumner who, as a Harvard law student, had cheered her appearances in Boston; the other was Samuel Gray Ward, son of a New York banker and a literary *flaneur*, who had bought a Berkshire farm and endeared himself to the entire community, both rural and intellectual, with amazing speed. Everybody called him Sam; Charles Sedgwick, who had negotiated the purchase of the farm, said Ward was as much beloved at the end of his first three months as if he had lived in Lenox his entire life.

To Sam Ward, Fanny wrote four letters during the spring of 1845. She spoke frankly of her hopes and fears: fears of her capacity to make her own way in the world, fears that Pierce would divorce her if she returned to the stage. All her hopes were fixed upon owning a home in Lenox. She had heard that Sam might be willing to sell her his house, or a corner of his property on which she might build. She had no money to invest in real estate at present, her allowance from Pierce having been paid so irregularly that she was practically destitute. Soon after the children's birthday, however, Fanny heard from England that she might receive a small legacy from a relative, possibly her Aunt Victoire De Camp, to whom, in lieu of Dall, she had given the income from her *Journal* of 1835.

In August, Fanny wrote to Ward that she would be seeing him very soon, and in going to Lenox, she renounced *de facto* the agreement with Pierce she had signed in December. A joyful welcome awaited her and an endorsement of what she had done. "Fanny should have tried for independence sooner," Catharine wrote to Mrs. Jameson.

The legacy Fanny had mentioned to Sam Ward had not materialized and she had to borrow money for her passage to England. After she had left, Charles Sedgwick wrote to his daughter, Kate Minot, saying how sorry he was she had not been with them that summer. "Fanny's presence," Charles wrote, "does so improve the quality of life and increase its power by her infinite variety of thought, feeling and expression, and she does so strangely link one to her in affection, almost as much by her mirth and joy, as by the deep sadness of her condition and her occasional despair." [6]

THE DESERTION

(October 1845–April 1848)

CHARLES KEMBLE had been plagued by sciatica and lumbago, but his most crippling ailment was an increasing deafness. To act, an actor must be sure of his cue. As a substitute for stage appearances, Charles had turned to dramatic readings of Shakespeare's plays, neatly tailored to a two-hour performance. A reading of *Cymbeline* had been commanded by Queen Victoria. Plebian audiences were more than gratified. On one occasion an American lady, who happened to be in London, was so overcome by emotion that she slipped out of her chair to the floor in a faint. Charles stopped reading, and looking over his spectacles, said, "Mam, this won't do." [1] A second admonition, "Mam, we are too much used to this sort of thing," brought no response. It was not until Charles said, "Mam, you are exposing yourself," without pinpointing the area exposed, that the lady jumped up and resumed her seat.

When Fanny reached London in October of 1845 she found her unsinkable parent had engagements for his one-man show at Brighton and at Highgate. He had an even more ambitious plan in mind, a tour of America, taking Fanny with him. Though her father's notion that, if he were on the spot, he could settle her differences with Pierce seemed fanciful, Fanny was willing to cooperate.

They would leave in a matter of weeks, but this, they were told by well-informed friends, would be hazardous. Texas had been annexed, and now another expansionist move, along the northern frontier, was in dispute, not with a secondary power, Mexico, but with almighty England. Feeling ran high in the States; "Fifty-four forty, or fight," was the cry, and Britishers were so unpopular that even an elderly gentleman reading *Cymbeline* might not find an audience, or, if he did find one, he might be heckled and insulted.

Fanny could not take the so-called Oregon Question too seriously. She discounted the rumors of war, and having received from Sam Ward an architectural drawing of a house she could build on his farmland in Lenox, she was greatly disappointed by the cancellation of the American tour. Her father, who knew her temperament well and who could see how tense and restless she was, offered her a trip to Rome, where she could spend the winter months with her sister Adelaide. Fanny left on December 20, going overland for the greater part of the way.

While traveling in trackless America, Fanny had bewailed the lack of cleanliness and the prevalence of expectoration. She found the same conditions obtained in France. In the United States, the spittoon had been the bane of her existence, but here, where spitting was at random, she saw what a useful purpose it served.

America was with her at every stage of her journey. When Fanny entered French churches, only to recoil from such pictured horrors as the Stations of the Cross, she thought of the burning Catholic churches of Philadelphia. In spite of the expense, she had felt it necessary to take a maid with her, since a woman traveling alone might be inconvenienced. How different the mores of the New World in this respect! There a woman could travel unchaperoned from Maine to Florida and be sure of constant help along the way, a fact that many women took advantage of, turning men out of the best seats in the coach and the best accommodations at the hotel.

As a young girl, and under the spell of Byron and Shelley, Fanny had dreamed of living in Italy, but her first sight of Rome, as she approached it in a slow-moving diligence, reminded her of a very different sort of wonder, of Niagara. The flora of the Campagna recalled the ilex and live oak of Georgia, and even the house of Adelaide and Edward Sartoris, when finally reached, atop the Pincio, seemed to Fanny exactly like the many dilapidated Southern houses she had visited; untidy, uncomfortable, but surrounded by beautiful flowers.

Adelaide and Edward Sartoris were kind to others and to one another. On arrival, Fanny was taken immediately upstairs to view two sleeping cherubs, whom Adelaide adored. She also adored her good-natured, but undistinguished, husband. They had many friends in Rome's extensive foreign colony, to whom they offered frequent musical entertainment, without, for Adelaide, the strain and stress of professionalism.

Fanny had brought writing materials with her and had begun to scribble as soon as she left England, thinking there would always be a sale for one more travelogue of Italy. Since her prospective readers would know she had lived in America, her frequent references to that country would add a further interest. Fanny made the round of sights. She relished the Roman carnival and mentioned disparagingly the bad manners of foreign tourists, the washing of beggars' feet in Holy Week, and the Italian attitude toward women, who were locked up every night when their men went out to enjoy themselves.

None of this was exactly original. Fanny, however, realized that the Rome she viewed was on the threshold of an awakening, dominated as it had been for centuries by foreign interests and by foreign powers. A new Pope had just been chosen. The old Pope, Gregory XVI, was an obscurantist, who would not allow the building of a railroad to the Eternal City and its lighting by gas. Pius IX endorsed both these improvements. He also released political prisoners, and it was thought he might actually introduce a representative form of government. Fanny wondered if

Prince Metternich might not take notice from his watchtower in Vienna. Her prose descriptions of events, of monuments and spectacles, were interlarded with outbursts of poetry, one of which was a tribute to Pio Nono, whose ceremonial taking over of the Lateran she had witnessed.

A far more heartfelt insertion was some verses Fanny wrote "Upon a Branch of Flowering Acacia." When, eleven years earlier, Sarah Butler was born, Fanny, who still lay on her bed, breathless from her labor, looked over at the open window of her room at Butler Place and saw that a spray of acacia had poked its way in. There was acacia also at her Roman window, and Fanny, sorrowing for her lost child, asked herself:

> Oh, was it all in vain,
> That night of hope, of terror and of pain.

No word had come from the children, but from friends who had been allowed to see them, Fanny heard that Sarah cried at mention of her mother's name; this became the subject of yet another poem. Fanny also heard of little Fan's having headaches and was worried to think they might be the result of the fall the child had had last summer when her arm was broken. To Harriet St. Ledger, Fanny wrote somewhat cynically that all the women who were pressing for equal rights seemed to be spinsters; if they had children who were in the despotic power of their husbands, they would not dare to clamor.

The Sartorises had taken a villa for the summer at Frascati, which, with its lakes and hills, Fanny saw as an Italian Lenox, though, being thickly sprinkled with human habitations, it was far less beautiful. She could not stay for a second winter in Rome and in early December was back with her father in London. Her manuscript was accepted promptly and would be published as *A Year of Consolation*, on its title page, a tribute to Edward Sartoris, Fanny's generous host.

But the news from America, except for some grapevine news of the children's good health, was unpropitious. While she was in Italy, Fanny's affairs had been handled by her Philadelphia lawyer, Mr. Gerhard, who had asked Pierce for a financial settlement, which could be handed on to the children; he had obtained the consent of Charles Sumner to act as trustee. If Fanny would renounce her dower rights in his estate, Pierce offered her a thousand dollars per annum, secured by a mortgage on Butler Place and on his house in town. The necessary documents, however, were not forthcoming, and Gerhard reverted to the idea of a divorce and alimony.

Pierce, apparently, was deep in debt. Fanny felt she should earn something, not only for herself, but for her girls, who might eventually find themselves at the mercy of their father's creditors. What was needed now was a steady, substantial income, and the only practical source for that was the theatre. To Sarah, who would be twelve her next birthday, Fanny wrote a letter giving her reasons for her return to the stage; she hoped, but hoped in vain, for an answer.

For various and sufficient reasons, success seemed dubious. Fanny was thirty-seven years old; she had put on weight, and had never, as she herself admitted, been really good-looking. If she tried for a London engagement, she might interfere with her father's readings, and there were two strong rivals entrenched in the capital: Jenny Lind, the Swedish Nightingale, and the great French *tragédienne*, Rachel. Fanny thought herself lucky to get an offer to appear in Manchester. She boldly demanded and received £500 for six performances.

Before the opening, and to soothe her trepidation, Fanny went to visit her scholarly brother John, who was living in a poor little country cottage and while working on an important contribution to learning, a history of English law, had to tutor boys for Cambridge to keep the pot boiling and a roof over the heads of himself and his family. Fanny thought John had made a noble choice of worldly poverty and intellectual wealth, but wondered if he would be able to survive. Would she survive, also?

During the past decade great changes had taken place in theatrical production; scenery was far more elaborate, the stage was was more brightly lighted. This called for a change in makeup. Fanny submitted, though with a poor grace, to being heavily rouged and whitened. If her face and figure had not improved, at least she felt that her voice had acquired greater authority, and the applause on opening night surprised and overwhelmed her to the verge of hysteria. The critics, too, were kindly; they said Fanny's acting had gained greater subtlety. After the Manchester run, there were other engagements in the provinces. When she was again in London, Fanny had a call from William Charles Macready, who was in need of star support in a series of Shakespearean plays: *Macbeth, Henry VIII, Hamlet, Lear, Othello.*

The offer was accepted, but once more with fear and trembling. Fanny respected Macready as an actor, while well aware of his limitations. He had no gift for comedy; he was not handsome enough for romantic roles, and all his associates complained of his egoism and physical violence.

"Macready is not pleasant to act with," Fanny wrote during the rehearsal period, "as he keeps no specific time for his exits and entrances, comes on while one is in the middle of a soliloquy, and goes off while one is in the middle of a speech to him. He growls and prowls and roams and foams about the stage in every direction, like a tiger in his cage . . . and keeps up a perpetual snarling and grumbling, like the foresaid tiger, so that I never feel quite sure that he has done and that it is my time to speak . . . I quail at the idea of his laying hold on me in those terrible passionate scenes"—Fanny had *Othello* in mind—"for in *Macbeth* he pinched me black and blue and almost tore the point lace from my head." [2]

Fanny had a deep-seated, sexual horror of *Othello*. She told Harriet St. Ledger that she would make a desperate fight for it, for she loathed the idea of being murdered in her bed. Nor would she allow herself to be chased about the stage, as she had seen the play, or opera, performed in Italy. Macready, however, tactfully let down the bed curtains before beginning the business of strangling, and Fanny-Desdemona was allowed to die in peace.

The Macready engagement went more smoothly than foreseen, though it did not pass without a characteristic entry in
Macready's journal. Fanny had told the stagehands to shift the
dining table in *Macbeth* so that she could circumnavigate it more
successfully. "I have never seen anyone so bad, so affected, so
conceited," Macready snarled. "She alters the stage arrangements
without the slightest ceremony and, in fact, proceeds not only
en grande artiste, but *en grande reine*." [3]

Macready also complained of Charles Kemble's constant attendance at the theatre and his applauding so loudly and knock-
ing with his cane whenever Fanny appeared that there were cries
of "Turn him out!" Charles probably did not hear the cries.
Because of his deafness he had had to decline a reading at Buckingham Palace of *Antigone*, with a background of choruses by
Mendelssohn. Fanny was asked to take her father's place, but she
also demurred on the score of inexperience and was glad to
escape exposure to the music of Mendelssohn, whom she had
known as a friend of Adelaide, and who had recently died, much
too young for one so gifted.

Her father's acknowledgment of his inability to read, however, gave Fanny the opportunity she had coveted ever since she
had begun to read informally to Elizabeth Sedgwick's schoolgirls in Lenox. Only a few weeks after her appearances with
Macready, Fanny took over one of her father's audiences at
Highgate and on April 3, 1848, repeated the experiment in London to great acclaim. The play was *The Merchant of Venice;* its
heroine, Portia, was, for Fanny, the brightest star in the Shakespearean galaxy. A way had opened before the granddaughter of
Roger Kemble which would lead her far. Fanny had once told
Theodore Sedgwick she would never return to the theatre, but
she was so instinctively dramatic that: "I cannot speak without
gesticulating and making faces. . . . I am fond, moreover, of the
excitement of acting . . . of realizing in my own person noble

and beautiful imaginary beings, and uttering the poetry of Shakespeare." [4]

Following the reading at Willis's rooms in King Street, St.
James, offers began to pour in, and Fanny took to the road. With
the intention of reading *Coriolanus* to the Literary and Scientific
Institute of Hull, Fanny arrived one day at the Hull railway
station and was met by a Mr. Frost, President of the Institute. In
passing through the station Fanny saw a bundle of rags lying in
a corner—or was it a bundle of rags? A wretchedly emaciated
boy was huddled beneath the tatters. Being timid, and as Fanny
put it, "a man by nature," Mr. Frost would have passed by, but
Fanny fell on her knees beside the boy, questioned him, and
learned he was homeless and had been abandoned by his parents.
He was here in the railway station because he had tried to spend
the night in the workhouse and had been turned away.

Fanny hailed a cab. With Mr. Frost still in agitated attendance,
she drove the boy to the workhouse, where she expostulated with
the management and "wept herself hoarse." Having made sure
her protégé would be taken care of temporarily, Fanny promised
to give a benefit performance so that the boy could be apprenticed to a trade; he had told her that he would like to be a sailor.

The Hull incident was only one of several rescue missions
Fanny had undertaken recently. These were the Hungry Forties
in Britain. While great fortunes had piled up, labor was cruelly
exploited and derelicts abounded. They drifted through the city
streets like ghosts, without even the energy to beg or to pick the
pockets of the rich. Fanny was particularly aware of the plight
of women and children. She bought buns and baked apples for a
boy who was ogling the contents of a bakeshop window, full of
goodies. She gave money to a stranded girl to get home to her
family, a job seeker, perhaps, whom she found asleep on a bench
in the park. When the girl was arrested as a prostitute, Fanny
went with her to the police station to weep and plead as aggressively as she had once wept and pleaded with her husband to
lighten the labor of his pregnant slaves.

When, early in 1848, the revolutionary movement surfaced in
France and soon after in almost every capital of the Continent,
London was filled with elegant refugees; one of them was Prince
Metternich, whom Fanny had seen as the reactionary power behind the throne in Italy. It was entertaining to read in the newspapers of the hairbreadth escapes of these personages, but Fanny
felt sure they had come to the only place in the Old World
where they could be reasonably safe. Dr. Channing had once
predicted that the day would come when responsible people
would be as shocked by poverty as now they were shocked by
slavery. "The crying sin of modern Christian civilization," Fanny
wrote, "the monstrous inequalities in the means of existence, will
yet be dealt with by the English, among whom it is more flagrant
than anywhere else on earth . . . I pray God it may be gradual.
. . . I have the same admiration for and confidence in, our national character that I have in the institutions of the United
States." [5]

On April 10, the day of the Great Chartist Meeting, which
might have been the signal for a bloody uprising, Fanny went out
in search of a revolution and failed to find one. Democracy, she
thought, would soon rule all the earth, and this would have a
profound effect upon the condition of women. Word came of
Fanny Appleton Longfellow's having given birth to a child, the
first to be born in America with the aid of an anesthetic. It was
not freedom from the curse laid upon them in the third chapter
of *Genesis* that women needed, Fanny said; it was freedom from
subjection to their husbands!

At this time also, the papers were full of the murder of a
French aristocrat, the Comtesse de Praslin, by her husband, but
Fanny was more concerned with the obscure case of a girl who
had stabbed the man who seduced her. She hoped the prisoner
would be reprieved, as had happened some years earlier in New
York. There the defendant took shelter with Elizabeth Sedgwick, who used to sit by her bed and sing to her when she could
not sleep for nightmare. "It will be long," Fanny commented,

"before women are justly dealt with by the social or civil codes of the Christian communities to which they belong. . . . With the world's progress, that reform will come." [6]

Fanny's springtime mood was confident. A year earlier she had written Sam Ward that she had enough money to buy land in Lenox, but not enough to build a house. At the end of her present season, she should be well on the way to her goal. Fanny planned a holiday in Switzerland with Harriet St. Ledger, who had deprecated herself as a traveling companion because she was old and stuffy. In reply Fanny described herself as not only old and stuffy, but also "fat and puffy." In August she would sail for America and in September would act in New York; if Pierce objected she would sue him for divorce.

But Pierce, who was so often dilatory and who may have learned of Fanny's intentions, was the first to have recourse to the law. On April 7, 1848, he presented to the Court of Common Pleas in Philadelphia a petition, asking for a divorce from his wife, Frances Anne, who had willfully, maliciously and without due cause, deserted him on September 11, 1845. Fanny's holiday with Harriet had to be canceled, canceled also a series of readings, worth £600, and an appearance with Macready at a fund raising benefit for a memorial to Sarah Siddons. Within a few days, Mrs. Butler was on her way to America to offer her defense and if possible, to gain possession of her children.

CHAPTER XVI

DIVORCE

(June 1848–June 1850)

In AMERICA, grounds for divorce differed widely from state to state. The laws of Pennsylvania in this respect were more liberal than elsewhere because of the local preponderance of settlers from Germany, where a marriage could be broken if a two-year desertion could be proved.

On arrival, Fanny went directly to Lenox. On June 19, 1848, she visited the Lenox Courthouse and deposited with its clerk, Mr. Charles Sedgwick, an answer to her husband's libelous plea, her main contention being that Pierce had known she was going to leave his house, and she had only left it because her life there was unendurable.

A more elaborate document was filed with the Court of Common Pleas in Philadelphia when the case came up in October. This defense which, when printed, ran to sixty pages, was the work of Rufus Choate, Boston's best-known lawyer and a theatre buff who considered Fanny the greatest actress he had ever seen. There was no direct mention in *Mrs. Butler's Answer* of Pierce's infidelities, but one of his letters was quoted, in which he mentioned, with appropriate indignation, a demand made by Adelaide Sartoris and Fanny's friend Mary Appleton Mackintosh, for the dismissal of Miss Hall, the governess, whose presence in

the household was an insult to Fanny. Emphasis was laid throughout the *Answer* on the alienation of the children and the inflic-
tion of mental, as opposed to physical, cruelty. A given instance
was Pierce's having sent Fanny a letter from Catharine Sedgwick.
When she opened it, as she thought she was supposed to do, he
accused her of having broken a clause of their signed agreement.

For one who was not a Pennsylvania lawyer, Choate pressed as
strongly as possible for the validity of the *Answer* as evidence;
this, however, was denied by the court. Judge King referred the
case to a trial by jury, which could not take place until the
spring. In the meantime, the contents of the *Answer* had become
known, not only to the readers of American newspapers, but also
in England. In the February issue of *Littell's Living Age*, an
article that had appeared in *The London Chronicle* was extensively quoted. It compared the ease with which divorce could be
obtained in Germany and Pennsylvania with the situation in England where an act of Parliament was necessary and the expendi-
ture of at least £1000. The letter trick Pierce had played on
Fanny was likened to the temptation offered to Saint Joan of Arc
when men's clothing was put down beside her in her prison cell.
The Sedgwicks were characterized as "one of the most ancient,
distinguished and respectable families in the United States," [1]
while Fanny herself was said to be a "female Byron," abnormally
sensitive to the restrictions of conventional life. "What might
not kindness, forbearance, gentleness and sympathy have made of
such a nature!" The *Answer* did not refer to an antislavery protest of which Fanny was the author, but the London article gave
Pierce's refusal to allow the publication of this work as prime
example of his tyranny.

While Choate was pleading her cause, Fanny had to go to
Philadelphia to appear in person and she felt as if she were going
to her execution. She had asked for funds to pay for her defense,
but she must have known how little chance there was of getting
them. While the wheels of the law stood motionless, she must get
to work—but not in Philadelphia. There, as Fanny told Sam

Ward, she was "a monster of iniquity," while Pierce had "glamor," and Pierce was still her husband and could persecute her. Fanny wrote to Kate Sedgwick's husband, William Minot, to ask if there was a chance of giving a series of readings in Boston.

There was, it seemed, a very good chance indeed. At about the time the February issue of *Littell's Living Age* appeared, Fanny also appeared at the Tremont Theatre. She was escorted to the stage by Charles Sumner, one of the tallest, the handsomest, and the most stately of the Brahmin brotherhood. Bowing deeply to her audience, Fanny said, "I will have the honor of reading to you *The Merchant of Venice*, by William Shakespeare." After this and other performances, there were small, select supper parties at the Revere House. There were readings also in Salem, New Bedford and, eventually, in Cambridge. There Fanny went to the dais on the arm of Henry Longfellow, and again the play she had chosen to open her series was *The Merchant of Venice*.

"I sat directly under her," Fanny Appleton Longfellow reported to a friend, "and thought her face never was so beautiful as in Portia's speeches. When it hardens to Shylock it becomes so altered it is like a different mask suddenly slipped on. She came home with us afterwards and we had a very nice little supper, with Hillard [a frequent visitor at Craigie House], Sumner, Stephen [Longfellow] and ourselves. . . . She [Fanny] was in great spirits, as she always is after reading, and seemed to enjoy it much. At the close, I presented her with a bouquet, and Henry with a sonnet, which he read. She was much overcome and could hardly recover herself. Her affectionate nature is easily touched by kindness, and the tears flow at once." [2]

The sonnet Longfellow read began, "Oh, precious evenings all too swiftly fled," and ended with an invocation to Shakespeare:

> How must thy listening spirit now rejoice
> To be interpreted by such a voice!

From Boston Fanny went to New York and to stay with the Sedgwicks. Devoured by jealousy, William Charles Macready walked out in the middle of one of Fanny's readings; but she took the town by storm, according to Philip Hone, who seventeen years earlier had invited a youthful Fanny, fresh off the ship from England, to dinner. In the interval they had met once at the Rockaway Hotel, where Hone asked Fanny to dance, and she apologized, in all sincerity, for her flippant description of his dinner party in her *Journal* of 1835, which had just been published. After the New York readings had begun, Kate Minot was informed by her Aunt Catharine Sedgwick that "the town talks of little else . . . fashionable people, old people, clever people, pious folk, the mourners, the Quakers—all are studying Shakespeare."[3]

But there was even better news for Kate. While Fanny was staying with the Sedgwicks and earning two thousand dollars a week, which, as Philip Hone remarked, was more than Shakespeare ever got, an offer came from Pierce: he would allow Fanny to have her children for two months of the year if she would withdraw her defense. Catharine strongly urged acceptance, saying that if it came to a trial, Pierce would bring all the women of Philadelphia to testify to Fanny's shrewish temper. Fanny, however, did not reply before she left for another engagement in Albany. The case, which had been scheduled for April, was again postponed to September, and there was time to bargain.

On her brief visits to Philadelphia, Fanny had seen her children, who now had a new governess. Miss Hall had returned to England with a letter from Pierce, addressed to her brother, exonerating her from all false and wickedly inspired aspersions. Word had got about that Sarah and Fan might go to Georgia with their father; this was protested, as a removal from the jurisdiction of the Philadelphia court, by Fanny's lawyers. Before she said yes or no to the proposed withdrawal of her defense, Fanny demanded the children's company for a month in Lenox, and she tried to make the month so memorable that they would insist upon it later as their due.

How reassuring, how comfortable it was to find her daughters so amiable and so affectionate! The years of separation seemed to have made little difference. "She loves them, and they love her," was Catharine's verdict.[4] Both the girls were intelligent, and though their mother could find flaws in their behavior, which she attributed to their upbringing, one of the most flagrant being a total ignorance of the value of money, she had no reason to fear for their future. From now on, Fanny told her friends, it would be a case of Ceres and Persephone; she pledged herself to work like a galley slave throughout the winter so that her summers would be a time of "roses and rest."

In September Pierce was granted an uncontested divorce. He entered into a legal contract to provide his ex-wife, who had relinquished all other claims upon him, with an annual income of fifteen hundred dollars. The children would spend two months of the year with their mother and could be seen by her at all times. They would be allowed to write to her, and she to them.

Following close upon the decree, Fanny resumed her maiden name and as Mrs. Fanny Kemble inaugurated a five-week engagement at the Samson Street Hall in Philadelphia with a reading of *As You Like It*. A delighted member of the audience was Sidney Fisher, who, as his diary relates, went to call on Fanny a few days later. She had, indeed, overstated the case when she said she was only a monster of iniquity in Pierce's home town. His conduct was considered "barbarous" by Fisher, and by Fisher's cousin, Joshua Francis Fisher, who, with his wife Eliza, had been Fanny's friends throughout. The Reverend William Henry Furness was, of course, a staunch supporter, so also was Lawyer Gerhard and his family, and many other individuals who had been Fanny's neighbors when she lived at Butler Place.

As a divorced woman, however, Fanny had made enemies whom she had never seen. After the decree was published, offers of marriage came from persons unknown, but there was much hostile criticism in the press, particularly in the South, where it was said she, as an abolitionist, had no right to accept alimony from a slaveholder. "Both parties are now free to marry again," a Northern newspaper commented contemptuously, "if anyone will have them, and Mrs. Fanny Kemble Butler is entitled to wear the breeches in her own right."

On a visit to Boston in 1849, a rising young novelist, Herman Melville, wrote of having attended some of Fanny's readings. She was a glorious Lady Macbeth, but her Desdemona was a mere boarding-school miss. "She is so unfemininely masculine that had she not, on unimpeachable authority, borne children, I should be curious to learn the result of a surgical examination of her person in private. The Lord help Butler. . . . I marvel not he seeks to being amputated off from his maternal half." [5]

The adjective "maternal" may have been a Freudian slip, for Melville had been on unsympathetic terms with his domineering mother. Seven years later he was living near Lenox and introduced into a novel he was writing, *The Confidence Man*, a repulsive female character named Goneril, who had been amputated off from her husband and who, like Fanny, was extremely athletic, similarities not purely coincidental.

While she was celebrating her first free Christmas, the Christmas of 1849, with Charles and Elizabeth Sedgwick, Fanny read aloud to them a new poem of Longfellow's, *The Building of the Ship*. She thought it had such dramatic possibilities, and its admonition:

> Thou, too, sail on, O Ship of State,
> Sail on, O Union, strong and great!

was so stirring that she read it shortly after to an audience of three thousand workingmen in Boston. The appeal of her appearances there was maintained in spite of distractions. The entire area was convulsed by the murder of a prominent citizen, Dr. George Parkman, the murderer being a member of the Harvard faculty, Professor John White Webster. Both, it was recollected, had been present at Fanny's reading of *Macbeth*. Had she, or, more precisely, William Shakespeare, suggested a bloody denouement?

Yet another Webster was in the news. On the day before Fanny's final reading in Cambridge, Massachusetts's mightiest orator delivered his Seventh of March Speech to the Senate of the United States. Seeking Southern support in a bid for the Presidency, Daniel Webster endorsed the compromise proposals of Henry Clay, which included a more stringent fugitive-slave law. Thousands of fugitives who had ridden the Underground Railway trembled. For Whittier, the bard of antislavery, Webster had become the vainglorious Ichabod—"so fallen, so lost." Charles Sumner, no mean orator himself, and soon to run for the Senate on a Free Soil ticket, compared Webster to Lucifer. Even Charles Sedgwick, who rarely spoke ill of anyone, wrote to a kinsman who lived in Syracuse, New York, that Webster "had acted like hell and inflicted a wound on the honor of the country which a generation of righteous men cannot repair." [6]

Fanny was cognizant of these opinions. She was so moved by the applause at the end of her final performance and by the righteousness of New England that she exclaimed to Fanny Longfellow, "I believe I love Boston better than any of you. I like to ride to Dorchester Heights and think how gloriously you beat us!" [7]

Fanny's personal problems, however, had not yet been solved. Sam Ward had offered to rent his house to her for five years, but she regretfully declined, saying her plans were too indefinite; if the girls were put out of her reach, she would go to England, where she could always find employment. Again Fanny had heard that Sarah and Fan might go to Georgia with their father, but an equally effective means of keeping them from her had been devised. While the girls were with her in Lenox, Pierce suddenly appeared in the village. He stayed for only a day, but the fabric of intimacy Fanny had been weaving was severely damaged, and there was, moreover, nothing she could do to prevent a repetition of the incident.

At the same time Pierce had privately printed, but fairly widely circulated, the statement of his case, originally prepared for counsel. It was twice as long as *Mrs. Butler's Answer*; it gave far more intimate details. In the foreword, Pierce disclaimed revenge. His object, he asserted, was "merely self vindication, a right belonging to everyone, and a duty which we owe not less to ourselves than to our friends, our kindred, and our children." Pierce's children were no longer babes; Sally was fifteen, Fan twelve, and they were quite capable of assimilating their father's point of view concerning their mother.

When Fanny definitely decided to go to England she rented the cottage she had bought in Lenox, and which she had named The Perch, to Nathaniel Hawthorne, who had given up his job in the Salem Custom House and come to live in the mountains. Fanny wrote to the children, promising a prompt return. The letters were never delivered. Somehow, Elizabeth Sedgwick learned that Sarah and Fan did not know where their mother had gone, or why she had suddenly vanished; Sarah was once more tearful at sound of her mother's name.

Elizabeth sent several letters she had received from Fanny to a Mrs. G. (probably Mrs. Gerhard) in Philadelphia. The girls went to hear Jenny Lind sing one afternoon and on their way home called on Mrs. G. They were overjoyed by what she had to show them.

"Pierce Butler," Elizabeth informed Samuel Ward, "is a monster."

During the winter Elizabeth's sister-in-law Catharine encountered Fanny's former husband at a wedding reception in New York. Though Pierce opened his lips as if to speak, Catharine passed him without a word.

CHAPTER XVII

AN INTERLUDE

(June 1850–May 1856)

FOR THE PAST ELEVEN YEARS Fanny had been too overwhelmed, too burdened, by the collapse of her marriage to think of the publication of her *Plantation Journal*. During those years the manuscript probably went back and forth with her across the Atlantic, while a copy remained in America, in the hands of Elizabeth Sedgwick. Elizabeth knew as well as Fanny that the premises against publication still obtained; even after the divorce, direct communication between Fanny and her children was difficult.

For friends and supporters of the Cause, the unique importance of Fanny's testimony may have dwindled. Lecturers, such as the Grimke sisters, Sarah and Angelina, daughters of a South Carolina planter, had given an insider's view of slavery; during the forties the slave himself was beginning to be heard. While Fanny was traveling south in 1838, Frederick Douglass was traveling north. He soon was in great demand at abolition gatherings. The Sedgwicks entertained him in Lenox, in memoriam Mumbet and brother Henry. Charles thought Douglass the most eloquent speaker he had ever heard, with the possible exception of Dr. Carl Follen. He urged Catharine and Theodore not to miss a Douglass lecture in New York.

Fearing capture by his former master, Douglass went to England, where he spoke to many sympathetic audiences. The British antislavery movement still lived, though its leaders now enjoyed the dubious privilege of standing above the battle. In 1852 a monster antislavery petition was sponsored by the Duchess of Sutherland and was styled "An Affectionate and Christian Address of Many Thousands of the Women of England and Ireland to their Sisters, the Women of the United States of America." It evoked a stinging rebuke from "Women of the South." The good Duchess was advised to visit the poor, the stricken, and the hungry of her own land and to "drop a single jewel from her hair into their lap." The Negroes of the South were said to live far more sumptuously than the destitute of London. This was the basic argument later elaborated by William Grayson in his *Hireling and the Slave*.

Though Fanny was still in England when the *Address* was being circulated for signatures, she did not feel free to add her name. An impetus to the effort had been given by the publication of Harriet Beecher Stowe's *Uncle Tom's Cabin*, which was read even more widely and eagerly, if that were possible, in the Old World than the New. Elizabeth Sedgwick sent Fanny a review which had appeared in *The London Times* on September 3, 1852. It charged that the picture of slavery was overdrawn and would do more harm than good. "Let us have no more Uncle Toms," it concluded, "engendering ill will, keeping up bad blood."

Fanny wrote a copious letter to *The Times*, refuting the charge of exaggeration; Mrs. Stowe had, in fact, "portrayed none of the most revolting instances of crime produced by the slave system." Fanny vouched for the truth of certain incidents, the lynching and the burning alive of blacks, which appeared in an earlier, more sensational, novel by Richard Hildreth, *The Slave, or Memoirs of Archy Moore*, published in 1836. An Englishman traveling in the United States, Fanny declared, could form no adequate conception of slavery. The manners of Southern gentlemen would be more likely to appeal to him than those of Northern businessmen, and his observations would be made, most likely, in Kentucky, Maryland, or Virginia, where slavery was less hideous than in the interior. The local planters there were brutal, sensual, and despotic. They fought duels; they carried on murderous feuds and had little respect for human life. There were also many absentee owners. Some of Fanny's experiences on an absentee-owned plantation were described: her arrival at Butler Island and the false and pitiful joy of its inhabitants, her visit to the hospital, the mockery of slave marriages.

The *Times* article had been signed "Dispassionate Observer." When Fanny discovered the author's identity and his importance in the eyes of the editors of the newspaper, she withheld her letter, since she was sure it would never be printed. The vindication of Mrs. Stowe and Uncle Tom was added to her manuscript as one more Letter to Elizabeth.

Fanny's stay in England lengthened. She heard that the girls were in boarding school and that the only visitors allowed them were friends of their father. She did not hear from them directly. Her reading engagements were satisfactory, though less remunerative than in the United States. Fanny was greatly aided in her nontheatrical career by her brother John's school and university friends, who were now established scholars or littérateurs. When Fanny read at Woodbridge, Edward Fitzgerald, not yet, but soon, the identical twin of Omar Khayyám, was present. As Fanny appeared he rose in his seat to bow profoundly, the rest of the audience following his example. William Makepeace Thackeray took his teenage daughters to hear Mrs. Kemble read the Falstaff plays. He shouted "Bravo!" and, less loudly to his girls, "Don't you see how admirably she forgets herself? How finely she feels it?" [1]

Thackeray was about to become a competitor of Fanny's. There were many such; attendance at readings of every sort had become a cultural fad on both sides of the Atlantic. Before Thackeray's first lecture of the series, later published as *The*

English Humorists, Fanny went backstage and found her old friend doubled up in an agony of stage fright, his manuscript strewn about the floor. She picked it up, sorted it, and, as an old hand tried to cheer him. "My dear soul," he said, "You couldn't have done better for me." [2] Since a tour of America was under consideration, Fanny wrote to the Longfellows and to Charles Sumner to give her friend a hearty welcome.

The expedition was deferred for almost a year, but in January 1853 Thackeray was in Philadelphia. On the day of his arrival Pierce Butler called at his hotel and left a card. Thackeray did not return the courtesy until the day he left. He had been afraid, he wrote to Mrs. Procter, whose friendship he shared with Fanny, that Butler might invite him to dinner, and the dinner would have choked him.

The only reason for Thackeray's call was to see Fanny's daughters and to be able to send word of them to England. In this, the visitor was frustrated. Fan was still in boarding school, but Sarah, now eighteen, was at home and actually upstairs in the elegant house inhabited by the Butlers. Thackeray had heard Sally was, like her mother, very clever, and that her father was devoted to her. A request to see the young lady was politely ignored. To Thackeray Pierce looked incredibly youthful, "not yet thirty," and he had heard that he was "very busy at money making."

"I saw no end of Puseyite books in his room, on tables and bookshelves," the report continued (Pusey being a leader of the High Church Oxford Movement in England), "by which I judge he is of that sort—successful, too, among the ladies (I don't mean anything wrong, you know) but specious, eloquent, winning, and a *petit maître.* He wouldn't bring Sally down, though, for all my asking, and I was obliged to go away." [3]

Earlier, in November, Catharine Sedgwick had enjoyed one of Thackeray's lectures, but she did not like his books. They seemed to her neither humane nor genial; she found his women "over sweet and pretty—with all the weaknesses of the weakest maternity." Fanny's first reaction to *Vanity Fair* had also been unfavorable, though she judged Thackeray's cynicism to be only skin deep; he was actually one of the kindest and the most sensitive of mortals. Her esteem, however, was not returned in full. Thackeray who once, in speaking of his school fellows, had said, "We were all in love with you," now found Fanny, the middle-aged divorcee, hard to bear. She was too unlike his ideal of a good woman, an Amelia Sedley, and she had none of the fascinations of a wicked woman, a Becky Sharpe. He learned to "admire but not endure" Fanny because she was so kind to his daughters.

During the winter of 1853 Fanny was again in Rome with Adelaide and Edward Sartoris. Thackeray's girls were there also and were joined by their father after his American tour.

Anne Thackeray, later a novelist in her own right, appreciated all that Mrs. Kemble did for her, but was puzzled and somewhat disconcerted by Fanny's passion in speaking of slavery; she seemed to Anne to have felt more vividly than any slave could what it meant to be a slave. Her eccentricities were also embarrassing to a properly conventional miss. Fanny would sing loud enough to be heard by all who cared to listen while she drove about Rome, and once when the driver asked her where she wanted to go, she replied, "*Al diavolo*," ("To the devil"). "I do not care what anyone thinks or chooses to say of me," Fanny told Anne, "It does not in any way affect the truth." [4]

Fanny's defiant attitude also impressed Elizabeth Barrett Browning, who was in Rome that winter, and who had been told the sad story of Fanny's marriage by her friend, Mrs. Jameson. Fanny was "a very noble creature, indeed," Elizabeth thought, "but somewhat inelastic, impliant to the eye . . . She thinks me credulous and full of dreams, but does not despise me for that reason, which is good and tolerant of her, and pleasant, too, for I should not be quite easy under her contempt." [5]

On the whole, the poets Browning, Elizabeth and Robert, and to a far greater degree, William Makepeace Thackeray, preferred the younger of the Kemble sisters. Everyone loved Adelaide; she was so good-natured and so hospitable; she gave delightful evening parties at which she sang and Fanny read; she arranged weekly picnics in the Campagna, with *conversazione* before and after luncheon. Though Rome was still occupied by foreign troops and still showed scars of its siege by the French in 1849, the life of the *forestieri*, the outlanders, continued much as usual.

For Fanny, it was both a pleasure and a satisfaction to find one of Elizabeth Sedgwick's schoolgirls in Rome, one in whom she had always taken a particular interest. Harriet Hosmer of Watertown, Connecticut, had been a star performer at Fanny's teenage Lenox entertainments, on which occasions she had worn tight yellow pants and spouted comic poetry. Here she was in Rome, well on her way to becoming a successful sculptor, sufficiently grounded in anatomy, accepted as pupil in the studio of John Gibson, himself a pupil of Canova, and one of the most revered artists and teachers of his day. Harriet led an emancipated life. She wore short skirts, a smock, and a man's cap to protect her curls from marble dust. Having vowed never to marry, she was considered a good fellow, "a chap," by the horde of male students. In spite of protests by the Roman police, she rode about alone on horseback wherever she chose.

Harriet intended a trip to England in the spring of 1854, but received word that her father had had financial reverses and could no longer send her a stipend. He wanted her to come home at once, but Harriet canceled all plans for travel, sold her saddle horse, and elected to stay in Rome during the hot summer months to work hard and to make her art pay. On behalf of her "dear little Capellina"—Fanny's nickname for Harriet was an Italian version of Hattie and also a reference to the sculptor's beret— Fanny approached an earlier Hosmer benefactor, a Mr. Wayland Crow of St. Louis and a frequent summer visitor to Lenox. Harriet was dear to her as a close friend of her daughter Sarah, Fanny wrote; her talent was indubitable, and just in case Mr. Crow had heard of Capellina's free and easy ways, Fanny reminded him that geniuses were often—and justifiably—odd.

Fanny herself could not neglect her profession. Much as she enjoyed being with Adelaide, her trips to Italy were an extravagance. During the summer of 1854, which Harriet Hosmer had hoped to spend in England, Fanny was giving readings in London, in Manchester, and in Leeds. She sometimes read gratis for an audience of industrial workers; a generous slice of her earnings went to a fund that was being collected for Anna Jameson, now well along in years and impoverished by the death of the husband who had refused to live with her, but had contributed to her support.

On her return to England, Fanny thought her father seemed well and "younger than ever," but her brother Henry, whose Irish regiment had gone off to fight in the Crimea without him, was ill and looked "a great deal more dead than alive." Henry's trouble was diagnosed at first as inflammatory rheumatism, but he was actually a mental case and in August became an inmate of an insane asylum, Moorcroft House at Hillington. Fanny, who had sometimes wondered if she might not be going mad herself, went to see her brother whenever she could between engagements. Thackeray also visited him and found him in a euphoric mood; Henry thought he was staying at a gentleman's country seat and told vainglorious, "long-bow" stories to prove he was the bravest man, the best rider, and the most favored of all by the fair sex.

Fanny's concern for Henry was soon deflected to her father, whose look of youth and health was deceptive. One day he seemed well, the next feeble and despondent. Because John Kemble, as well as Adelaide, was living abroad, Fanny was alone with Charles when he died, after a brief illness, on November 4, 1854. Edward Sartoris, however, had thoughts of abandoning Italy and running for parliament, and Fanny was anxious for her sister and brother-in-law to be in England to look after Henry when she left for America.

Already, and all through the ensuing year, Fanny's eyes were fixed on a certain date, May 28, 1856. On that day Sarah Butler would be twenty-one years old and could do as she chose. Many a word concerning Sarah had come from Thackeray, from Harriet Hosmer, from Elizabeth Sedgwick and others, but lately Fanny had been hearing directly from both her girls, and all that she heard was encouraging. As reunion day approached, her excitement mounted.

When, early in May, Fanny landed in Boston, she was met by Sarah, who was "so handsome and so clever" that her mother longed to show her to all her English friends. One house party after another filled the Lenox cottage. There were dances; there were mountain-climbing expeditions, some as far afield as the Presidential Range. Fanny found that Sarah was a good musician, a far better pianist than she. Many evenings were happily devoted to the playing of duets.

In the autumn, however, Sarah elected to go back to Philadelphia, and Fanny went about her business. As in England, there were friends to smooth her way. Before going abroad, Fanny had met a Charles Baldwin Sedgwick, who lived in Syracuse, but who often came to visit his kinfolk in Lenox; "Dear Sir and Cousin," Fanny addressed him; his wife was her "dear Dora." During Fanny's repeated tours of upper New York State and as far west as St. Louis, Charles of Syracuse provided tips on hotels and travel routes, newspaper clippings and letters of introduction. He even saw to it that here and there a riding horse was available. In Boston and its environs, Fanny was entertained by the Longfellows and became familiar with their academic circle; with Motley, the historian; Agassiz, the naturalist; and with James Russell Lowell.

As she moved about, Fanny viewed the spectacle of burgeoning America with awe and with distrust. New cities were building, new lands were being opened up, new railroads were pushing out across the continent. Yet another financial panic was on its way, preceded by something new in panics, a frenzy of speculation. Stocks changed hands so rapidly that businessmen had to be informed by conservative commentators that the New York Stock Exchange was not a gambling hell.

And one of the more reckless gamblers was Pierce Butler, whom Thackeray had heard was very busy making money only a few years earlier. In June of 1856, while Fanny and Sarah were enjoying the Berkshires, diarist Sidney Fisher was told by his brother Henry, a financier, of Butler's gigantic losses. By the end of the year things had come to such a pass that a syndicate was formed to take over the management of the Butler estate. Henry Fisher, Pierce's brother-in-law, George Cadwalader, and a third man of affairs undertook to pay Pierce a small income for an indefinite period, that is to say, until his debts had been paid.

The debts amounted to half a million dollars, Fanny was told, perhaps too high a figure. She lamented nevertheless "the ruin of my girls earthly prospects through their father's insane gambling." [6] The girls would have to live in a second-rate boarding-house, since the elegant Philadelphia mansion, which Thackeray had visited, had been put up for sale. Butler Place might be cut up into small lots and thus disposed of. As for Fanny, her alimony allowance never had been paid and she had been much too proud and scornful to demand it. Now she seriously considered bringing a suit for the sake of her children.

CHAPTER XVIII

THE BIRTH OF A COPPERHEAD

(February 1859–September 1861)

As a result of the panic of 1857, there were hunger and noisy labor demonstrations in cities of the North. The Southland suffered less, though there the price of cotton went down, while the price of slaves rose to fantastic heights. Even in Philadelphia there was talk of the slave trade's revival.

To the caretakers of the Butler estate, it seemed wise to retain the Georgia plantations as a source of future income, but a sale of the plantations' human livestock was a quick and easy means of raising money. To this scheme, Pierce Butler offered resistance. More and more, he had come to identify himself with his grandfather, who had been such a successful planter and such a kind master. A kind master did not sell his slaves! Pierce's conviction that a paternal possession of one's fellow man was just had been strengthened, no doubt, by his conflict with Fanny and by the many pleasant winter months he had spent in the islands. On one of his recent trips, Pierce had taken Sarah with him to renew her childhood memories of the plantation and to give her a taste of Southern hospitality.

But now the bare, cold facts of necessity had to be faced. In February 1859 Pierce left for Savannah, Georgia, to be present at an auction of 436 men, women, and children who had lived all

149

their lives either on Butler Island, or at Hampton Point. This was only half of the plantation work force. After the death of John Butler, who had gone with a Philadelphia regiment to Mexico and had died, not of wounds received in battle, but of dysentery, there was a division of the slave community, part of it going to John's widow Gabriella in trust for her only child, a daughter, and part to Pierce.

Slightly in advance of Pierce's departure, a young man named Mortimer Thomson, who was a reporter for *The New York Daily Tribune*, also headed for Savannah. *The Tribune*, whose editor, Horace Greeley, carried a multiplicity of banners for reform, had been printing news items which illustrated the inhumanities of Northern racism; a poor old woman, for example, had been denied a seat in a New York bus and when she protested, was pushed off into the snow. The Savannah sale seemed well worth covering, since it was one of the largest that had taken place recently in "Star Spangled America." The breakup of an old family estate was also unusual.

On arrival, several days before the sale, Mr. Thomson found the Savannah hotels crowded with speculators from North and South Carolina, Virginia, Georgia, Alabama, and Louisiana. The slaves had been brought in from the islands and were housed in the stables of a racecourse, three miles outside the city. Thomson hid his identity and joined parties that went out to look the prospects over. The buyers were, on the whole, a repellent breed, though various types were represented, from the out-and-out bully, who boasted of managing niggers with a whip or branding iron, to sleek, elderly, gold-rimmed-spectacled individuals, who might have been mistaken for pillars of the church, but who went about pestering the black women with indecently intimate questions. To pull open a mouth to look at the teeth, to pinch a muscle to test its firmness, or to command a slave to trot about to make sure he was not lame was standard procedure.

The sale was to last two days. On the opening day, March 2, Pierce Butler appeared. Thomson noticed that most of the blacks seemed glad to see him, and to some he gave a gloved hand to shake. It had been advertised that the lot would be sold by families. A family, however, consisted, as a rule, of a man and woman and perhaps two young children; larger relationships were not taken into account. The groups or individuals were led to the block by a smiling mulatto, who seemed to think the whole affair a joke. The auctioneer, a beefy, red-faced man, kept everyone in good humor by many a jest and quip.

Thomson, who had read *Uncle Tom's Cabin* and who had the true reporter's eye for personal detail, told of a pair of lovers parted, of a father pleading unsuccessfully for the purchase of his older children, of a young girl, under whose shawl was hidden a baby only two weeks old. The highest price paid for a family was in excess of six thousand dollars, and though an older man and woman without offspring went for a mere $250 apiece, a carpenter named William was considered a bargain at $1750.

Throughout the two day's chaffer a cold rain fell, and a bar which had been opened on the lower floor of the building was well patronized. On the final day a basket of champagne was broached, a free treat for all. The sun came out. The moment for parting had come. Again Thomson's attention was focused on Pierce Butler. Pierce stood at the door of the stable, with a bag of silver coins on a table beside him. To each of his former slaves he gave four shining silver quarters, a gift which, as Thomson remarked, he could well afford, since the proceeds of the sale had amounted to $303,850. Thomson was only surprised that no charge had been made for the dingy and wretchedly inadequate clothes which the slaves wore. In the North one did not need to throw in the harness when one sold a horse!

The tone of Thomson's article, which appeared in *The Tribune* soon after the Savannah sale, was symptomatic of the deepening hostilities that prevailed in the nation. Fanny had returned to a torn and angry America. A guerilla war—some already called it a civil war—was being fought in Kansas. On May 20, 1856, a proslavery force, armed with five cannon, devastated the prairie town of Lawrence. On the same day Charles Sumner delivered his *Crime Against Kansas* speech in the Senate. It was laced with invective against Southern senators and provoked an attack upon him by a Southerner, who came up behind him as he sat at his desk and bludgeoned him. The attacker was hugged and kissed by Southern ladies, but a roar of protest came from Northern moderates, as well as radicals. The nonviolent antislavery faction felt, as Lydia Maria Child expressed it, that their pacifist principles "were shivering in the wind."

Fanny must have read the *Tribune* article, though her only mention of the sale that has survived was made many years later, after Pierce had been accused of taking time by the forelock in disposing of his plantation workers. Fanny refuted the implication that her former husband had foreseen the downfall of slavery in 1859; she gave him credit, however, for being pained and mortified by the step he had been forced to take.

Panic and depression had cut the income from Fanny's savings in half, but as long as her earning power persisted she could give her girls luxuries which their father could not, or should not, afford. In the summer of 1859 young Miss Fanny Butler, who had just achieved her majority, went with her mother on a European tour that included Switzerland, France, England, and Scotland.

Both of the Butler girls were comely, but they differed greatly in appearance, the elder being tall, willowy, and blonde, the younger a petite brunette. As a child, Fan had been delicate and slow to develop. She had outgrown her weaknesses. In physical stamina and in fervent appreciation of the beauties of nature, Fan rivaled her mother. She was an ideal companion on Alpine paths or in the English hunting field.

For Fanny it would have been a double pleasure to have had both her daughters with her, but there was a very good reason for Sarah's having stayed at home. That summer she was married to Dr. Owen Jones Wister, a descendant of German Quak-

ers who had come to the New World early in the eighteenth
century, a young man who, according to Sidney Fisher, had a
large practice and was very much liked. Fanny made the acquaintance of her son-in-law as she disembarked with Fan in Boston.
After only two or three days of united family life, the three
young folk went their way, and Fanny was once more alone.
She had had to accept the fact that, however rewarding her con-
tacts with her daughters were, there were large areas of their
lives she was forbidden to enter. She could be fairly sure that
they loved her, but they also loved their father.

For this reason, perhaps, and at this time, thoughts of Pierce
rankled. Fanny's friends, the Sedgwicks of Syracuse, had read
her *Journal* of 1835 and wanted to know who all the people were
whose identities were concealed by the use of dashes and initials.
Fanny provided them with a copy in which the full names had
been written in, in pencil. While she was in Lenox and had some
spare time on her hands she told them to send the book back to
her so that she could interleave it with further information. What
Fanny wrote of Pierce was, to say the least, uncharitable. The
Englishman who had introduced him to her and to her father was
one of "the most profligate and unprincipled men I have ever
known." A friend of Pierce's youth told her he was mad and
said, "Since you have married that man there must be *something*
good in him!"

Fanny also informed the Sedgwicks of the illicit love affair,
which had occurred at the time of Sarah's birth, and giving the
name of the young woman involved, the daughter of Pierce's
doctor, asked that the page be torn out of the book after it had
been read. Even Fanny's view of public events echoed her animosity. A crisis impended, a "yawning chasm," but the South,
Fanny felt, had been hopelessly corrupted by slavery, while the
North had been demoralized by its greedy, insatiable pursuit of
wealth. On either count, Pierce Butler stood indicted.

*   *   *

If Fanny could be said to have a home in the fifties and early sixties, it was at her Perch above the lake in Lenox. There had been sad changes in the Happy Valley. Charles Sedgwick was dead and had been carried to his grave by a group of farmworkers who demanded the right of paying tribute to their best friend. Theodore Sedgwick had also died. Though Elizabeth still continued with her school work, her health had begun to fail, and more and more of Catharine's time was spent near Boston with her beloved niece, Kate Minot.

Catharine had recently published yet another novel, *Married, or Single*, in which she championed the right of feminine self-determination; she had, however, reached an age when the past is more vivid and more authentic than the present. For the Minots' little daughter Alice, Great Aunt Kitty was writing her reminiscences of the long ago, when the house at Stockbridge was full of young people, when the mailbag came only once a week, and when, to keep a fire smoldering on the hearth in winter, a great log was dragged up to the door by a horse and rolled in across the floor, making a sound like thunder.

Fanny came and went as her working schedule allowed. Her stay in Lenox in the summer of 1860 was broken by a visit to Germantown, to which she was drawn by a "grandmotherly yearning." Sarah had given birth on July 14 to a son, Owen Wister, who, according to Sidney Fisher, first saw the light of day under unusual circumstances. No preparation for the event had been made; there was no one in the house but Dr. Wister and an inexperienced servant girl, and there was even no layette for the baby, Sarah having been "fractious" and refusing to take a proper interest.

Mother and child, however, were doing well by the time Fanny arrived. To pay his respects to Mrs. Kemble, Fisher made a special trip by the horsecars out to Germantown. He now wholeheartedly approved of Fanny; she was "a woman of genius, and of noble impulses, and kind feelings." [1] They talked animatedly of many things; of books and authors, of English country life and politics—for who could avoid the subject of politics in 1860?

Philadelphia was having its full, uproarious share of town meetings, stump oratory, and torchlight processions. A great effort was being made by all parties to attract the vote of recent immigrants, and Fanny was afraid only that in the universal hubbub the voice of the New England Puritan farmer, whom she considered "the most intelligent man of his class in the whole world," would be drowned out.[2]

On November 6 Abraham Lincoln was elected to the Presidency, having been nominated on a ticket which did not promise to do away with slavery, but only to prevent its extension. Fanny was expecting to spend the greater part of the winter in her cottage and for domestic help would depend upon some young ex-convicts in whom Charles Sedgwick had taken an interest. Until late November Fan was also in Lenox, having come up from New York where she had danced at a ball with the Prince of Wales, whose visit to the United States was giving a little light-hearted and much-needed diversion to the nation.

Fanny was amused to hear her daughter say casually that the Prince "seemed to be a nice little fellow, who danced rather well." This was not the moment to be overawed by royalty. On December 20 South Carolina seceded from the Union, and "the perilous state of the country" was occupying the thoughts of Sidney Fisher, who was planning to write an article on secession, on how to make it "safe and easy, since secession is to be."

In the next of his diary paragraphs, Sidney mentioned Fan in giving the gist of a conversation he had had with her father. "Butler is eager for secession," Sidney wrote, "and has just returned from Georgia, where he says there is no difference of opinion. He said that he came here only to *buy arms*"—Sidney underlined the words—"and intends to return immediately and join the army. He will take his daughter Fanny with him and has bought a rifle for *her*, too, for he says even the women in the South are going to fight. What madness, yet one cannot help admiring the knightly spirit these southern men are displaying." [3]

There was no doubt in Sidney's mind that Pierce Butler should now be classified as a Southerner, his daughter also. Whether Fanny Butler got her rifle and whether she went South with her father in midwinter is uncertain; there is evidence, however, of yet another Southern journey which actually took place three months later.

On March 26, 1861, only seventeen days before the firing on Fort Sumter, Sidney went to call on his cousin Joshua Francis Fisher and his wife Eliza. Eliza was a birthright Middleton of South Carolina. She was leaving the following day for Charleston to visit her relatives while still the way was open. "Her escort," Sidney chronicled, "is to be Pierce Butler, who will be accompanied by his daughter Fanny. Odd changes sometimes occur in people's relations to each other, and that Mrs. Fisher should travel with Butler is one of the oddest." [4]

Because of their friendship for Fanny senior, and the fact that Joshua Francis had taken Charles Sumner's place as her trustee, the Fishers had been loud in denunciation of Pierce. They had even refused to speak to him until, a year earlier, they had wanted to invite Sarah and Fan to a party and felt they couldn't do so without including the young ladies' father. "Butler went to the party," Sidney rounded out his narrative, "and, as he well knows how to do, if he pleases, made himself acceptable to Mrs. Fisher. The acquaintance being thus renewed, secession, I suppose, has proved a bond of sympathy."

To travel innocuously with a party of ladies may have suited Pierce's purpose, and by the latter part of June, Fan was safely back in Lenox. In the interval much had happened. The seceding states already had a constitution, which had been praised for its renunciation of the principles of Thomas Jefferson by Vice-President Alexander Stephens in a speech at Savannah. "Our new government," Stephens had said, "is founded on exactly the opposite ideas . . . Its cornerstone rests upon the great truth that the Negro is not equal to the white man, that slavery, subordination to the superior race, is his natural and moral condition." [5]

After the bombardment of Sumter, Lincoln called for seventy-five thousand volunteers. In the evening one heard the tap of a drum along the streets of remote and peaceful Lenox, summoning the young men out to drill. Fanny saw the Stars and Stripes flying from the flagpole of many a lonely farmhouse. In July came news of the disaster at Bull Run, of which a scathing account was given in *The London Times* by William Howard Russell, who had won his reporter's accolade in the Crimean War. Fanny feared intervention by a foreign power; England and Europe would be glad to see the New World divided and impotent. She disliked the brag and invective of American journalism, but felt sure that the Northern Americans, whom she knew so well, were brave enough to fight successfully.

In August Sarah came up for a holiday from her maternal duties. She was as fond of her baby, Fanny later remarked, as she could be of anything that so closely resembled an animal and that did not appeal to her intellect.

But Sarah's stay and Fan's were curtailed. On August 15, Simon Cameron, Secretary of War, ordered a Philadelphia marshal to arrest Pierce Butler on a charge of treason. He was taken to Fort Hamilton in New York Harbor. The girls left at once to visit him.

"Knowing Mr. Butler's southern sympathies," Fanny wrote to her English friends, "I think the charge very likely to be true." She thought that Pierce would be detained until the conclusion of the war, since he would not take an oath of allegiance and "was inimical both on public and private grounds to Mr. Lincoln and his ministers." [6]

Sidney Fisher was not surprised by the arrest and thought it a good thing that Pierce Butler should be locked up; he would find plenty of congenial company in prison. Southern sympathizers were making a great deal of trouble in Philadelphia by their talk, but so far the government was lenient to suspects. In September Sidney's brother Henry went to Washington to plead successfully for Pierce's release. Pierce had maintained his innocence under questioning, and no incriminating data was discovered in his papers. He evaded the oath of allegiance, however, by saying that if he took it he might lose his property in Georgia. The plantations now were his and his alone, John Butler's heir, a daughter, Mrs. Julian McCallister, having died without issue. Pierce promised to commit no act hostile to the United States and would only be allowed to travel on a passport issued by the State Department. It was urged in the prisoner's behalf that he had two daughters who were northern women and distressed by his plight. One of them was married to a staunch Republican.

CHAPTER XIX

A FAIR AND ACCURATE ACCOUNT

(September 1861–July 1863)

FANNY HAD HOPED that Pierce's incarceration would make Fan completely dependent upon her and available for a trip to Europe in the summer of 1862. Fan apparently did not make up her mind to leave her father and to fall in with her mother's plans until the last moment. After a few weeks of Switzerland in July and August, Mrs. Kemble and Miss Butler went to England, where a cottage was rented for the winter at the gate of an estate in Hampshire, now the home of Adelaide Sartoris and her family.

Before leaving America Fanny had spent some time in Washington in close communion with the Sedgwicks of Syracuse. Charles Baldwin Sedgwick was now a New York congressman and one of the more radical group, the power of which had increased after the rout at Bull Run. The antagonistic account of that battle that appeared in *The London Times* was only one of a series of attacks upon the Union. When in October of that same year, the Southern emissaries, Mason and Slidell, were forcibly removed from a British steamer by an overzealous Navy captain, the incident was represented as a deliberately hostile act. Fanny was relieved that the *Trent* affair did not result in war, but her anxiety smoldered and was fueled by the bad news

which came throughout the summer of 1862: the defeats in
Virginia, the invasion of Maryland, the threat to Pennsylvania.
These were "terrible and sorrowful events," Fanny wrote to
her trusty friend, Joshua Francis Fisher. "I am grieved at the
tone of our press upon the subject of your national troubles and
am frequently surprised and pained by the total absence of
sympathy with the northern cause." [1]

On October 4, 1862, the news of Lincoln's first and somewhat
tentative Emancipation Proclamation reached England. Word
had also come of the enrollment of a black regiment. Lincoln,
The Times declared, was calling for a slave revolt throughout the
South. Some gorgeously purple prose was employed a few days
later to describe the American President rubbing his hands with
glee while the flames shot up and shrieks resounded through the
night. Less lurid, but equally damaging, was a speech delivered
at Newcastle-on-Tyne by the Chancellor of the Exchequer,
William Ewart Gladstone, whose family had made an enormous
fortune from slave labor in the West Indies. Gladstone declared
that Jefferson Davis had created both an army, a navy, and a
nation; he gave the impression that recognition of the Confederacy was not far off. If that was the intention of the British
Cabinet, Charles Francis Adams wrote in his diary, his stay in
London would be brief. The American Minister had had the
temerity to threaten war if the South was recognized.

To Charles Greville, the diarist who had taken such an unsympathetic view of her marriage difficulties and who had asked
various questions concerning the Lincoln Proclamation, Fanny
wrote a lengthy letter, which showed she had been a good lis-
tener during her Washington stay, since it represented the views
of the lawmakers with whom she had consorted. In reviewing
the events leading up to the war, Fanny bewailed Northern
racism and the long tolerance of Southern hegemony in the
Congress. She mentioned the Texas question, which William
Ellery Channing and Theodore Sedgwick had attacked so elo-
quently; she touched upon the emergence of the Republican

party, the bloodletting in Kansas, the attack upon Charles Sumner, and the "strange and piteous" episode of John Brown's raid.

Like Gladstone, Charles Greville had a connection with the Indies. Early in life he was gifted with a lucrative and completely sinecure government position as Secretary to the Island of Jamaica. One of the questions he put to Fanny must have been coupled with a statement that emancipation would lead to sloth. Fanny assured Greville that the Southern states of America were not tropical, that frosts occurred in Florida, and food did not drop from the trees, as in Jamaica. To eat, the freed slave would have to work, and if he was paid for his work the entire agricultural community would benefit. Eventually the black man would come to own the land he cultivated; citizenship was inevitable and could be dealt with by later legislation.

Fanny realized that no definite plans could be evolved at present and while the war continued, but she had heard of thousands of blacks having followed the Union armies and being employed as laborers and soldiers. These people, she wrote, who had been armed and already enjoyed a more invigorating diet than boiled rice and hominy, would never be the same again. The only insurrection to be feared was if the freedom granted was withdrawn. Then there would be a revolt in every state, in every county, on every plantation, a struggle as fierce as it would be futile, for its only end could be the total extermination of the resubjugated slave.

Greville was not the only individual to whom Fanny tried to give what she considered "a fair and accurate account" [2] of the American situation. She also had a talk with Lord Clarendon, a liberal peer and a former foreign minister. These persuasive efforts probably took place in the period between Lincoln's first proclamation and his second, which was issued on January 1, 1863, for soon after that event was made known in Britain Fanny reached for a larger audience. There was no reason now why the *Plantation Journal* should not be published. Both of Fanny's daughters were of age; one of them was married to a

staunch Republican, as the petition for Pierce's release from
prison had stated, while the other was with her mother in England.

In handing over her manuscript to Messrs Longman, Fanny
gave it a topical significance. From the first *The Times* had
maintained that the conflict between the States had nothing to do
with slavery; Fanny put on her title page a quotation from the
speech of Alexander H. Stephens in which the Vice-President of
the Confederacy pointed to slavery as the cornerstone of their
new government. A few passages of text of the *Journal* were
omitted as being too personal, and the letter to Greville and the
earlier letter to *The Times* concerning *Uncle Tom's Cabin* were
added as appendices. The substance of the book, however, which
was affectionately dedicated to Elizabeth Sedgwick, stood as it
had stood for more than twenty years. Fanny's brief preface was
dated London, January 16, 1863. It reads:

"The following diary was kept in the winter and spring of
1838-9 on an estate consisting of rice and cotton plantations in
the islands at the entrance of the Altamaha, on the coast of
Georgia.

"The slaves in whom I then had an unfortunate interest were
sold some years ago. The islands themselves are at present in the
power of the Northern troops. The record contained in the
following pages is a picture of conditions of human existence
which I hope and believe have passed away."

"The islands themselves are at present in the power of the
Northern troops"—this, also, was something of which Fanny
must have heard talk in Washington as a *fait accompli*. Her
friend, Charles Baldwin Sedgwick, was a member of a congressio-
nal committee appointed to investigate corruption in the United
States Navy, the pressing and important task of the Navy being
to blockade the southern coast. In November of 1861 Forts
Beauregard and Walker, guarding the entrance to Port Royal
Sound, were bombarded by a Northern squadron. When a toe-

hold for the Union had thus been established midway between Charleston and Savannah, St. Simon's Island and Fernandina in Florida were also occupied. Heavily fortified by the Confederates in the earliest days of the war, St. Simon's defensive force had been withdrawn to guard Savannah and its entire civilian population evacuated to the mainland.

The Sea Islands, indeed, had become the focus of political as well as of naval strategy during the early months of 1862. On Port Royal, and to a lesser extent on St. Simon's, hundreds of black folk had begun to collect as soon as the Union forces took over. From these refugees from coastal plantations whose proprietors had fled, a black regiment was recruited by Major General David Hunter, who had asked for the assignment as Commander of the Department of the South in order to speed the program of the radical group in Congress, a group in which Fanny's friends, Charles Sumner and Congressman Sedgwick of New York, were prominent. Hunter even went so far as to put his minute, insular domain under martial law and to issue an order on May 11, freeing all slaves in South Carolina, Georgia and Florida. The order was promptly voided for fear of offending the loyal, slave holding states, and President Lincoln's first reaction to the proposed arming of black men was unfavorable.

The question of armament, however, and the question of emancipation were closely related, even as Fanny had suggested in her true and accurate account to Charles Greville. The radicals continued to exert their pressure. Sumner called for a proclamation on the 4th of July, but Lincoln waited until after a minor military success, the retreat of Lee's army to Antietam, was reported in September. In the hundred days that followed many doubted a second proclamation and many—Congressman Sedgwick was one—feared a lack of implementation, a fear which Fanny had dramatized in her premonition of a slave revolt on every plantation if freedom was granted, then later cancelled.

In England both of the proclamations had their effect. After that of January, 1863, there were massive labor meetings at

which republican sentiments were tossed about. Young Henry
Adams, son of the American Minister, went to a rally which was
held in London's Exeter Hall. He was exhilarated by the groans
and hisses that followed every mention of the South. "Emancipation and reunion" were so wildly cheered that Henry wrote to
his brother, Charles Francis jr., who was with a Massachusetts
regiment at Port Royal, that the Queen's crown might be tottering on her head. The British Empire had itself been challenged
—"these are lively times, oh, Hannibal." [3]

The Times of London, however, continued, as Adams put it,
"to scold like a drunken drab," and Fanny was not yet reassured.
The Adams family might be excluded from certain social circles,
but they had constant encouragement from such liberals as John
Stuart Mill and the great Quaker parliamentarian, John Bright;
they were invited to dine with the Duke of Argyll, whose wife
was the daughter of the Duchess of Sutherland, author of the
great appeal to American women to abolish slavery. Fanny, on
the other hand, was embedded in a nest of Southern sympathizers, not the least fervent of whom was her daughter, Fanny
Butler. Like young Henry Adams, Fanny saw the issue in terms
of class struggle. A Sonnet on the American War which she
wrote during this time of dark uncertainty begins with the lines:

> She has gone down—they shout it from afar,
> Kings—nobles—priests—all men of every race,
> Whose lagging clogs Time's swift, relentless pace,
> She has gone down, our evil boding star!

Needless to say, America could only be "an evil boding star" to
reactionaries.

In May, while a motion for recognition of the Confederacy, in
concert with other European powers, was being debated in Parliament, Fanny's book appeared. It caused little stir. Many of the
weeklies and all but one of the small circulation, but influential,
quarterlies ignored it. The Athenaeum, to be sure, was favorably
impressed by its antiaristocratic tone, and so was The Spectator.

The London Review of Politics, Society and Literature, however, while admitting that Fanny's account of slavery was "beyond the power of imagination to conjure up," also praised "the pluck and good sportsmanship" of the Southern war effort.

The most virulent hostility shown was that of *The Saturday Review.* In its issue of June 13, a strongly antifeminist reviewer was "amused" by the mere idea of a lady criticizing the system which prevailed on her husband's plantation. Fanny had apparently enjoyed letting her readers know she had first learned to dislike her husband as a slaveholder. And some of the details she revealed were fit only for a medical publication! The *Journal,* in short, was unworthy of a place in the drawing room and inappropriate for "the amusement of a family group." [4]

But if Fanny's book had fizzled, so had the debate in Parliament. The British government was playing a waiting game. Its hands-off policy toward the United States did not crystallize until after the Union victories at Gettysburg and Vicksburg were announced. Even while these engagements were being fought, in July, Fanny was writing to an American friend that she would be glad to leave England where so much that she heard of America was painful to her.

CHAPTER XX

OUR FOREHEADS IN THE DUST

(June 1863–June 1865)

THE AMERICAN FRIEND to whom Fanny wrote that she would be glad to leave England because of anti-American propaganda was John Murray Forbes, a shipping and railroad magnate who had come abroad on a secret mission to prevent the building of Confederate ironclads in Liverpool. Forbes was one of the Boston friends Fanny had made in her early days in America. He was a great admirer of her art as reader and preferred it to her art as actress. Fanny's rendering of the witches' scene in *Macbeth*, he said, made his eyebrows stand on end and push against the rim of his spectacles. When the *Journal* appeared, Forbes urged an American edition, something which Fanny had thought would be unnecessary. The arrangement for the publication by Harper & Brothers in New York was entrusted to Forbes's cousin, Francis George Shaw, a transplanted New Englander who was living on Staten Island.

Shaw's wife Sarah had given comfort to Fanny during her days of domestic trial. In 1853 she and her family were in Europe and Fanny saw much of them in Italy. At that time the Shaws' only son, Robert Gould, was in a Swiss boarding school and came to spend the holidays with his parents at Sorrento. Fanny thought him, as so many others did, as beautiful as an angel, and he, in turn, was fascinated by the stories she told of her life on the Georgian islands.

In June, 1863, Robert Gould Shaw was on his way from Port Royal to St. Simons.

A new chapter had been added to the history of that off-shore paradise. After the crew of a single Union gunboat, the *U.S.S. Pocahontas*, had taken possession of the island on March 9, 1862, the influx of blacks, which had taken place on a larger scale farther up the coast, began. These so-called contrabands of war, most of whom were male and few of local origin, were set to work planting corn, cotton and potatoes under naval super-vision. The population swelled to five hundred, but a sense of security was lacking. The contrabands lived in fear of being kid-napped by small groups of confederate guerillas, who came over from the mainland at night. The leader of a posse which dared to follow a trail of these marauders into a swamp was shot at close range and killed.

Since the naval garrison was too small to police the entire area, help was asked from Port Royal, and for three months, from August to November, St. Simons was under the protection of General Hunter's black regiment. This force, however, was also recalled as the pinch for manpower was felt and thousands of troops were sent north to the support of McClellan in Virginia. Once more the territory where Major Butler had founded his cotton kingdom was denuded of its inhabitants. At the time of the first evacuation personal effects and household furniture were loaded onto scows; now the crews of the gunboats removed everything that could be of any possible use to the War Depart-ment: farm implements, wagons, live stock. Some of the contra-bands were sent north to Carolina, others south to Fernandina, Florida.

Thus the island on which Robert Gould Shaw landed in June 1863 seemed to him as empty of human life as the seabeach of Prospero's isle. He had come as colonel of a new black regiment, the Fifty-fourth Massachusetts, which had been recruited in Boston with the aid of such abolition stalwarts as Wendell Phillips and Frederick Douglass. Its first assignment to active duty was to cooperate with a unit of Hunter's Volunteers in a raid on the mainland community of Darien. The citizenry of Darien had also fled, but had left much behind them. Shaw was shocked when he heard the Commander of the Volunteers, a bushwacker named Montgomery, telling his men to take what they wanted and to then set fire to the town. Only a Negro church and the cabin of a free black man were spared.

Before and after this episode, which Shaw protested and considered a disgrace to his fledgling soldiers, some pleasant days were spent on St. Simons. The regiment was bivouacked on a plantation somewhat south of Hampton Point, at Pike's Bluff. Shaw had time to explore widely and noted how abundant deer and other wild creatures had become after their chief enemy, man, had departed.

But not all the enemy had gone. Shaw did not fail to visit the Butler plantation, thinking how strange it was that he, who had only heard of its existence years ago and thousands of miles away, should be seeing it now, deserted and in conquered territory. In the old manor house, which Major Butler had built to face the river and which Fanny had considered a hopeless ruin in 1838, a few black people were living.

Who were they, and where had they come from? Shaw did not question them closely, but some with whom he chatted must have been sold at Savannah in 1859. They told him of that catastrophe; they spoke of it, with unconscious poetry, as "the weeping time." From some inland plantation, perhaps from a hundred miles away, they had returned to the only place they could call home. How great their pleasure was when this attractive young soldier told them he knew "Miss Fanny!" Would Miss Fanny come back, they asked; would she bring her children with her?

Shaw also visited a small chapel, encrusted with pink lichen, which stood near his encampment. He did not know its history.

Pike's Bluff Plantation belonged to the Hazzard family, which had feuded with the clan of Wylly, and the result of the feud, the shooting of a Wylly by a Hazzard, Fanny had recounted in her *Journal* as spot news, though it had actually occurred just before she came to the islands. Though protected by the decision of a jury and by the code of honor, which Fanny despised, the Hazzards were cold-shouldered by their neighbors, so much so that they ceased to attend the island church and built themselves a family chapel, surrounded by a family burying ground. One of the leaders of the guerilla bands that had made secret expeditions to St. Simons in the preceding summer was William Miles Hazzard, who, after being pursued from one hiding place to another in the swamps by black soldiers, wrote to a friend that "if you want to know hell before your time you have only to be hunted about for ten days by a gang of niggers."[1]

Shaw noticed that the pink chapel had been vandalized, the gravestone leveled; he tried with his men to set things to rights. Recently Miles Hazzard had heard of the desecration and had made another nocturnal expedition to the island to see with his own eyes. He wrote a scathing, vituperative note, vowing vengeance, and left it stuck up on a stick, but that, too, had disappeared before Shaw's visit.

The Fifty-fourth Massachusets was soon back at Hilton Head, the center of military and naval operations. General Hunter had been succeeded by a new commander, Gillmore, an engineer and artillerist, who intended to threaten Charleston by getting control of the batteries on two islands to the south of Fort Sumter. Robert Shaw begged to take part in this endeavor, which would show the mettle of his men and erase the stigma of the Darien raid.

On July 11, at dusk of a cold, rainy day, the attack on Battery Wagner on Morris Island was made. The black troops had only just arrived in the combat area and were exhausted by lack of food, sleep, and even water for the past forty-eight hours. They approached the battery along a corridor of sand, waves rolling in on one hand, bursts of fire from the fort on the other. The outer ramparts had just been reached when the big guns opened up. For a moment, before he pitched forward into the dark, Shaw was seen standing on the parapet, waving on his men to follow him. Out of his regiment of six hundred, 270 died or were wounded in this luckless, suicidal adventure. The worth of black soldiery, however, had been established for all war-minded Americans, and Shaw, who was buried in a mass grave with his men, had become a hero, immortalized in bronze for future generations.

"How I wonder how it fared with those you love in all these late disasters," Fanny wrote to John Murray Forbes, who had left for home, his mission done. Fanny had had no word whatsoever and was particularly worried for Frank Shaw's son and "for all the precious, precious lives offered up for sacrifice to redeem your land. Oh, what a country it ought to be hereafter, ransomed at such a cost!" [2]

The idea of redemption, with its biblical overtones, gave a little, but only a little, comfort to those who had first envisioned the end of slavery by peaceful means, by an appeal to the conscience of the individual slaveholder. Fanny had to weep eventually, not only for Robert Gould Shaw, but for many others. One of those she mourned was Elizabeth Sedgwick's son Will, who died at Antietam, leaving a young wife and two small children, for whom Elizabeth, ill and impoverished, had to provide. As the war lengthened, Fanny felt that only a Dante, or a Milton, could do justice to the suffering it had caused. Her fears of intervention, to be sure, had been allayed by the English reaction to Gettysburg. There the true voice of the nation had spoken, she wrote; compared to it, the voice of aristocracy was like the buzzing of gnats.

Though Fanny resented the accusation of her *Journal*'s being fiction or its having been subsidized, she did not overestimate its effect on public opinion. It may have seemed ironic to her that the publication of her book in America, which was coeval with the victories of Grant and Meade, the assault on Fort Wagner, and the vicious race riots in New York, which took the lives of hundreds of blacks, should have caused so much comment, most of which was favorable. "The most powerful antislavery book yet written," was the verdict of *Harper's New Monthly Magazine*. George William Curtis in *The Atlantic*, termed it "a permanent and most valuable chapter in our history." Curtis also took account of the fact that Fanny had produced another American *Journal* in 1835 and compared the brilliant girl of that youthful tour de force with the mature and sobered woman of 1838. Her power to convey emotion had magnified. "There is no writing for effect," Curtis added. "There is not a single sensational passage . . . A sadder book the human hand never wrote."

As in the case of the earlier *Journal*, other publications were brought out to shine by its reflected light. A Judge Woodward and a Bishop Hopkins gave their views on slavery, illustrated by passages from Fanny's work. The description of the Savannah auction of 1859 which Mortimer Thomson had written for *The Tribune* was reissued in pamphlet form as *A Sequel to Mrs. Kemble's Journal*. Within the year, Fanny was quoted as an authority on the effect of slavery upon women in the report of a commission, appointed by War Secretary Stanton, to look into the status of the Freedman, ex-contraband of war: his disabilities, his prospects for the future. The Board of Inquiry was made up of three distinguished investigators, Robert Dale Owen, Samuel Gridley Howe, and Colonel James McKaye. Their study was broad in scope; it became the blueprint of the Freedman's Bureau Act of 1865.

Fanny was probably unaware of these tributes to the value of her observations, for, though she had told John Murray Forbes that she would be glad to leave England, she stayed on while Fan went back to America and again returned to her mother in the spring of 1864. Proximity to Adelaide, her dear and only surviving sibling, meant much to Fanny; both of her brothers, John and Henry, had died during her latest absence in America.

In England, also, there was work to do and money to be earned. Fanny gave readings and contributed an article, "On the Stage" to *The Cornhill Magazine*, a new periodical, the first editor of which had been William Makepeace Thackeray. Fanny's essay picks out her mother as the most gifted of her entire family, from a dramatic point of view, but denigrates acting, as an art "that requires no study worthy of the name; it creates nothing; it perpetuates nothing."

Eighteen sixty-three also saw the publication of a collection of Fanny's dramatic works. To see in print the text of *An English Tragedy*, the play that William Charles Macready had thought so powerful, but had failed to produce, must have been a welcome sight to Fanny, for she considered it the best thing she had ever written. And when the City of Richmond fell on April 3, 1865, Fanny was again moved to poetic utterance:

> Thy work is done, God terrible and just!
> Who laidst upon our hearts and hands this task;
> Now, kneeling with our foreheads in the dust,
> We venture Peace to ask!

These plodding, but heartfelt, lines were dashed off while Fanny was traveling in a train to London from her Hampshire retreat. She took the poem to the office of *The Spectator* to see if it would be accepted and there learned of Lincoln's assassination. Fanny's cry of anguish was so loud that it brought the editor-in-chief out of his inner sanctum on the run. She was too overcome to speak; she had to be helped downstairs and put into a cab.

Somewhat earlier, Fanny had been heartened by an account of a testimonial luncheon given by the Union League Club of New York City to Goldwin Smith, an Oxford don who hoped to foster international good will by attracting American students to English universities. The simile of Mother England and Daughter

America was one which Fanny had often used, but, she added on this occasion, a mother and daughter did not always see eye to eye; she knew that from personal experience.

To her sculptor friend, Harriet Hosmer, she of the short skirts and masculine headgear, Fanny wrote soon after Lee had surrendered at Appamattox Courthouse. Harriet had recently been in America, where her work was exhibited in New York; she had also gone to Lenox to see her beloved teacher, Elizabeth Sedgwick, so near to death that she told Harriet she would soon visit her "on spirit wings." Their dear friend, Fanny told Capellina, should have lived to see this day and to rejoice in "the victory of the righteous cause for which her young son gave his life. I have had rather a difficult task in sympathizing with my daughter's grief at the overthrow of the Southern Confederacy, while rejoicing with every thought and feeling of my own in the victory of the North. Surely, there never was a more signal overthrow of the devil and all his works in the world's history since it began!" [3]

✠ *PART THREE* ✠

CHAPTER XXI

ONCE MORE THE ISLANDS

(March 1866–March 1869)

MANY YEARS after the Civil War, Frances Butler Leigh, as she then was, said that she had never read her mother's *Plantation Journal;* if she had done so, she might have ceased to love her mother.

The child of warring parents, Fan had never been allowed to choose between them. In her day, family loyalty was a force to be reckoned with, and in her particular case, family loyalty was under constant strain, dragged first in one direction, then in the other. Since Sarah's marriage to a Union sympathizer, Fan had been her father's sole companion, his comrade, and, no doubt, his confidante on his expeditions to the South; she had, however, chosen of her own free will to spend most of the war years with her mother. After the war she embarked on an attempt to revive something which her mother had hoped would die as swiftly and as painlessly as possible.

In March of 1866 Pierce Butler and his daughter left Philadelphia and once more headed for the islands, for Pierce was now free to travel where he chose. After his release from Fort Hamilton, he had tried to sue the former Secretary of War, Simon Cameron, for trespass, assault, battery and false imprisonment; the case was dismissed by order of President Lincoln. In private

Pierce might call Lincoln and his administration a gang of des-
peradoes, but, except for frequent visits to prisons and hospitals
where southerners were held, he did not over emphasize his
sympathies in public. By maintaining an office at 424 Walnut
Street he continued to function more or less as a business man
until, with peace, another line of endeavor opened before him.
In January 1866, Sidney Fisher was told by Dr. Wister that his
father-in-law had received an offer of twenty thousand dollars
a year for his land in Georgia, but had foolishly declined and had
decided to go down and work the place himself, in which case,
the Doctor said, he would probably make ducks and drakes of it.

What Sidney Fisher, and the Doctor also, perhaps, did not
know was that Pierce had received word from the Freedmen's
Bureau that some of his former slaves had returned to the plantations and unless he came to care for them, they would be sent
elsewhere to avoid starvation. It would be unfair to Pierce not to
give him credit for a sense of responsibility in this matter, a sense
which Fan came to share profoundly. She was sustained by her
taste for adventure throughout a journey, more rigorous than
the one she had made as a babe in arms in 1838. South of Washington, train service was, to say the least, erratic; hotels, if any,
were dilapidated, filthy, rat infested. At Columbia one picked up
the trail of devastation which General Sherman and his army of
sixty thousand bummers had cut through the Carolinas.

When Savannah was reached it was so late in the season that
Pierce left at once for Butler Island to plant a crop, leaving Fan
to gather together some household gear, for there was not a stick
of furniture left in what had once been a fairly comfortable habitation. Fan tried in vain to salvage the belongings that had been
removed by the overseer when the islands were evacuated and
he went "up country" with the slaves. She had to buy new beds
and chairs and tables; her father was amazed by the cozy effect
she was able to create with chintz curtains at windows, most of
which were cracked or broken, and a picture of General Robert E. Lee in the living room.

Pierce had found a full work force on the island. He had been affectionately greeted, even by those who, once upon a time, were sold to pay his debts. Fan wrote Sarah that she must have shaken at least four hundred welcoming, black hands. Over and over, she had said, "But now you are free." The answer always was, "No, Missis, we not free. We belong to you as long as we lib." There was no danger of immediate death, for a sharecrop bargain had been struck, and until the crop was harvested, Massa Butler had promised to supply the necessities of life. Necessities were few. Small individual truck gardens had been planted, there were fish and oysters and turtles in the river, wild turkeys in the undergrowth. The threat of starvation had been overstated.

When, however, it came to getting the rice seed into the soil and the necessary cultivation, which followed after, Pierce and Fan found the efforts of their partners in agriculture languid. They would only work for half a day, and it took a good deal of coaxing and scolding to get them to do that.

On St. Simons, the situation was even worse, for there the plantation workers had, as Fan put it, eaten of the Tree of Knowledge. During the past three years a vigorous, but all too limited, effort had been made to educate the black man and to raise his consciousness to freedom level. A corps of New England schoolteachers, divinity students, and what today would be called social workers, had labored valiantly at Port Royal. Land for the landless was an important part of their program, and after capturing Savannah General Sherman had issued a field order, setting aside all the coastal region, from Charleston to the St. John's River, as a resettlement area for the thousands of suffering, homeless freedmen who had followed his army on its march to the sea. Though no acreage had actually changed hands on their island, the St. Simonians had been led to believe that the land would be theirs, that the owners late their masters would never return. The Butlers' sharecrop offer was accepted without overt hostility, but without enthusiasm.

Fan considered the man who had raised false hopes, an agent of

the Freedmen's Bureau, "a miserable creature." As she viewed
the unplanted fields and the desolation of empty manor houses,
as she thought of the indifference of the North to the sufferings
of the South, her anger swelled. Of those who had been dispossessed and beggared by the war, few of the living had returned.
In July, Fan and her father went to the funeral of one of their
former neighbors who had died on the mainland, and whose
body was brought to be buried in the cemetery of the island
church. This was James Hamilton Couper, the son of the old
Scotchman whom Fanny senior had so enjoyed visiting a generation earlier, and whose plantation she had thought the best
that one could hope from slavery. The Butlers rode to the funeral
in a rickety cart, drawn by a mule. The coffin was transported
on a farm wagon, the family having trudged behind it two miles
from the landing place. To enter the church, one had to walk up
a plank, the steps having disappeared; the pews were scarred with
hieroglyphs; one saw the sky through a rent in the ceiling.
"Standing there," Fan wrote to Sarah, "I said to myself, 'Some
day justice will be done and the Truth shall be heard above the
political din of slander and lies, and the Northern people shall
see things as they are, and not through the dark veil of envy,
hatred and malice!' " [1]

Fan realized how fortunate her father was to have funds in the
North on which he could draw. In spite of difficulties, he seemed
to be well pleased with his present way of life, for he was now,
in the true sense of the term, a planter; in him the family voca-
tion had come full circle. When a Northerner who had rented
the Couper place and was working it even less successfully than
Pierce remarked to Fan how fond her father seemed to be of his
people, his workers, Fan said proudly, "Yes, this is a relationship
you Northerners cannot understand and will soon destroy."

Though Fan went back to Pennsylvania for the summer, Pierce
stayed behind and began to build an addition to the Butler Island
house. It was there that he spent most of his time during the ensuing year, only coming down to Hampton Point for weekends

to rest from his exertions. To see that others did their daily stint, he found to be a strenuous occupation.

On Butler Island, however, the danger of catching "country fever" was greater than on St. Simons, where ocean breezes kept the mosquito population down. Just before she left in the summer of 1867 Fan had a touch of fever, from which she rapidly recovered. It was not until after she was gone that Pierce fell seriously ill. There was a doctor at Darien, the town that Robert Gould Shaw had seen put to the torch in 1863, now in process of rebirth as a lumbering center. Pierce got a young black, with the odd name of Liverpool, to paddle him across the river, but it was too late; the doctor could do nothing for him.

The death of Pierce Butler was copy for Sidney Fisher's diary. He heard of it in September when he returned from a trip to Saratoga for his health, for Sidney, now a married man and more than middle aged, was a sufferer from gout. At the same time the diarist was told that Mrs. Fanny Kemble was in America and was staying with her daughter, Mrs. Wister; everyone was going to call upon her. Sidney urged his wife Elizabeth to join the procession to Germantown, but, though she said she would, she dreaded it almost as much as going to a dentist to have a tooth pulled. Fanny, whom Elizabeth had never met, was awe inspiring.

In this opinion, Sidney concurred. His epitaph on Pierce Butler had been that Pierce had wasted his life and had thrown away great advantages. Fanny, on the other hand, had come through grievous trials unscathed. She was a "grand creature, full of intellect and passion," who had distinguished herself as an actress and a writer, and now was amassing great wealth as a reader of Shakespeare. A giant of a woman! No wonder that "ladies of ordinary experience" should quail at thought of appearing before her! [2]

Fanny intimated to her visitors that now she had come to stay. She no longer needed to avoid Philadelphia and its environs for fear of meeting Pierce. Her daughters' grief for their father, she

could respect. Sarah was much depressed, and Fan had left for
the plantations, in spite of the entreaties of her sister and all her
friends. She had said the Negroes would abscond as soon as their
master was dead, even though a contract had been signed for the
coming season. Dr. Wister had consented to go with her to help
her in getting things in working order.

But no good would come of it—Fanny was sure of that. Her
daughter, she wrote to England, had "simply deferred the settlement of the question which it is most important to have speedily
settled: namely, whether these poor people [the blacks] can be
made to understand that freedom means leave to labor or leave to
starve. She being down there has not helped to make them realize
their new position as laborers, but has simply tended to prolong
the dependent feelings of the old relations . . . An estate cannot
be made to depend upon a woman's coaxing or scolding the culti-
vators . . . Personal influence is one thing and the laws of labor
another." [3] A somewhat similar opinion had been reported to the
War Department by the Commission appointed to study the
needs and potentialities of freedmen.

Only until Dr. Wister's return did Fanny stay in Germantown. She soon set out on a tour of readings. In New York, one
of her listeners was George Templeton Strong, who, like Sidney
Fisher, kept a diary of impressive bulk and content. Strong was
as much afraid of Fanny as was Sidney's wife Elizabeth, but put
a bold front on his fear. Mrs. Kemble, he declared, was "a trucu-
lent amazon." He had actually been in the same drawing room
with her when she was visiting the Sedgwicks of Syracuse in
Washington, during the war, but had not dared to speak to her.
This did not interfere, however, with Strong's appreciation of
her art. The night he heard her read in New York, the play was
Cymbeline. When Fanny came to the line of greatest emotional
value, the gentle rebuke of Imogen to her husband, "Why did
you throw your wedded lady from you?" her voice sank to such
a tender, compelling whisper that Strong was moved to think it

a pity that Mrs. Kemble, the woman, not the interpreter of Shakespeare, was such a "tartar."

On her springtime round, Fanny went as far south as Washington; she had no desire, nor had she been urged, to cross the Mason-Dixon line. After a month's respite, she was off again, up through New England, and to the west, to Chicago and Detroit. The public was reminded that Mrs. Kemble had been reading for almost twenty years. Those who had heard her in the early days wanted to hear her again; the younger generation was urged not to miss this opportunity, since this might be a farewell tour.

Fanny gave good value, it was felt, without superfluous frills. She tried to match her costume to the mood of the play she was projecting. Her only stage prop was a red screen before which she sat at a table, her book opened before her, a substantial, a commanding figure. What a satisfaction it was, one comment ran, when every part in a comedy or tragedy, even the least important, was so well played! An even greater compliment than that of George Templeton Strong was paid to Fanny by a little girl, who, when Shylock was sharpening his knife to cut off Antonio's pound of flesh, cupped her hands over her eyes and shrieked, "No, I do not wish to see it! I will not see him cut the man!"

After six months of endeavor, Fanny had earned twenty thousand dollars; she had also "read away" for charity a quarter of that sum. The expense of traveling and of accommodations, however, had been heavy; it seemed to her preposterous. Again, as in the fifties, Fanny was struck by the great changes which were taking place in America. When she had come here, some thirty-odd years earlier, the United States had seemed like a remote district of England which she had never visited. Now it was a foreign land; its inhabitants might be German, or almost any other nationality. "It is difficult," she wrote, "to conceive anything more interesting and exciting than the aspect of these extraordinary people in their new world." The New World was not, perhaps, the ideal habitat for an elderly Englishwoman, but, Fanny added, "my children are Americans, and the gain to my happiness and peace of mind in no longer being divided from them by the Atlantic is indescribable." [4]

Yes, America was now her home. In the interval between her two tours, part of Fanny's time was spent at the Lenox Inn and part in a house she had thought she might never see again, Butler Place. The farm had been rented to various tenants; the house was much run down. When Fan came up from Georgia in the early summer, she did as excellent a job of interior decoration as she had done for her father on Butler Island. To Fanny, it seemed almost incredible that she should be tranquilly living in what she frankly termed "my former purgatory." The room she occupied was the room where Fan and Sarah were born. They had left the house, "the richest girls in America"—this was a slight exaggeration—but, though no longer rich, they, and their mother, too, had managed to return.

The return of Fan in the autumn to the plantations was, to be sure, disquieting, but it could be explained as a declaration of independence, and that Fanny could both understand and applaud. Except for the fact that the blacks were "pursuing idleness, and happiness" Fanny had little idea of the problems her daughter faced. Perhaps she did not want to know them.

CHAPTER XXII

DAUGHTERS AND THEIR MOTHER

(September 1869–September 1873)

WHEN FANNY BUTLER had written to her sister, saying that some day the Northern people would be forced to see things as they are, she may have intended a personal rebuke. Both Sarah and her husband had been strong supporters of the Union cause. Dr. Wister would have enlisted if he could have found anyone to take over his practice. Sarah had wielded a patriotic pen throughout the war. She wrote a posthumous memoir of a Germantown volunteer, Walter Symonds Newhall, which was published by, and sold for the benefit of, the Sanitary Commission. One of her neighbors in Germantown, James Miller McKim, was the editor of *The Pennsylvania Freeman*, an abolitionist paper, to which Sarah contributed a poem, *The Boat of Grass*, describing the escape of a slave from an island plantation and his joy when, from his hiding place in a swamp, he catches sight of a Union gunboat. Her voice quavering with emotion, Sarah's mother had included *The Boat of Grass*, coupled with Whittier's *Barbara Frietchie*, in one of her readings.

Fan was glad that her brother-in-law should see something of the South with his own eyes when he went with her to Georgia after her father's death in 1867. The Doctor was surprised, though possibly not as indignant as Fan, when he, who had voted for President Lincoln and was a member of the Republican party, had to take the oath of allegiance to insure his wife's interest in the Georgian property.

Of his success as planter, Pierce Butler had given a too cheerful picture to the Doctor and also to one of the Doctor's patients, Sidney Fisher; his affairs were in confusion. The first crop of rice had been planted so late that the yield was meager. The workers were now in their second year without having received any reward in cash. To each, Pierce had given a passbook in which was noted the cost of items—clothing, for example—which would have to be deducted when a distribution of profits was made. After Dr. Wister had left her, Fan sat up, night after night and until two or three in the morning, to balance these accounts. She subsequently went over the result with each individual. None were satisfied. They had expressed a profound sorrow for Massa's death; they could not believe that he had cheated them. Massa's daughter was to blame!

A running battle began between the chatelaine of Butler Island-Hampton Point and the Government of the United States. The life of the Freedmen's Bureau had been prolonged, over President Johnson's veto, and by the Bureau all agreements with workers had to be scrutinized. On March 2, 1867, a Reconstruction Act was passed, putting all the South, with the exception of Tennessee, under martial law. Fan heard of wild promises being made by Northern politicians: not only votes for black men, but good seats in the theatre and seats beside white persons in street and railway cars.

An election for a black senator was to take place at Darien in 1868. Only those who had never borne arms against the Union could vote, and Fan was determined that none of her personnel should take part in what she considered to be a farce. She ordered all to stay away from a meeting held in Darien and even wrote asking the help of General Meade, the satrap of Georgia, Florida, and Alabama, to enforce her authority. The General knew Fan personally, and his reply was kindly. He refused, however, to give her control over voters enfranchised by the Fourteenth Amendment to the Constitution. At 6 A.M. on election morning the rice and cotton fields were empty.

The conflict between Fan and her people, for so she considered them, was all the more harrowing because it was fought day by day, season by season. Some of the workers who had accumulated a few hundred dollars by their years of toil bought land of their own and went to live elsewhere. Others continued to occupy their cabins and refused to work at all; they hunted and fished for food. Manners worsened. Folkways were abandoned. The women ceased to wear the brightly colored head handkerchiefs which Fanny thought so becoming; the men sometimes failed to remove their hats when speaking to her, an omission which always brought an angry command to "take off your hat immediately!"

Fan could not abandon those whom, she thought, her father had loved so well, but out of her frustrations, scorn and something close to hatred developed. She imported a school teacher from the North and did a little teaching herself when she had the time. The mulattoes, she thought, were definitely better at book learning than the pure bred blacks; the latter were "incapable of advancement." [1] She found comfort in a book by a Frenchman, Paul Du Chaillu's *Travels in Africa*, which asserted that Negroes did well enough if forced to work by whites, but when left to themselves were of no account. Not to Sarah, but to a Southern friend, Fan confided her suspicion that the enslavement of the black race was the will of God. She had some cabins near her house moved so that she could neither see, hear, nor smell their inhabitants.

In the winter of 1869 the ancient bugaboo of slave revolt was disinterred. Its bare bones were fleshed by rumors of rape and murder. One of the Hampton Point blacks had killed a man and was being protected from arrest by a black sheriff. Fan was not ordinarily timid, but she took to sleeping with a pair of loaded pistols underneath her bed.

During the winter, however, Fan entertained some visitors, one of whom saw her as a snow white queen, reigning benignly over a kingdom of sable subjects. The Honorable and Reverend James Leigh, an English clergyman of aristocratic lineage, had met Fan in New York, and after traveling from coast to coast in America came to Georgia to see her again. During his stay Leigh held a religious service in the schoolhouse for the subjects of Queen Fan and preached a sermon on what he considered an appropriate text, the conversion of the Eunuch of Ethiopia by the Apostle Philip.

Fan was urged to come to England. She was able to do so only because she had engaged a new agent who she thought would rule the plantations with a firm hand. She had also found a promising schoolteacher, a black theological student from Pennsylvania. In June of 1870 Miss Butler crossed in one of the new, fast, transatlantic steamships, and chaperoned by her sister, Mrs. Owen Wister, visited Stoneleigh, the ancestral home, near Birmingham, of the Reverend James Leigh. A proposal of marriage was made and accepted. The marriage, however, did not take place until a year later, in London, in St. Thomas' Church, Portman Square, with the mother of the bride, who had had no part in Sarah's wedding, as a prominent and a well-pleased witness.

For more reasons than one, it was satisfactory to Fanny to have her daughter married to an Englishman. Though she and her latest son-in-law had never met, they had a number of mutual aristocratic acquaintances. As a youth, on his way to Cambridge, Leigh was tutored by the private chaplain of Lord Ellesmere. When asked to dine at the nobleman's table, he listened silently to the conversation of Charles Greville, his brother Henry, and their mother, who was a sister of Lady Ellesmere. Leigh was rather shocked by what seemed to him the ill-natured gossip of his elders. He valued kindliness above wit and was as much a friend to all mankind as had been Charles Sedgwick of Lenox.

Fanny took an immediate liking to James. The fact that he was a cricketer and an all-round athlete was also endearing.

After the London wedding, the Leighs made a triumphal entry into the village of Stoneleigh, of which James, who had been given the family living, was vicar. Schoolchildren paraded, a drum and fife corps played, tea was served in a tent. The wedding gift of the community was a handsome silver inkstand.

Fan was well fitted to play the part of vicar's wife. She and her father had nursed into being and kept alive a small Episcopalian church near Butler Place. This was an activity on which Fanny senior looked askance. When in London, she continued to attend a Unitarian chapel and avoided high church services in which there was too much singing and chanting to suit her taste. Now, however, she was prepared to take a more tolerant view, though she was still glad to tell her old friend, Harriet St. Ledger, that Sarah was "a rather indifferent Episcopalian."

To be separated from Sarah, to have her heart again divided, was trying to one who had come so late into full possession of her children. In the autumn of 1872 Sarah, her husband, and her son Owen, who was now twelve years old and who, to differentiate him from his father, was nicknamed Dan, came to spend the better part of a year in Europe. Dr. Wister had not been well and having recently received a legacy, was able to take a prolonged holiday from his profession. After Dan had been put to school in Switzerland, the Wisters went to Rome, and Fanny with them.

Rome had been visited many times since the writing of Fanny's *Year of Consolation*. One of her stays there had coincided with that of Charlotte Cushman, with whom Fanny had been intimate during the purgatorial year of 1844 and her brief intention of suing Pierce Butler for divorce. Fanny knew that Charlotte's feelings were hurt when she was asked to abandon her efforts to collect evidence of Pierce's misconduct; in Rome, she tried to make amends. Charlotte, then famous and in mid-career, played royal parts. Fanny offered her a crown, a bit of dramatic regalia still, *mirabile dictu*, in her luggage. Recalling Charlotte's many gifts of flowers, Fanny wrote, "You must permit me to send it [the crown] to you, as some small recompense for those far more beautiful things, with which in the early days of our acquaintance you adorned my room." [2] With Fanny, an act of contrition never came too late.

But during the season of 1872–1873, Charlotte Cushman was not in Rome, and her career was all but over. Others there were of the *forestieri* who showed signs of age; this was even true of Harriet Hosmer, who was only forty-three. A youngish man who met Harriet at dinner thought her "a remarkably ugly little gray haired boy, adorned with a diamond necklace."

The youngish man was Henry James, who had come abroad for another respite from Cambridge, Massachusetts, but had not yet made up his mind that the only milieu in which he could work was Transatlantica. Nor was he yet what one might call a professional writer, in spite of a published novel and a number of tales and sketches. Most of James's time in Rome was given over to social activities. One day he went to a party given by an American lady and there met Mrs. Owen Jones Wister, who invited him to her at-home two nights later.

Sarah was thirty-eight, only five years younger than Harriet Hosmer, and eight years older than Henry James. She was very handsome, slender, animated, her head crowned by a coiled abundance of russet hair. James thought her beautiful and was intrigued when she asked him to visit the Villa Medici with her the following day. For two hours, Sarah talked "uninterruptedly, learnedly and even cleverly." Other American women in Rome might seem charming to James, but they lacked Sarah's literary, cultivated mind.

A typically Jamesian flirtation ensued. On either hand it was conducted with the greatest circumspection. There were visits to other villas than the Medici, famous for their treasuries of art. There were wonderful rides in the Campagna, in which Dr.

Wister sometimes joined, both Sarah and her sister Fan being excellent horsewomen.

Mrs. Wister was mentioned so frequently in James's letters to Cambridge that his mother became somewhat worried. She had heard that Sarah was "too conscious of her own charms to be dangerous—but beware!" [3]

James was reassuring. He went so far as to tell his family that Sarah was a bore and to say he was glad he was not Dr. Wister. His Roman notebook, however, records many rendezvous which he could have avoided or have failed to keep. His final judgment on Sarah was "a fine person—but not 'easy,'" most of the uneasiness apparently being in the mind of the novelist.

Some months after the last Campagna ride with Sarah, James wrote a story, which he titled *Madame de Mauves*. It has to do with the thwarted love affair of an American man and a married woman. Madame de Mauves is also an American and though unhappy with her dissipated and unfathful French husband, she rejects a liaison on the score of conscience; her decision is accepted with "awe." Here are the themes, so pregnant for James, of sex frustration and of American innocence and European depravity. Though the scene is laid in Paris and its environs, the protagonists walk on garden paths which might surround the villa of the Medici. The heroine of the story does not resemble Sarah Wister, but her admirer, uncertain of whether or not he should make love, suggests a vague self-portrait of the author.

As to the title of the piece, it too has reference to what James later looked back upon as a romantic period in his life. In Sarah's salon, James was introduced to Sarah's mother, "the terrific Kemble." He remembered the glimpse he had had of Fanny many years earlier when she was riding on a road near New York City and reined in her horse to speak to some workmen. "Why, it's Fanny Kemble," one of the grown-ups in the carriage had said, and the little boy in the carriage, who was Henry James, realized he had seen a person of great importance. Seeing her again in Rome, James thought Mrs. Kemble's "splendid handsomeness of eye, nostril and mouth were the best things in the room." Again at the Wisters, he listened rather impatiently to the reading of a five-act play which one of the aging *forestieri*, William Wetmore Story, was trying out on Fanny. Though his ears were engaged against his will, "my eyes," James wrote, "were for our distinguished companion, in whom the whole matter was mirrored, commented, silently represented." [4] A disproportionate amount of James's nostalgia centered about the elderly lady who, that season in Rome, seemed to be always dressed in shades of lavender or mauve.

When James got down to writing his story, not in Italy, but at Bad Homburg, Fanny was in England and was staying at Stoneleigh Vicarage. The Wisters had gone back to America so that young Dan could be entered at St. Paul's School. The Leighs were preparing to follow. Fan's marriage had been delayed for a year, and until 1871, because she had had to return to Georgia to quell a revolt against the plantation manager she had left in charge. Now there was further trouble. A black man had been installed at half the white man's salary, but word came that the rice mill and principal buildings on Butler Island had been destroyed by fire, almost certainly a case of arson. The loss amounted to fifteen thousand dollars, plus all the seed for the ensuing crop. A minor, but far from negligible, calamity was the black schoolteacher's having given up studying for the ministry, taking a political job as assessor of taxes, and "leading astray" one of the girls on the plantation.

Fan wept bitterly and said this was the end; she could do no more; the property would have to be abandoned. James Leigh, however, comforted her and evolved a plan for action.

During the past year, Leigh had developed a concern for the plight of agricultural workers in England. As children they might be able to earn a shilling, sixpence a week by frightening away the crows from a seeded field. In the full flush of manhood, their weekly wages amounted to twelve shillings, and in old age they were supported by the parish dole. Strikes had occurred, and James was active in arranging meetings between the workers and their employers. So popular was he with the former that he was widely and affectionately known as Jimbo Leigh. James's plan for Georgia was to import English laborers to the American Southland. As a starter, he engaged eight, whose passage over and back would be guaranteed and who, in return, promised to stay for at least two years.

The Leighs took passage on the *Celtic* in September, and Fanny with them. She had no intention now of being left behind and told the many friends with whom she had renewed acquaintance recently that this crossing might be her last.

CHAPTER XXIII

OLD WOMAN'S GOSSIP

(September 1873–January 1877)

ACCORDING TO PIERCE BUTLER'S WILL, his real estate was entailed; none of it could be sold. The headquarters now of the Leighs would be in Georgia, the Wister family would live at Butler Place, and just across the road was a small house, York Farm, which Fanny could rent from her daughters. York Farm had been the last Northern home of Pierce. He was living there at the time of the Lincoln assassination, when the mild prejudice against copperheads turned overnight to savagery. Windows were draped with black in mourning for the President, but not the windows of York Farm, which, standing close to the highway, could be seen by every passer-by. Dr. Wister learned that a gang of superpatriots intended to attack the house of his father-in-law, but a pacifist neighbor got wind of the affair and put a stop to it.

Until York Farm could be renovated, in the spring of 1874, Fanny took an apartment in Rittenhouse Square. She had brought with her from England a maid, Ellen, to whom she was tenderly attached, as one of the "bravest and least selfish creatures I ever saw." The latest proof of Ellen's unselfishness was her willingness to come to America for a year or more though she was engaged to be married. When the move to the country was made, Ellen took complete charge of the household, which consisted of four persons, in spite of the fact that Fanny no longer considered herself affluent and felt she could not afford to keep a carriage.

For at least a dozen years, Fanny had, from time to time, spoken of herself as old. She was sixty-four when she took over York Farm. Her days on horseback were over, though she could still walk for miles on roads that were deep in mud or glazed with ice and snow. A tendency to doze of an evening over her book annoyed her, and she complained of an occasional loose tooth or aching joint. Toll of the years was most evident in the loss of friends. One of the last duties Fanny had had to perform before she went to England was to write a eulogy of Catharine Sedgwick, who had died in 1867, and a collection of whose letters, gathered by her niece, Kate Minot, was about to be published. Fanny hardly knew what to say about a friend who was so closely connected with so many joys and sorrows. She could only write that Catharine was "one of the most charming, most amiable and most excellent persons I have ever known." [1]

Possibly Fanny, still comparatively vigorous, overemphasized her disabilities in writing to Harriet St. Ledger, who needed companionship in infirmity. The slim young woman, whom Fanny had once likened to Atalanta, was almost eighty; her eyesight had failed; she could only write by proxy. From Harriet, Fanny received a huge box of her own letters, thousands of them, written over the years and carefully preserved. This was treasure trove. Before leaving England Fanny had started to put together some personal memoirs, and here was the stuff of memory itself, fresh from the event. Fanny went over the box carefully, removing and destroying all that she found painful. The labor of transcription was so heavy that she later learned to operate "a printing machine," in other words, a typewriter.

Eventually the Editor of *The Atlantic Monthly*, William Dean Howells, heard of Mrs. Kemble's memoirs and made her an offer, which was gladly accepted. No longer equal to the wear and tear of barnstorming, Fanny appreciated any addition to her income. She did not want to put a solemn interpretation on her work, and the recollections of her girlhood began to appear in *The Atlantic* in 1875 as "An Old Woman's Gossip." Fanny's first suggested title, "Elderly Female Twaddle," was rejected by the editor.

But while she was re-creating the past, the present seemed to Fanny to be rushing by her and to leave no mark. She was sometimes depressed, sometimes elated, but her swings of emotion were less wide than formerly. She had only to look over at Butler Place and see Sarah moving about to experience a sense of *deja vue*. There she had been herself, and there she had been wretched. She could thank God that things had, on the whole, turned out so well, that after so much turmoil she had found a measure of tranquillity.

A few of Fanny's friends remained in the neighborhood, or came out from Philadelphia to visit her. While she was in Rittenhouse Square, Horace Howard Furness, son of her onetime Unitarian pastor, William Henry Furness, came frequently to spend an evening with her and to talk of the theatre. He was in the forefront of Shakespearean scholarship; the first volumes of his Variorum Edition had begun to appear. Fanny was delighted she could give Furness what were—supposedly—a pair of Shakespeare's gloves; they had come to her by the death of a Siddons cousin, Celia Combe, the wife of a famous phrenologist. At the same time Fanny received five Kemble portraits which were installed at Butler Place.

Lapped about as she was by family, much of Fanny's happiness came from her grandchildren. She now had two. When the Leighs came up from the South in 1874, a baby girl was born at York Farm while a July thunderstorm was roaring and crackling about the house. Christened by her father Alice Dudley Leigh, the baby seemed delicate, a pale wraith of a child. She was, however, perfectly healthy and perfectly good humored; she almost never cried. During succeeding summers, Alice occupied a room directly over her grandmother's, and the sound of small feet pat-

tering back and forth, and eventually of a small voice announcing, "Go see ganny now," was delightful.

Dan (Owen) Wister, on the other hand, was well on the way
to adulthood. Fanny wondered if he might not be lacking in
"animal spirits," a common American failing, which he shared
with his mother; she found him very companionable, however,
and the day in autumn when he left to go back to his boarding
school was always a day of mourning. Dan had many talents. He
might be an engineer, a writer, or a composer; he was gifted
musically and played the piano well; poems he had written appeared frequently in his school paper. When he was sixteen, Dan
projected an opera, for which his grandmother would write the
libretto and he the score.

With so much to keep her busy and so much to be thankful
for, Fanny could only find serious fault with one feature of her
present existence. She constantly wished that the Georgian plantations could be sold. They were as great and as menacing a lia-
bility as Covent Garden, the decrepitude and insolvencies of
which had darkened Fanny's youth and childhood.

When the Leighs reached Butler Island in the autumn of 1873
they found the workers they had imported from England already
there. All eight of them were living in a single room in the long
disused hospital building. Unhandy, homesick, and frequently
drunk, they were not welcomed by their black co-workers, few
of whom remained to man the rice fields. Fan was much annoyed
by the Britishers' untidy living habits and suspected that most of
them had come to America to escape the burden of supporting
their wives and children. At the end of their first season, two had
absconded, and four others left for the North, having refused
the offer of well-paid lumbering jobs in Darien.

Although the scheme which Jimbo Leigh had conceived to
solve the labor problem was a failure, he himself was a great success on the plantation. From the very first day, the title of Massa
was accorded him, and when his baby daughter Alice came to

spend her first winter in the South, she was Little Missis, and as such, extravagantly petted. James accepted his wife's theory that the blacks were children who, if kindly treated and not led astray by unscrupulous agitators, were easily managed. He fitted up a chapel in a room of the overseer's dwelling and began to prepare fourteen boys for confirmation. Their basic religious beliefs were difficult to ascertain. James liked their singing of hymns, but thought their "shouts" heathenish and likened them to tribal dances he had seen on a visit to North Africa. Ever a good fellow and ever an enthusiastic athlete, the Vicar of Stoneleigh promoted sporting events and canoe races to enliven holidays.

Some years earlier, after a caterpillar infestation had ruined the entire cotton crop, cultivation ceased at Hampton Point. When James Leigh went to inspect what had once been the more opulent of the two Butler plantations he found that the mansion house had burned and only an aged pair, Uncle John and Mum Peggy, were living in one of the tumbledown cabins. Leigh was accompanied on this expedition by James Couper, son of the James Hamilton Couper, whose funeral in the devastated church had made such a deep and lasting impression upon Fan. Couper also wanted to see his family estate, no longer rented and unvisited by its owner for sixteen years. There, the house was still standing, but there was nothing in it. The quarters, except for a single inhabitant, a decrepit mammy, were also empty, and the overgrown garden, dominated by the palm tree which Couper's grandfather had planted so long ago, had become a jungle.

Fan, however, had always preferred St. Simons to Butler Island, and James' tour of inspection was prelude to part of each season being spent at Hampton Point. For Fan, this healthier and more beautiful spot had rich associations with the past. In Philadelphia she had read some of the old plantation records, dating back to the days of her great-grandfather. A memento of those days existed in a silver loving cup that the Major had given to his head driver, Morris, who when a tidal wave swept over the islands in the year 1804 saved the lives of his gang by driving them into a shelter with his whip. The cup had been preserved in Morris' family, even during the weeping time, and some of his virtues were inherited by his descendants. When one of them died in 1866 Pierce paid tribute to him as having "the sense and judgment of a white man." Now, however, the strain had run out, and the latest Morris offspring, who had been sent north to a school for blacks in Pennsylvania, proved to be such a troublesome boy that he had to be returned to the plantation, where he ran amok one day with an axe and tried to drown himself in the river.

Though Fan considered the islanders were becoming progressively ignorant and degraded, her relations with them had mellowed. With the dwindling of the work force, malcontents had disappeared. The Freedmen's Bureau was no more, as of 1872, and it was no longer necessary to sleep with a pistol underneath one's pillow.

In the autumn of 1875 the Leighs went down to Georgia by sea, a less fatiguing way of travel than by rail. Fan was again pregnant. Shortly after Christmas she had a miscarriage and came close to dying. The devotion of her black nurse, who lay all night on the threshold of her room, the concern and the joy of all in her recovery, caused Fan to speak and to write of "my dear people." When Sarah came down to console her sister and showed some disappointment because the blacks seemed to have changed so little since antebellum days, Fan said, yes; their rebellious fling was over; they had come back to their senses and their manners.

With sorrow, Fan realized that this would be the last full season she would pass in the islands. James Leigh had received from one of his brothers-in-law, Sir Charles Adderly, the offer of a living at Leamington in Staffordshire, and the offer was too good to refuse. He had, nevertheless, enjoyed his stay in Georgia and felt that much had been accomplished. His Sunday school class had been confirmed by Bishop Beckwith; he had served a church in Darien and another on St. Simons after its consecration at Easter in 1876.

The following Christmas James went down to share a last festival with his black parishioners and to wind up his and Fan's affairs. Butler Island would continue to be worked by an agent, but one could no longer expect a substantial return. Rice was being grown even more extensively than heretofore in Louisiana, and in May, 1875, a Savannah firm had failed with a thousand dollars' worth of the island crop in its possession.

Fanny Kemble had always found her daughter Fan a cheerful and pleasant companion, but she had long ago given up discussing public affairs with her. With the Wisters, Fanny could talk of politics and lament the trend of events. Their thinking and hers was influenced by reading *The Nation*, a journal which had come into being after the war and which was given a helping hand in Philadelphia by Sarah's abolitionist friend and neighbor, James McKim. It was the aim of *The Nation*'s editor, Irish born Edwin Lawrence Godkin, "to maintain true democratic principles and to work for the equality of the laboring class in the South," in other words, to work for the black man. Fanny could not understand why, when blacks could vote and sit in legislatures, there were still no black children in Pennsylvania's public schools and why a servant who had been with her for a short time in Philadelphia was denied even a gallery seat at the theatre. "Charles Sumner," she remarked, "had gone to his grave [in 1874] leaving incomplete his Bill of Rights." [2]

The manipulation of the Southern vote, the rising tide of racism in the South were deplorable, but, more and more, *The Nation* came to focus its attention upon the corruption of the Republican regime, so firmly in the saddle; the paper's constant faultfinding earned it the sobriquet of "the weekly Day of Judgment." When the Grant administration was attacked, Fanny stated her belief that the President was essentially an honest man, deceived by his advisers, though this may have been due in part to the fact that Grant's daughter Nelly had recently been married, with a good deal of White House splendor, to Algernon, son of Adelaide Sartoris. Fanny felt she was on surer ground in declaring the American people far superior to their politicians and their financiers. A similar faith in democratic dogma had been the solace of her years in England while the Civil War was being fought.

A day was coming, a great day, a hundredth birthday for democracy. Well in advance of the Centennial Year, Fanny was asked to read in the Philadelphia Opera House to raise money for buildings to house the Centennial exhibits, which would demonstrate to the World the forward leap of American industry and American invention. She had had to decline because her voice would no longer carry in a sizable auditorium.

Though the Wisters showed an appropriate interest in the forthcoming celebration and Fan, as a Southerner, showed no interest whatsoever, Fan's English husband proved to be the best participant and sightseer. James Leigh attended all the ceremonies, which began on July 1, 1876, with orations delivered in Independence Hall by descendants of the Founding Fathers, "some of the early settlers," as James termed them, with naïve irreverence. On Sunday, the 2nd, a service was held in Christ's Church, at which Whittier's *Centennial Hymn* was sung. Monday was marked by a solemn procession of foreign representatives, and on the Fourth, after a monster military parade, the *Declaration of Independence* was read by a grandson—James was not sure which—of a Lee of Virginia, the programme concluding with the singing of *Old Hundred* and of Handel's *Hallelujah Chorus*.

Not to miss a single event, James also dropped in on a suffragist meeting. Its intention was to remind the public that women had asked for independence, but their demand had not yet been granted. The gathering was chaired by Lucretia Mott and Elizabeth Cady Stanton. Lucretia Mott was an old friend of Fanny's and still a neighbor on the Old York Road. Fanny was impressed that Lucretia, aged eighty-three, should have the energy to issue what William Makepeace Thackeray had once called "a woman-ifesto," but to Harriet St. Ledger she confided that; "I suppose my own individual superabundant sense of independence and the unfortunate circumstances which have given full scope to its exercise, prevent me from sympathizing as I ought." [3] To yet another correspondent of these years, Frances Cobbe, who was active in the British suffrage movement, Fanny wrote that laws were all very well, but what she coveted for women was a better education and a greater sense of individual worth.

James Leigh did not want his mother-in-law to forego that feature of the Centennial that was most appealing to the public, the exhibits. At Fairmount Park, there was an Art Building, an Agricultural Building and—more crowded than any other—a Machinery Hall. Here were displayed sausage makers, potato peelers, sewing machines, and typewriters, one of which Fanny already possessed. She was pushed about in a wheelchair by James to view these marvels; the one by which she lingered longest was the great engine that powered all the rest, enshrined in a circular boudoir of green baize, silently, ceaselessly at work, a god of the future, demanding worship.

To Leigh it seemed rather odd that the President of the United States was not on hand for the opening festivities of the Centennial; to Fanny it was a good omen that Grant should not be running for a third term. Throughout the summer, the Hayes-Tilden campaign seemed a jog-trot affair, but toward its close its pace accelerated. For the first time, Dr. Wister failed to cast a Republican vote, the Democratic candidate, the New Yorker, Samuel Jones Tilden, having distinguished himself by tilting at the Tweed Ring and other political skulduggery. When the polls were closed, it seemed as if Tilden had won, but fraud and intimidation of black voters were claimed by the Republican Committee. Recriminations became so raucous that Fanny was only glad the Union showed no sign of breaking; she marveled that the temper of the electorate was "so moderate, so temperate, so law abiding." [4]

The result of the contest was still in doubt, and the decision had been handed over to an Electoral Commission when, on January 28, 1877, Fanny left for England with the Leighs. For the past eight months she had been preparing for departure, realizing that this was, indeed, farewell. Three years earlier she had told English friends she might never return, but now the liklihood of her coming again to America seemed far more remote.

When, in the spring, faithful Ellen went home to be married to an Italian and to live in Italy, the household at York Farm was broken up. Fanny went to spend the summer in Lenox. Her cottage there, The Perch, had been sold and so she stayed at the Inn, the proprietor of which was William Curtis. As a boy, Curtis was a fishing companion, a rower of the then Mrs. Butler's boat on the lake. Later he drove the omnibuses which Fanny hired to take her schoolgirl friends on excursions to the mountains. Later still, Curtis married a teacher in Elizabeth Sedgwick's school, and now, the father of grown sons and daughters, he was a man of substance. The rise of this uneducated, but industrious and astute individual seemed to Fanny a peculiarly American phenomenon.

The town of Lenox had also prospered. Its houses were well kept; sidewalks lined its dusty roadways. Fanny walked under trees that her dear Elizabeth Sedgwick had planted and that now gave shade. Elizabeth herself was a shade, but there were still Sedgwicks in the town and in Stockbridge who were Fanny's friends.

There were friends also in Boston, which Fanny visited on her way to and from the mountains. While staying with Kate Minot she made an expedition to Mount Auburn Cemetery. It was a long time since she had sought out Dall's grave, to prostrate herself upon it and to beg for some small share of her aunt's hallowed disregard of self.

A year earlier Fanny had given orders for a tombstone to be placed. When she asked to be guided to the spot, she was given a map, but had the greatest difficulty in following it as she threaded her way through a maze of marble. The green hillsides had disappeared beneath a sheath of stone. The only landmarks which Fanny could recognize were the treetops under which she and Pierce Butler had sat when he was urging her to be his wife.

CHAPTER XXIV

SOME GREAT OBJECT

(January 1877–January 1893)

THE LEIGHS had been fortunate enough to find a picturesque old house at Stratford-on-Avon, which had been the medieval hospital for the Monks of Worcester Abbey. Its only drawback was that it was ten miles from James's parish church at Leamington. Fanny would have liked nothing better than to live in Shakespeare's birthplace, or in some other semirural setting, but for a woman who had celebrated her sixty-eighth birthday, the mechanics of living would be simpler in London. She need not breathe its smog-laden atmosphere the year round, since she intended, as long as she was able, to make summer excursions to the Swiss Alps, to France, or Northern Italy.

A house on Connaught Square was the first of several which Fanny inhabited during the ensuing years, and being a householder, she had to face up to the servant problem, which had been a constant plague to Sarah Wister in America. On both sides of the Atlantic, a more subtle revolution than that expressed in riots and window-breaking had begun. Fanny was amazed by the manners and the attire of the cooks and parlormaids she interviewed. They stood up close to her with their hands clenched in the pockets of their jackets; before she could say a word, they wanted to know how big the house was, how many servants were kept, and whether there would be a man to do the heavy work. And the wages they demanded! A story was going the rounds of a lord who remonstrated with a butler for asking £100 a year; his son and his son's friends, he said, all of whom were curates, got less than that! "Poor young gentlemen," was the unperturbed reply. "I really feel very sorry for them!"

Callers had begun to seek out Fanny even before she was settled in Connaught Square. Here, as in America, the ranks of the elderly had thinned, but the younger generation came to pay their respects and welcome her return, as never before. Of Kemble children and grandchildren, there was no lack. With one of them, Fanny became intimate; this was Harry Kemble, the son of her brother Henry, who had never emerged from Moorcroft House, the lunatic asylum to which he was consigned in 1853. When, some four years later, Henry died, his family were surprised to find that he, who had always been a spendthrift, had money in the bank, £3,000, and two young orphaned children, a boy and a girl; since they were illegitimate, he had never introduced them to their relatives.

For Adelaide Sartoris to take little Jenny Kemble into her home, and for Fanny to see that Jenny's brother went to school seemed a proper sharing of responsibility. Harry had caused no trouble to his aunt, nor had he been a serious financial burden. Now almost thirty years old, he was well launched in the family profession. Though Fanny did not think him a good actor, and with her usual frankness, told him so, she perhaps no longer knew the requirements of the stage. Harry could always be sure of a leading role at the Prince of Wales Theatre; he earned an excellent salary. "I like him very much," Fanny told an old friend of the family. "He is very affectionate and kind to me, and his Kemble face and Kemble voice, which are both very like his father's and my father's, are dear and pleasant to me." [1] She was sometimes afraid that her emotionalism might be distasteful to Harry, who tended to be both reticent and reserved; she was pleased when he proved his liking for her company by joining her in Switzerland for one of her holidays.

Other attentive youngsters showed their devotion by keeping in constant touch with Fanny. There was Anne Thackeray Ritchie, who, like her father, considered Fanny a little difficult, but nonetheless lovable and entertaining. There was the suffragist, Frances Cobbe, a prolific writer on a wide range of subjects, from the "Theory of Intuitive Morals" to "Darwinism and the Duties of Women." Fanny had urged Miss Cobbe to spend a winter with her at York Farm, where she would have been a congenial companion for herself and also for Sarah Wister. The philanthropist, however, could not be lured away from her many activities, which included not only the woman's suffrage movement, but schools for the under-privileged and an incipient crusade against animal vivisection.

But of all Fanny's devotees there was none to compare with Henry James. Since their meeting in Italy, Fanny had seen James once in America, when he came to visit Sarah in 1875 and crossed the road from Butler Place to York Farm to hear her read aloud a play by Calderon. On that occasion Fanny was so stirred by the climax of the drama that she hurled the book across the room. She still thought of James only as a friend of Sarah's, however, when she invited him to join her for the Christmas of 1877 at Stratford. He was dark, handsome, and bearded; he seemed thoroughly to enjoy the trimming of the Christmas tree, she wrote, and all the other observances of the day, one of which was attendance at a service in Shakespeare's church.

Having decided now that London was his home, James came often to spend the evening with Fanny. When he was away in America, called thither by the illness and death of his parents, Fanny wrote to tell him how much she missed him, and how grateful she was for his friendship. The letters might be signed "Your old Gossip," or "Catherine of Russia." She teased him sometimes. She twitted him on his love for children—other people's children—and when he tried to read aloud to her, complained of his hemming and hawing. He was writing some of the best contemporary prose, she told Sarah, but his novels were overloaded with analysis; all very well, in its way, but much too much of it.

One evening—the date was February 20, 1879—Fanny told Henry James a story that was soon transformed into a novel, *Washington Square*, which was serialized in both *The Cornhill Magazine* and *The Atlantic Monthly*. Its heroine is, in the words of James's notebook, "a dull, plain, commonplace girl," a presumptive heiress, who is jilted by her suitor when her father disapproves of the match and threatens to disinherit her. For James, this was merely a situation, a nexus of events from which he could develop and analyze his characters; for Fanny, it was a reaching back into the past, a slice, though not cut from the quick, of her own life. The dull, plain girl of her story had died that day of pneumonia at the age of sixty-one. Her name was Mary Ann Thackeray, a relative of William Makepeace Thackeray, who, when they were all boys and girls together, introduced her to the Kemble household. As for the hero-villain of Fanny's anecdote, he was her own brother Henry. When Mary Ann confided in her and asked her whether she should defy her father and marry against his wishes, Fanny warned her that Henry might make a very good husband to an heiress, but not to one whom he had to support for the rest of his life on an officer's pay. Nine years after the jilting Mary Ann got her inheritance and when Henry renewed his suit rejected him, a denouement which Fanny found satisfactory.

It was also satisfactory to Henry James, the novelist. There was no part in *Washington Square* for a replica of Fanny Kemble. To fictionalize her would involve what James termed "the terrible question of art" and its relation to a superabundant reality.

The year of *Washington Square*, 1879, was for Fanny heavy laden. In August, Adelaide Sartoris died, Adelaide with whom

Fanny had always been in such close harmony and on whom she had depended for companionship. She was now alone, the last of her ilk, and loneliness, as she reiterated to Henry James, was one of the heaviest burdens of old age.

Fanny had given up her trip to Switzerland that summer, not only because of her sister's illness, but also because Fan was expecting a baby in October. The Leighs were now living in Leamington; in the autumn Fanny went to stay at a hotel in the neighborhood. During the Stratford sojourn, she had hoped Fan would give birth, on April 23, Shakespeare's birthday, to a boy who would be christened William, a hope which was not fulfilled. The child who was born in Leamington on November 2, 1879, was a boy, but he was christened Pierce Butler Leigh. Fanny felt she could not go to the church to hear "that evil name" uttered.[2]

The old wound gaped. Some of Fanny's associates thought she had learned to live at peace with the past, and she could sometimes speak of it in lighter vein. A pair of ladies who came from Georgia to England and visited Fan heard Mrs. Kemble say her opinion of slavery was unchanged, but she regretted certain passages in her *Journal*. When it was written, she was young and passionate and such a fanatic that she wondered why her husband didn't strangle her. A sonnet Fanny wrote for her friend of many lonely hours, Henry James, welled up from a deeper emotional level as she lamented her own failure to achieve in marriage "love, joy and hope, honor and happiness." Down the years a sense of guilt had pursued her; this was only one of the many occasions when it caught up with her.

The poor little baby who had received the evil name did not survive. Its short life of a year was full of suffering, and before and after the birth, Fan's state of mind was noticeably abnormal. Her letters to her sister in America expressed so many paranoid grievances and reproaches that Sarah thought of breaking off the correspondence altogether. A cruel and mortifying conversation took place between Fan and her mother, the setting Paris, the subject, the forthcoming publication of Fanny's second volume of memoirs.

Fanny's contributions to *The Atlantic Monthly*, "Old Woman's Gossip," had been published in book form, both in England and America, as *Records of a Girlhood*. The book was rapturously received. *Temple Bar Magazine* characterized it as the kind of reading one could relish out-of-doors, lying underneath a tree; it was sure to please "the young and old, the clever and the stupid, the sinner and the saint"; its beautifully lucid style needed "no Browning society to elucidate it." Mr. George Bentley, Fanny's London publisher, was anxious for more and was willing to pay handsomely for it. From the first, Fanny had intended to continue her reminiscences beyond the date of her marriage, of which she would say very little. Nor would the word, divorce, appear. The book would end with an unmotivated return to America in 1849 and the buying of a house in the Berkshires, that "beautiful and beloved region."

But Fan had no faith at all in her mother's sense of discretion. She would never forgive her, she said; she would never see her or speak to her again, if there was a single disparaging word in the book concerning the man for whom she had named her child. The Wisters were urged to protest the publication of *Records of Later Life*, for which an American edition was planned. "The success of her first book has roused her vanity," Fan wrote. "She wants to keep herself before the public." [3]

Whether or not the Wisters protested, Fanny's only reply to them and to Fan was that she, and she alone, must take responsibility for her work.

A year later, in 1883, Frances Butler Leigh also appeared before the public as an author. Her *Ten Years on a Georgia Plantation* shows some signs of hasty writing, but it may have been long in the making; during the Christmas festivities of 1877, Fan told Henry James she was forever homesick for the islands. The narrative of her experiences is prefaced by a poem, *Brothers Again, Suggested by Decoration Day, 1877*. The poem is signed

O.W., and is almost certainly the work of young Owen Wister, who in 1877, the year in which local government was restored to the South and a policy of white supremacy throughout the nation was confirmed, was seventeen years old. Fan's book testifies to the inevitability of these developments, just as her mother's *Journal* testifies to a contrary point of view and calls for a broader conception of brotherhood. As her father's daughter, and without a single mention of her mother's name, Fan had had the final word in the agonizing controversy which had begun before she was born.

But there was, of course, a surface reconciliation. Fanny could not ignore Fan's suffering in the loss of her child, and she was drawn repeatedly to Leamington by the charms of her granddaughter, who had reached an age to be delighted by the gift of a donkey cart and thrilled by a picnic outing of her father's choir boys.

In 1883 James Leigh was called to a London parish, and again the parishioners he served most faithfully belonged to the working class. He was so impressed by the obvious connection between poverty and the abuse of alcohol that he took the Pledge himself and established coffee houses, where workers—hopefully—would drop in of an evening, or on their way home from shop or factory.

Fanny had moved to Hereford Square. There she was visited at regular intervals by Fan, but to Sarah a sad account was given of these visits: "Fanny and I have but little real intercourse with one another," Fanny senior wrote. "She comes to see me from a sense of duty and is kind and affectionately indifferent in her manner to me, but I have never been able to forget her furious outbreak of temper in Paris and am much too afraid of challenging another of the same sort to speak to her with any freedom about anything. Her servants and her clothes are the principal subjects of her conversation—when it is not the rice crop—and I say but little of what I think and feel about anything to her. . . .

Our intercourse is one of the tragical consequences of life—to me the most tragical." [4]

To fend off senility, one must continue to flex the muscles of the mind. Fanny spent long hours every day at her writing table. She wrote letters to Sarah, her "dearest dear," containing chitchat of books and of the theatre. From Sarah, perhaps, for now she never read the newspapers, Fanny heard of strikes and of great struggles between labor and capital; she felt that these conflicts could be better resolved in America than in Europe. When a new legacy of letters came to her after the death of Harriet St. Ledger and that of a friend of her brother John, Arthur Malkin, with whom she had carried on a long correspondence, Fanny confected a third volume of memoirs, *Further Records*. As a record, it is somewhat confusing, since its author had never been careful about dating what she wrote and could not be bothered now by the drudgery of reading proof. Her poems were reissued and also *Notes on Some of Shakespeare's Plays*, prefaced by the essay, "On the Stage," which she had contributed to *The Cornhill Magazine* in 1863.

From time to time, Fanny worked on something that was of even greater interest to her since it was something new, a novel. Its title, *Far Away and Long Ago*, announces escape from the present; its verbiage, unlike the memoirs, is that of an earlier century, an unconscious reminiscence, perhaps of the kind of novel Fanny had read as a child. "Towards the northern boundary of the County of Berkshire in the State of Massachusetts," runs the opening sentence, "is a lovely valley, locked in by mountains, crowned by forests and watered by the playful windings of a clear, rapid stream. Few spots on earth can boast of a more perfect union of all the elements of nature."

To the Happy Valley come James Morrison, a Lancashire ironworker, and his wife, just as industrialism is about to invade the region. For a few pages it seems as if a sociological study is intended, but the narrative line follows a zigzag course among a fairly large cast of characters. There is a kindly philosopher, Judge Selbourne, who, with his happy, well-adjusted helpmeet, might be Charles and Elizabeth Sedgwick. There is an Indian woman, named Mumbett, the last of her tribe, who lives in a forest cabin. There is also a Calvanist divine, the Reverend Caleb Killigrew, who might be one of those whom Catharine Sedgwick held up to scorn in her *New England Tale*.

All of these are of, so to speak, local origin, but the autobiographical element, which all critics like to ferret out in fiction, is supplied by Mary Morrison, the daughter of the English ironworker, born in America and therefore very unlike her angelic sister Susan, born in England. Mary is moody, irritable, and proud, a creature of the wild; her fate is as melodramatic as that of some of the non-Shakespearean heroines whom Fanny had impersonated on the stage. Mary loves William; William loves Susan, and when he is forced by a snowstorm to spend the night alone with Mary in Mumbett's cabin, in all innocence, the Reverend Killigrew tries to blackmail the girl into marriage. She spurns his advances, rushes off to the top of Monument Mountain, and after confessing her love to William, who has followed her, falls and strikes her head against a stone. William blames himself for her death, develops brain fever, which blots out all memory of the event, and marries Susan. When, some years later, the truth is revealed, William dies promptly of heart failure. Susan and her mother, Mrs. Morrison, return to England and in the comfortable monotony of their existence there, look back upon what happened far away and long ago as the substance of a dream.

For Fanny, the dream of America had never faded, though now it had thinned to a landscape, a backdrop for fantasy. It was no longer the scene of the emotional and moral struggles which had marked her so deeply and marked her for its own. Fanny frequently told Henry James that she was the most English of Englishwomen, but the remark was always made in French, as if to mock at its validity—"*Je suis la plus anglaise des anglaises.*"

Far Away and Long Ago, affectionately inscribed to Elizabeth Rackeman, a daughter of Elizabeth Sedgwick, was published in 1889, Fanny's eightieth year. On November 27 her birthday was fêted by eight of her youthful kinswomen, a delightful, a sparkling occasion. Not long after, however, Fanny gave up her house in Hereford Square and went to live with the Leighs. Economy, as well as failing strength, may have necessitated the move. She would miss their evenings together, Fanny wrote wistfully to Henry James.

A few years earlier Fanny had suffered what might have been a slight stroke when, on a trip to Italy, she made an expedition into the mountains to be present at a christening, that of a child who had been born to her former maid Ellen and Ellen's Italian husband. Faithful Ellen was nevertheless able to come back to London to care for her dear Mrs. Kemble after Fanny was installed at the Leighs, to wait upon her and to write at her dictation the letters that still went to American friends; Sam Ward was the recipient of one of these, and John Murray Forbes of another, two men to whom Fanny had formerly written in the full heat of conflict.

On January 15, 1893, Ellen was helping her patient to get ready for bed when Fanny gave a little sigh and died. Fan was in America. James Leigh, who was very fond of his mother-in-law and who felt he had suffered a great loss, sent at once for Henry James to come to the house and to handle interviews with the press. A few days later James wrote a letter to Sarah, describing the funeral which had taken place at Kensal Green Cemetery, where Fanny was buried beside her father. The day was mild. Only a few of the devotees were present, but they had remembered their old friend in masses of flowers. Her hands full of blossoms, Ellen stood beside the grave, and James noticed how forlornly pale she looked.

"I am conscious of a strange bareness," James wrote to Sarah, "and a kind of evening chill, as it were, in the air, as of some great object that had filled it for long and left an emptiness." [5]

CHAPTER XXV

FAIR AS A LILY

THE SECOND and successful Atlantic cable had been laid immediately after the American Civil War, and notices of Fanny's
death began to appear simultaneously in British and American
newspapers. Henry James was asked to write a more extensive
article than these for *Temple Bar Magazine* by its editor and
Fanny's publisher, George Bentley. The result was later included in James's *Essays in London and Elsewhere*, a tender and
perceptive tribute to his "sublime Fanny."

The most ample American portrait was the work of an even
older friend, Colonel Henry Lee of Boston, in *The Atlantic
Monthly*. Lee had been one of the Harvard students who waited
at the stage door of Boston theatres in the early thirties to see
Fanny emerge. He had also waited outside the Tremont Hotel
to see her mount her horse and thereafter could never pass the
building without looking up at its windows, hoping for a glimpse
of "her radiant face." This encomium and the obituaries in general lightly skimmed over the subject of Fanny's marriage and
the eloquence of her anti-slavery testimony. It was Fanny, the
ravishing young actress, or Fanny, the writer of entertaining
memoirs, "the last and most intellectual of the Kembles," as *The
New York Times* put it, who was recalled.

Even while she was alive, however, a saga of Fanny Kemble had begun to develop, which paralleled and travestied the thousands of words which were written and printed concerning her. For guides in Swiss resorts, Mrs. Kemble was the English lady who went singing through the mountains. In Lenox, Massachusetts, Fanny's sharp or witty sayings were perpetuated by word of mouth, one of the perpetuators being William Curtis, the proprietor of the Lenox Inn, who had been Fanny's fishing gillie as a boy.

In Georgia, oddly enough, where she had made so brief a stay, the accumulation of Fanny's anecdotes was impressive. When her *Plantation Journal* was published in 1863 it was read by many of the New England abolitionists who had come south to educate the blacks of Port Royal. One of them made a special effort to seek out and question a Butler slave among the refugee population. The nearest the lady could come to finding one was a woman who had been a nursemaid to the Butlers' neighbors, the Hazzards, and who remembered Fanny as a "very great and most beautiful lady." In her account of the interview, the teacher tried to reproduce the local dialect, which the Northerners found so fascinating and so baffling. "She [Fanny] tell Mr. Butler if he give up the slavery she would likes to live there, but she couldn't stan' that; but he wouldn't 'grees to that so she goes 'way and gets a dewoce." [1]

On St. Simons the saga's longevity was assured by the continued interest that Fanny's descendants took in the plantations. They were visited by James Leigh, by Fan, and less frequently, by the Wisters, though Fanny's grandson Owen sometimes used them as a holiday retreat. In 1901 Fan and her daughter Alice came over from Jekyl Island to inspect the properties. Butler Island was still being worked, after a fashion, but Hampton Point was a wilderness of undergrowth, its buildings collapsed and sinking back into the earth. When, in 1905, Alice Leigh was married to a distant cousin, Sir Richard Butler, Fan sent money for the black community to celebrate the event. She herself rejoiced in it because her father would have so approved.

In 1916 one who was not a relative, but who greatly admired Fanny Kemble, did some research among Fanny's black constituency. Mrs. Amelia Watson's chief informant was Celia Davis, born on Butler Island in 1824, and therefore fourteen years old in the year of Fanny's sojourn. Thumbnail sketches of the entire family and of the former overseer, Mr. Roswell King, Jr., were drawn. Massa John Butler, Pierce's brother, was tall and had a bald head. He died in Mexico, "where money grows on trees; the buckras kill him." Massa Pierce was small and dark and good to the people. He took the Missis' boy Jack north to see a doctor, but Jack died. He also handed out candy and vermifuge to the children. Mr. Roswell King, by contrast, was a great big man, "a no good man; not a bit. He used to lick people, lick them until he kill them in the barn; we chillen peep."

The "chillen," of whom Celia Davis was one, did a good deal of peeping and saw Miss—or Missis—Fanny, the chief object of their curiosity, do some very extraordinary things. She dipped her baby in the river and when someone protested, said it would make the baby strong. She walked so fast along the dykes of Butler Island that no one could keep up with her, and as if that was not enough to tire her out, she did setting-up exercises in her bedroom; the peepers thought she had gone crazy when they saw her waving her arms and legs about. When she called for Jack, she always said, "Come now, Jack, my dear."

But it was Fanny's clothes, her wonderful clothes, that could never be forgotten, even by a nonagenarian: her black broadcloth riding habit, her low-necked dresses, all of them of silk and a different one for every day in the week. A more sophisticated and a younger testifier, much too young to have peeped with Celia Davis, declared Fanny was "the most beautiful among women. She was fair as a lily. To see her one would imagine one was beholding an angel."

How Fanny, who so honestly summed up her personal advantages and disadvantages, would have smiled at this apotheosis! She had once predicted, overoptimistically, that it would take one hundred years for the leprosy of slavery to be cured, and the last one of the Butler slaves died in 1936, only two years short of the date which she had set. The lone survivor for many years was Liverpool, who had once rowed stroke on the big plantation barge, the Water Lily, and who, in 1867, had paddled Pierce Butler, sick unto death with fever, over to Darien. When Fan was managing the plantation single handed she found Liverpool a trouble maker, and he got little sympathy from her when the overseer knocked him down and cut his forehead.

But time heals all. Fan gave the aging Liverpool her photograph, and Fan's daughter, Lady Butler, gave him a rose to wear in his buttonhole and contributed to his support. Another benefactor was Mr. Henry Ford, who had a liking for relics of the past and who used to spend his winters at Richmond Hill Plantation. Liverpool claimed to be more than a hundred years old— and of course remembered Fanny! Eventually he became a tourist attraction. A promoter charged admission to see him after a high fence had been built about his cabin.

There were a few people in 1936 who remembered an aged Fanny Kemble, but behind Liverpool's fence disappeared the only surviving eye which had seen her as a young woman, hurrying along the dykes of Butler Island, distraught, deeply troubled, and yet feeling herself at one with the beauty which surrounded her. Part of herself, Fanny had once foretold, would live on after she was gone in "the winds that blow and the trees that grow and the waters that flow." [2]

NOTES AND COMMENT

ABBREVIATIONS USED:

Frances Anne Kemble, *Records of a Girlhood—Girlhood*
Frances Anne Kemble, *Records of Later Life—Later Life*
Frances Anne Kemble, *Journal (August 1, 1832—July 17, 1834)—Journal, 1835*
Frances Anne Kemble, *Journal of a Residence on a Georgian Plantation in 1838–1839—Journal, 1838*
Massachusetts Historical Society—M.H.S.
Historical Society of Pennsylvania—H.S.P.
Official Records of the Union and Confederate Armies—ORUCA
Official Records of the Union and Confederate Navies—ORUCN

CHAPTER I. MY SUBLIME FANNY

1. James, 83
2. Edel, II, 351
3. James, 100
4. Ibid., 106
5. Ibid., 107
The material for this opening chapter is derived from *Essays in London and Elsewhere* by Henry James and from Book 6, Volume III of Leon Edel's *Henry James, The Conquest of London.* The *Sonnet to a Friend of Many Lonely Hours* is more fully considered in Chapter XXIV.

CHAPTER II. ENGLISH BORN AND ENGLISH BRED

1. *Girlhood,* 26
2. Ibid., 82

3. *Later Life*, 619
4. Driver, 48

Chapter II, also III and IV, are based on Fanny's *Records of a Girl-hood*, published in 1878, and consisting for the most part of letters she had written to Harriet St. Ledger, whom she met as a young girl and who was her friend for more than fifty years. In one of her last letters to Harriet, Fanny wrote, "Those that we love never alter unless we cease to love them. I am ever as ever yours, F.K." Harriet was interested in philosophical and sociological questions and the letters to her are more "serious," while those to another correspondent, who was a professional writer, Mrs. Anna Brownell Jameson, are more "worldly." Fanny had been first attracted to Mrs. Jameson by reading her *Diary of an Ennuyée*, based on her experiences as a governess, and this may have led to Fanny's offer to her father to adopt that profession after the downfall of Covent Garden. A subsequent series of letters was incorporated into Fanny's *Records of Later Life*, which is drawn upon heavily for the account of the years preceding her divorce. Fanny had apparently written with great frankness to her friends, but the intimate portion of the correspondence was deleted and the originals destroyed before publication.

CHAPTER III. THAT DREADFUL PLACE

1. Hone, I, 77
2. Wister, F.K., 12
3. Ms. Diary, C. Sedgwick—M.H.S.
4. Ms. Letters, C. Sedgwick—M.H.S.
5. *Girlhood*, 164
6. Donald, 103
7. *Journal, 1835*, I, 106
8. *Girlhood*, 543

The Edinburgh Review (Vol. LV, p. 479) describes America as "emphatically the new world" in a scathing appraisal of Mrs. Trollope's book, which was published early in 1832.

The anecdote of the Quaker boy's repeated visits to the theatre is taken from Chapter VIII of *The Boyhood and Youth of Joseph H. Choate*, though not told here precisely in the words used.

Fanny's Indian pundit was Rammohun Roy, philosopher and pacifist, who gave her a copy of the *Sakuntala* to read.

CHAPTER IV. A RACE WITH ATALANTA

1. *Girlhood*, 552
2. *Journal, 1835*, I, 131
3. *Girlhood*, 135
4. *Journal, 1835*, II, 28
5. *Girlhood*, 567
6. *Journal, 1835*, II, 22

7. Ms. Letters, C. Sedgwick—M.H.S.

8. Driver, 224.

One of the Romeos who was considered as Fanny's acting partner was her handsome younger brother Henry, but his attempts to play the lover were so ludicrous that he was laughed off the family boards and never got as far as a tryout in the theatre.

Catharine Sedgwick's unpublished diary, in possession of the Massachusetts Historical Society, gives an account of the Kemble party's stay at West Point, where they visited an American "relative," Gouverneur Kemble, who lived in the neighborhood and owned an iron foundry. The rest of the trip is described in Fanny's *Journal, 1835*. Here individuals are indicated only by initials, but the Columbia University Library owns a copy in which the full names have been inserted, and thus we learn Fanny's first impressions of Pierce Butler. As told in Chapter XVII, Fanny gave the book to the Charles Baldwin Sedgwicks of Syracuse and it was presented to Columbia by a member of their family.

CHAPTER V. PHILADELPHIA NABOB

1. Fisher, 94, 109
2. Johnson, J., 469
3. Ibid., 469
4. *Later Life*, 16

The diary of Sidney George Fisher, which has been edited by Nicholas B. Wainwright and published by the Historical Society of Pennsylvania as *Philadephia Perspective*, pictures the upper-crust society of its day. Its author, a keen observer of human nature, in spite of his conditioned snobbery, is, on the whole, an ardent admirer of Fanny Kemble.

The speeches of the Constitutional Convention of 1787 have been preserved verbatim and, of course, include those of Major Pierce Butler. Printed copies of the Constitution have also survived, with his shrewd marginal comments, and have brought high prices at auctions of memorabilia.

The Major's son Thomas returned to America after his father's death and tried unsuccessfully to claim his full share of the family fortune; correspondence on the subject is in the H.S.P. collection. Thomas built himself a house, which Joshua Francis Fisher says was so expensive that he could never afford to live in it. It still stands at the corner of Walnut and Thirteenth streets and is the home of the Philadelphia Club.

Dr. James Mease, Pierce's father, was author of a history, chiefly topographical, of Philadelphia; it was published in 1811 and republished in 1831. After the death of Pierce's mother the Doctor married for a second time and conducted a school on Seventh Street, below Spruce, which was carried on by his wife after his death in 1848. Fanny's only reference to him (*Later Life*, 13) is to say that his picture was painted by Sully at the instigation of his sons.

CHAPTER VI. THE DANGEROUS EXPERIMENT

1. Butler, 9
2. *Later Life*, 25
3. Ms. letter, Berg Collection
4. Driver, 77
5. *Later Life*, 30

Mr. Butler's Statement was printed in 1850, after the divorce was granted, and was intended as a retort to his wife's *Answer* to her husband's plea for divorce, most of which had appeared in newspapers. The *Statement* was apparently widely circulated, as there is a fairly large number of copies in existence. Most of the unpublished letters in the Berg Collection are addressed by Fanny to her lifelong friend, Sarah Perkins Cleveland. They are particularly valuable as giving evidence of Fanny's early dissatisfaction with her marriage, only indirect reference to which has been allowed to stand in her published letters. A lack of harmony on the honeymoon was noted by Fanny Appleton, later Mrs. Henry W. Longfellow, who met the Butlers at Newport in the summer of 1834 (Wagenknecht, 13).

Catharine Sedgwick's unpublished diary tells of her and Kate's visit to Butler Place.

CHAPTER VII. THE HAPPY VALLEY

1. Dewey, 66
2. Driver, 165
3. Brown, 226
4. *Later Life*, 41

Catharine Sedgwick's memoirs, written for her great-niece, Alice Minot, give a charming picture of the Sedgwick family and of life as lived off the beaten path in early nineteenth-century America. It is included in her *Life and Letters*, by Mary E. Dewey.

Harriet Martineau tells the story of Mumbet in her *Retrospect of Western Travel*, which is still, after more than a hundred years, entertaining reading. Fanny does not mention the tale in her letters, but many years later (see Chapter XXIV) she introduces a character, Mumbett, who is an Indian; into her novel, *Far Away and Long Ago*; she may have thought that Mumbett was an Indian name. The tombstone of the authentic Mumbet, or its replica, with the inscription recut and legible, has been placed among the Sedgwick graves in the Stockbridge Cemetery.

The English clergyman who visited Channing in 1834 and chided him for not having spoken out against slavery, the Reverend E. S. Abdy, seemed to be one of the few persons whom Channing failed to charm. Their interchange was far from friendly, but Abdy was glad to record that before he left the country Channing had preached an antislavery sermon.

Apparently the Butler brothers had never visited the plantations, except, perhaps, as very small children. There is a reference in the unpublished reports of the overseer, Roswell King, owned by the Historical Society of Pennsylvania, to his having for a short time corresponded with John and with an older brother, Thomas Mease, who died in 1823.

CHAPTER VIII. AN APPOINTED TASK

1. *Later Life*, 71
2. Ibid., 101
3. Ms. letter, C. Sedgwick—M.H.S.
4. Ibid.
5. Brown, 234
6. *Journal, 1838-9*
7. Ms. letter—Berg Collection

The disgrace of Baron de Ros is mentioned in the *Diary of Charles Greville*, of whom Ros was an intimate friend. Greville wept when he heard of the affair. His criticism of Fanny's relations with her husband and of her politics is mentioned in Chapters XII and XIX. It is hard today to credit Catharine Sedgwick's remark that an angel might have written Fanny's *An English Tragedy*, but she herself considered it the only one of her works that was worth anything at all. This was at some time in the eighties and at a moment, no doubt, of deep discouragement (Ms. letter, F.K. to Mrs. Field—Columbia University Library).

Mrs. Jameson's literary labors resulted in various books on art, travel, and history, the most successful of which was *Sacred and Legendary Art* (1848), frequently reissued.

CHAPTER IX. SOUTHWARD

1. *Journal, 1838–41*
2. Ibid., 48
3. Ms. Reports of Roswell King—H.S.P.
4. Roswell King, Jr.

The letters to Harriet describing the journey to the islands are included in Fanny's *Records of Later Life*, as well as in the *Plantation Journal*.

The reports of Roswell King to Major Butler and to the Major's daughter Frances (H.S.P.) are written in a beautiful Spencerian hand, and except for a persistent spelling of get as "git," are painstakingly grammatical. His son Roswell King, Jr., who had gone to school in the North, had far more book learning and was apparently considered an authority on the cultivation of sugar as well as of rice.

CHAPTER X. FOR ELIZABETH

1. *Journal, 1838*, 216
2. Ibid., 84
3. Ibid., 69
4. Ibid., 111
5. Ibid., 142
6. Ibid., 146
7. Ibid., 210
8. Ibid., 344

The *Journal* speaks for itself. It is written with vehemence and an ardor that sets it apart from Fanny's other works and carries over from the description of events to the description of the natural beauty of the islands. One has the impression that most of the *Journal* was written on the spot and very little added in revision.

CHAPTER XI. A DISEASED MIND

1. Butler, 34
2. Ibid., 39
3. *Later Life*, 158
4. Fisher, 86
5. Butler, 48
6. *Later Life*, 185
7. Ibid., 203
8. Butler, 13

Henry James remarks that Fanny always had a good reason for everything she did. The concept of a diseased mind as one in which reason no longer prevails was unacceptable to the novelist and heralds a new era in psychology.

Marie Therese had always been difficult to live with and earlier in life had had a breakdown which completely prostrated her. Its symptoms suggest hysteria.

CHAPTER XII. HOUSES IN PICCADILLY

1. *Later Life*, 243
2. Ms. letter—Berg Collection
3. *Later Life*, 293
4. Butler, 15
5. *Later Life*, 308
6. Butler, 67
7. Ibid., 79
8. Greville, C. II 546

Lady Dacre and her husband were liberals, and through them Fanny, as a girl, met the liberal statesmen of her era.

Charles Cavendish Fulke Greville was born in 1794 and so was fifteen years older than Fanny. She had met his mother, Lady Ellesmere, and his brother Henry long before she met him, and though she recognized his intelligence and personal charm, she never really liked him. When she once said that she didn't care for gossip, he exclaimed, "Good heavens, what *do* you care for?" A grandson of the Duke of Portland and a great grandson of the Duke of Warwick, Greville was, in Fanny's eyes, the aristocrat par excellence. For forty years Greville was clerk of the Council in Ordinary and served under three sovereigns, George IV, William IV, and Victoria. Fanny was shocked by the cynicism of his *Diary*, published in 1874, but this was merely an expurgated version of what was published in 1938.

CHAPTER XIII. ENEMIES AND FRIENDS

1. Ms. letter—Berg Collection
2. *Later Life*, 405
3. Macready, 204
4. Ibid., 207

Channing's *Duty of the Free States* and his final sermon appear in Volume V of his collected works. The theological opinions of Channing were so well known in England that many years after his death his spirit appeared to Elizabeth Barrett Browning at a spiritualist seance. When E.B.B. asked the manifestation of Channing if he now thought differently on the subject of the divinity of the Lord Jesus Christ, he replied that God had indeed been manifest in the flesh, but when asked if he had actually seen the face of God, the answer was an affectionate, but scandalized, "No, no, no, child!" (Ward, I, 291.)

The connection of the Sedgwick family with William Cullen Bryant was close. Catharine was the first to encourage his talent, and her brothers facilitated his removal from the Berkshires to New York. He was, of course, an ardent antislavery man.

A series of notes Fanny wrote to Charlotte Cushman are owned by the Library of Congress. Most of them belong undoubtedly to this period, but they are so sketchy as to dates that it is hard to arrange them in sequence.

Mr. Butler's Statement is drawn upon heavily in this as in all other chapters dealing specifically with Fanny's marriage problem.

CHAPTER XIV. A POINT OF DEPARTURE

1. Butler, 116
2. Schott, 5
3. Fisher, 162
4. Ibid., 168
5. Wagenknecht, 111
6. Sedgwick, Charles, 232

A statement of his action in regard to the duel was published by James Schott. This seemed to be standard procedure in such affairs. Later, in 1864, Pierce himself published a statement concerning a duel which misfired. He tried to call out a business associate, Andrew Mehaffey, who ignored the challenge and said he was too busy to attend to it. Dueling was on the way out; murder at ten paces had been rendered obsolete by wartime murder en masse.

Fanny's verses suggestive of Pierce's infidelity are omitted from later editions of her poems. They appear only in that of 1844.

Fanny's letters to Samuel Ward are preserved in ms. at Harvard in the Houghton Reading Room.

CHAPTER XV. THE DESERTION

1. Leach, 249
2. *Later Life*, 642
3. Macready, 247
4. *Later Life*, 319
5. Ibid., 650
6. Ibid., 654

The murder of the Comtesse de Praslin is the subject of Rachel Field's *All This and Heaven Too*. Both Elizabeth and Charles Sedgwick were interested in prison reform and in the reform of insane asylums.

An unpublished letter in the Berg Collection (F.K. to Sarah Perkins Cleveland, April 19, 1848) tells of Fanny's plan to act in New York. She must have received an offer of which Pierce may have heard, thus hastening his plea for divorce.

CHAPTER XVI. DIVORCE

1. *Littell's Living Age*, Feb., 1849
2. Wagenknecht, 149
3. Dewey, 313
4. Ms. letter, C. Sedgwick—M.H.S.
5. Oliver, 489
6. Sedgwick, Charles, 299
7. Wagenknecht

The original article on which that in *Littell's Living Age* is based appeared in *The London Chronicle*. One suspects that it was written by a personal friend of Fanny's.

Fanny's letters and those of Charles and Elizabeth Sedgwick to Sam Ward are in the Harvard Library, Houghton Reading Room.

Mrs. Butler's Answer goes over much of the ground covered by *Mr. Butler's Statement*, but from an opposing point of view. Copies of *The Answer* are extremely rare; there is one in the Rare Book Room of the Library of Congress.

Egbert Oliver's reading of "maternal" in Melville's letter concerning Fanny (*New England Quarterly*, Vol. 18, p. 489) is given as "matrimonial" in the edition of Melville's letters published in 1960 (p. 78). The word is, however, sufficiently blurred in the manuscript letter (New York Public Library) as to admit of a dual interpretation.

Shortly after Macready walked out of Fanny's reading, he was involved in a riot which grew out of his rivalry with the American actor, Edwin Forrest, a symptom of the uneasy relations between England and America during this period. On May 10, 1849, the Astor Place Theatre was wrecked, sixteen people killed and twenty-two injured.

Pierce's one-day visit to Lenox is mentioned in an unpublished letter to the Charles Baldwin Sedgwicks in the Library of Columbia University. It is dated Sunday, August 19.

CHAPTER XVII. AN INTERLUDE

1. Ritchie, 78
2. *Later Life*, 619
3. Thackeray, III, 251
4. Ritchie, 86
5. Browning, II, 159
6. Ms. letter—Berg Collection

The rebuke of the Women of the South to the Duchess of Sutherland was voiced by Mrs. John Tyler, widow of President Tyler.

The Mrs. Procter to whom Thackeray wrote in 1853 was the wife of Bryan Waller Procter, whose nom de plume was Barry Cornwall; she was mother of yet another poetizer, Adelaide Anne Procter. Her sharp tongue earned her the title of "Our Lady of Bitterness." Though she and Fanny had occasional spats, they remained friends until her death in 1892.

Harriet Hosmer's statues were much admired and sold well; one of them, a "Puck," was bought by the Prince of Wales. A pet of the Brownings and of the entire foreign community, Harriet loved both Adelaide and Fanny and in 1869 considered the latter to be "really the most wonderful woman I know." (Carr, 279.)

The Brownings, though impressed by Fanny's high mindedness, were surprised that her verses were so mediocre.

CHAPTER XVIII. THE BIRTH OF A COPPERHEAD

1. Fisher, 360
2. Ibid., 335
3. Ibid., 375
4. Ibid., 383
5. Rozwenc, 45
6. *Further Records*, 335

The copy of her *Journal, 1835* that Fanny gave the Charles Baldwin Sedgwicks, now in the Library of Columbia University, is an index of her state of mind during the 1850s. The page she asked her friends to tear out was left in the volume.

The Prince of Wales was in Philadelphia on October 10, 1860, and the New York ball at which Fanny Butler danced was held at the Academy of Music on October 12.

Eliza, the wife of Joshua Francis Fisher, must have been a relative of the Butlers through their grandmother, Polly Middleton, but she was not intimate with the family; Polly's husband, the old Major, had never been popular with his wife's kin.

The account of Pierce Butler's arrest and subsequent freeing is given in ORUCA, Series II, Vol. 2.

CHAPTER XIX. A FAIR AND ACCURATE ACCOUNT

1. Ms. letter, H.S.P.
2. Forbes, II, 26
3. Adams, I, 251
4. Lombard, 335–343

Fanny in her letter to Charles Greville mistakenly states that Charles Sumner delivered a phillipic against Congressman Brooks of South Carolina. Brooks's attack on Sumner was motivated by what Sumner had had to say concerning Brooks's uncle, Senator Butler of South Carolina, in the *Crime Against Kansas* speech. Sumner was out of the Senate for three and a half years; part of his convalescence was spent in the home of the Reverend William Henry Furness.

General Hunter's means of recruitment and his handling of the first black regiment, the South Carolina Volunteers, came under attack, even from those who approved of the move, one of the attackers being Charles Francis Adams, Jr. (See *A Cycle of Adams Letters.*)

Humane though he was, Lincoln could not shake off the conception of the black race current in the Kentucky of his childhood. He at first predicted that if the blacks were given arms their weapons would be taken from them by the enemy. Later, at the end of the war, he said that the war could not have been won without help from "the sable arm."

The idea that Fanny's book had a great effect upon English policy during the war was fostered in Georgia, where a route sign on Route 17 on Butler Island, now a bird sanctuary, proclaims this to be the case (*Journal, 1838*). A negative and well substantiated view is expressed in an article by Mildred Lombard in *The Georgia Historical* Society *Quarterly* for December 1950.

CHAPTER XX. OUR FOREHEADS IN THE DUST

1. Higginson, 213
2. Forbes, II, 51
3. Carr, 212

Shaw's expedition to St. Simons and his story of the Darien raid are told in letters to his family, the originals of which are owned by the Massachusetts Historical Society. The account of the Fort Wagner attack and of his death is taken from Peter Burchard's *One Gallant Rush* (130 ff.).

The war history of St. Simons is documented in ORUCN, Series I, Vol. 6 and Vol. 13. The report of the Commission appointed by the War Department to study the needs of freedmen is in ORUCA, Series III, Vol. 4.

Sidney Fisher mentions (470) Fanny Butler's being in Germantown in April 1864, and about to leave for a year in Europe with her mother.

CHAPTER XXI. ONCE MORE THE ISLANDS

1. Leigh, F.B., 45
2. Fisher, 533
3. *Further Records*, 341
4. Ibid., 342

Fan's book, *Ten Years on a Georgia Plantation*, is drawn upon for this and subsequent chapters.

Mrs. James Dent and Mrs. Joseph Wilder, two Georgian ladies who visited Fan in England, were told she had never read her mother's journal (Lovell, 211). When Sidney Fisher heard of the book's publication in 1863 (456) he thought its raison d'être was to annoy Pierce Butler. Fisher spoke of it later with Mrs. John Butler, Fanny's former sister-in-law, (458) who said its picture of slavery was not overdrawn. She herself was a Southerner, but had not approved of secession.

The doctor whom Pierce sought out was probably Dr. Holmes, whom Fanny met in 1838 and whom she considered shrewd and intelligent. He is mentioned in Betsy Fancher's *The Lost Legacy of Georgia's Golden Isles* as having published an article in *The Darien Lumberman* testifying to Pierce's kindness as master and to Fanny's love for her husband.

Fanny's American tours of 1868 were indeed her last. The account of them is taken from an entry in George Templeton Strong's *Diary* for April 1868 and Leota Driver's *Fanny Kemble*.

Into Fanny's *Further Records* went some last letters to Harriet St. Ledger, written in the seventies, and also letters to Arthur Malkin, a boyhood friend of her brother John, most of them written before or during the Civil War. The book was published in 1891 when Fanny was in her eighties and got scant attention from her in proofreading, so that the dating is obviously faulty.

CHAPTER XXII. DAUGHTERS AND THEIR MOTHER

1. Leigh, F.B., 92
2. Mrs. Cushman Correspondence, Library of Congress
3. Edel, Leon, II, 214
4. Ibid., 127

Sarah Wister's *Memoir of Walter Symonds Newhall* was published anonymously; its authorship is established by Sidney Fisher (178). Some years later Fanny said her daughter was busy writing articles for *The Atlantic Monthly,* urging higher education for women, something of which she, herself, approved.

James Leigh's cheerful book of reminiscences, *Other Days,* tells of his visit to America, his wedding, and of his later life in Georgia. There are frequent references to "dear James" in Fanny's correspondence.

Book 3, Volume II of Leon Edel's life of Henry James describes James's association with Fanny and Sarah.

CHAPTER XXIII. OLD WOMAN'S GOSSIP

1. Dewey, 417
2. *Girlhood,* 543
3. *Further Records,* 190
4. Ibid., 208

Fanny's *Further Records,* James Leigh's *Other Days,* and Fan's *Ten Years on a Georgia Plantation* are the sources of this chapter.

Fanny mentions in her *Plantation Journal* (317) the silver cup given to Morris by the Major, but falsely attributes its having been presented for services rendered during the War of 1812. Yet another descendant of Morris, Dan, a mulatto, went with the Leighs to England and though flattered and cherished there, insisted on returning to St. Simons.

According to George Templeton Strong, the launching of *The Nation* was discussed at the Union League Club during the war. Godkin had toured the Southern states in 1856 and reported his impressions to the London *Daily News.* James McKim asked Sidney Fisher, who died in 1871, to contribute to *The Nation.* As further recommendation to Fanny and the Wisters, Arthur Sedgwick, a son of Theodore, was one of the editorial staff.

CHAPTER XXIV. SOME GREAT OBJECT

1. *Further Records,* 225
2. Ms. letter, Berg Collection
3. Ms. letter, H.S.P.
4. Ibid.
5. Edel, II, 329

The origins of *Washington Square* are established in an article by Bruce Dickins in *The Times Literary Supplement* for October 3, 1961.

Ten Years on a Georgia Plantation was published only in England. Fanny's sonnet to Henry James was probably written after she realized Fan's deep-seated animosity.

CHAPTER XXV. FAIR AS A LILY

1. Pearson, 271
2. *Later Life*, 178

Manuscript letters in H.S.P. mention visits of the family to the plantations. Fanny Leigh suggested to her sister Sarah Wister in 1906 that Hampton Point should be cleared and used for pasture.

Mrs. Amelia Watson's reports of conversations with former Butler slaves, held in 1916, are preserved in the Lenox, Massachusetts Library.

Liverpool is mentioned in Wightman's *Early Days in Coastal Georgia* and also in Lydia Parrish's *Slave Songs of the Georgia Sea Islands*. No longer an agricultural center, St. Simons had by that time become a pocket of survival for folk lore, and in its purest form, the only art which was allowed to flourish under slavery.

BIBLIOGRAPHY

Abdy, E. S. *Journal of a Residence and Travels in the United States of North America*. 3 vols. London, 1835.

Adams. *A Cycle of Adams Letters*. 2 vols. Boston, 1920.

Anonymous. *Walter S. Newhall, A Memoir*. Philadelphia, 1864.

Armstrong, Margaret. *Fanny Kemble, A Passionate Victorian*. New York, 1938.

Birdsall, Richard D. *Berkshire County, A Cultural History*. New York, 1959.

Bobbé, Dorothie. *Fanny Kemble*. New York, 1931.

Brown, Arthur W. *Always Young for Liberty, A Biography of William Ellery Channing*. New York, 1956.

Browning, Elizabeth Barrett. *Letters of Elizabeth Barrett Browning*. 2 vols. New York, 1897.

Burchard, Peter. *One Gallant Rush, Robert Gould Shaw and His Brave Black Regiment*. New York, 1965.

Burt, Nathaniel. *The Perennial Philadelphians*. New York, 1963.

Butler, Pierce. *Mr. Butler's Statement*. Philadelphia, 1850.

——— *Statement and Correspondence in Regard to a Duel*. Philadelphia, 1864.

Carr, Cornelia. *Harriet Hosmer, Letters and Memories*. London, 1913.

Channing, William Ellery. *Complete Works*. 6 vols. Boston, 1849.

Chapman, Maria Weston. *Right and Wrong in Massachusetts*. Boston, 1840.

Child, Lydia Maria. *An Appeal in Favor of that Class of Americans Called Africans*. Boston, 1833.

Choate, Joseph H. *The Boyhood and Youth of Joseph H. Choate*. Privately printed, 1917.

Cobbe, Frances Power. *Life of Frances Power Cobbe by Herself*. 2 vols. Boston and New York, 1895.

Cornish, Dudley Taylor. *The Sable Arm*. New York, 1966.

Craven, Pauline Marie Armande Aglae. *La Jeunesse de Fanny Kemble*. Paris, 1882.

Davis, David Brion. *The Problem of Slavery in Western Culture*. Ithaca, 1966.

Dewey, Mary E. *Life and Letters of Catharine M. Sedgwick*. Boston, 1872.

Donald, David. *Charles Sumner and the Coming of the Civil War*. New York, 1960.

Driver, Leota S. *Fanny Kemble*. Chapel Hill, 1933.

Dumond, Dwight Lowell. *Antislavery, the Crusade for Freedom in America*. Ann Arbor: University of Michigan Press, 1961.

Edel, Leon. *Henry James*. Vol. I, Vol. II. Philadelphia and New York, 1953, 1962.

Erskine, Mrs. Steuart. *Anna Jameson, Letters and Friendships*. London, 1915.

Fancher, Betsy. *The Lost Legacy of Georgia's Golden Isles*. New York, 1971.

Fisher, Joshua Francis. *Recollections of Joshua Francis Fisher, Arranged by Sophia Cadwalader*. Printed privately, 1929.

Fisher, Sidney George. *A Philadelphia Perspective, the Diary of Sidney George Fisher*. Philadelphia, 1967.

Fitzgerald, Edward. *Letters to Fanny Kemble*. London, 1895.

Follen, Eliza Lee. *Life of Charles Follen*. Boston, 1844.

Forbes, John Murray. *Letters and Recollections*. Boston, 1899.

Forten, Charlotte L. *The Journal of Charlotte Forten*. New York, 1953.

French, Mrs. A. M. *Slavery in South Carolina and the Ex-Slaves, or the Port Royal Mission*. New York, 1962.

Genovese, Eugene D. *The Political Economy of Slavery*. New York, 1965.

Gibbs, Henry. *Affectionately Yours, Fanny*. London, 1945.

Greville, Charles. *The Greville Diary*. 2 vols. New York, 1938.

Greville, Henry. *Leaves from the Diary of Henry Greville*. 2 vols. London, 1883.

Grylls, R. Glynn. *Trelawny*. London, 1950.

Higginson, Thomas Wentworth. *Army Life in a Black Regiment*. East Lansing: Michigan State University Press, 1960.

Hone, Philip. *The Diary of Philip Hone*. 2 vols. New York, 1927.

James, Henry. *Essays in London and Elsewhere*. New York, 1893.

Johnson, Guion Griffis. *A Social History of the Sea Islands*. Chapel Hill, N. C., 1930.

Johnson, Joseph. *Traditions and Reminiscences, Chiefly of the American Revolution*. Charleston, 1851.

Johnston, D. C. *Outlines Illustrative of the Journal of F . . . . . . A . . . . K . . . . .* Boston, 1835.

Kemble, Frances Anne. *Answer of Frances Anne Butler to the Libel of Pierce Butler Praying a Divorce*. 1848.

—— *Far Away and Long Ago*. New York, 1889.

—— *Francis I.* London, 1832.
—— *Further Records.* New York, 1891.
—— *Journal (Aug. 1, 1832–July 17, 1834).* Philadelphia, 1835.
—— *Journal of a Residence on a Georgian Plantation in 1838–1839.* New York, 1960.
—— *Notes on Some of Shakespeare's Plays.* London, 1882.
—— *Plays by Fanny Kemble.* London, 1863.
—— *Poems.* New York and London, 1844, 1859, 1866, 1883.
—— *Records of a Girlhood.* London, 1878.
—— *Records of Later Life.* 1882.
Klingberg, Frank J. *The Anti-Slavery Movement in England.* New York, 1927.
Korngold, Ralph. *Two Friends of Man, the Story of William Lloyd Garrison and Wendell Phillips and Their Relationship to Abraham Lincoln.* Boston, 1950.
Lader, Lawrence. *The Bold Brahmins.* New York, 1961.
Leach, Joseph. *Bright Particular Star, the Life and Times of Charlotte Cushman.* New Haven, Conn.: Yale University Press, 1970.
Leigh, Frances Butler. *Ten Years on a Georgia Plantation Since the War.* London, 1883.
Leigh, James W. *Other Days.* London, 1921.
Lestrange, A. G. *The Literary Life of the Reverend William Harness.* London, 1871.
Lovell, Mrs. Caroline Couper. *The Golden Isles of Georgia.* Boston, 1932.
Mabee, Carleton. *Black Freedom, the Non-Violent Abolitionists from 1830 through the Civil War.* New York, 1970.
Macready, William Charles. *The Journal of William Charles Macready.* London, 1967.
Martineau, Harriet. *Society in America.* London, 1837.
—— *Retrospect of Western Travel.* New York, 1838.
Massey, G. Valentine. *The Mitchells and Days of Philadelphia,* New York, 1968.
Melville, Herman. *Letters of Herman Melville.* New York, 1960.
Morse, John T. Jr. *Memoir of Colonel Henry Lee.* Boston, 1905.
Nye, Russell B. *William Lloyd Garrison and the Humanitarian Reformers.* New York, 1955.
—— *Fettered Freedom.* New York, 1963.
Official Records of the Union and Confederate Armies. Series I, Vol. 28; Series II, Vol. 2; Series III, Vol. 4.
Official Records of the Union and Confederate Navies. Series I, Vol. 6, Vol. 12, Vol. 13, Vol. 14.
Parish, Lydia. *Slave Songs of the Georgia Sea Islands.* New York, 1942.
Pearson, Elizabeth W. *Letters from Port Royal.* Boston, 1906.
Pierce, E. L. *Memoirs and Letters of Charles Sumner.* 3 vols. Boston, 1877.
—— *The Records of the Federal Convention,* Ed. Max Farrand. 4 vols. New York, 1937.

Ritchie, Anne Thackeray. *Chapters from Some Unwritten Memoirs.* New York, 1895.

—— *Thackeray and His Daughter.* New York, 1924.

Rose, Willie Lee. *Rehearsal for Reconstruction.* New York, 1964.

Rozwenc, Edwin C. *Slavery as a Cause of the Civil War.* Boston, 1963.

Rushmore, Robert. *Fanny Kemble.* New York, 1970.

Schott, James. *Statement in Relation to a Duel.* Philadelphia, 1844.

Sedgwick, Charles. *Letters from Charles Sedgwick to His Family and Friends.* Boston, 1870.

Sedgwick, Elizabeth Dwight. *A Talk with My Pupils.* Boston, 1863.

Sedgwick, Henry Dwight. *The Practicability of the Abolition of Slavery.* New York, 1831.

Sedgwick, Hubert M. *A Sedgwick Genealogy.* New York, 1961.

Sedgwick, Theodore. *Thoughts on the Proposed Annexation of Texas.* New York, 1844.

Simpson, Benjamin. *Lives of Eminent Philadelphians Now Deceased.* Philadelphia, 1804.

Spindler, George W. *Karl Follen, A Biographical Study.* Chicago, 1916.

Stampp, Kenneth M. *The Peculiar Institution.* New York, 1956.

—— *The Era of Reconstruction, 1865–1877.* New York, 1965.

Stern, Philip Van Doren. *When the Guns Roared, World Aspects of the Civil War.* New York, 1965.

Strong, George Templeton. *The Diary of George Templeton Strong.* 4 vols. New York, 1952.

Tappan, Lewis. *A Sidelight on Anglo-American Relations, 1839–1858, Furnished by the Correspondence of Lewis Tappan and Others With the British and Foreign Anti-Slavery Society.* New York, 1927.

Taylor, Susie King. *Reminiscences of My Life in Camp.* Boston, 1902.

Tennyson, Hallam. *Alfred Tennyson, A Memoir.* London, 1897.

Thackeray, William Makepeace. *Memoirs and Letters.* 4 vols. London, 1945.

Thomas, Clara. *Love and Work Enough, the Life of Anna Jameson.* Toronto, 1967.

Thomson, Mortimer. *What Became of the Slaves on a Georgia Plantation? A Sequel to Mrs. Kemble's Journal.* New York, 1863.

Wagenknecht, Edward. *Mrs. Longfellow, Selected Letters and Journals of Fanny Appleton Longfellow.* New York, 1956.

Ward, Maisie. *Robert Browning and His World.* Vol. I, *The Private Face.* New York, 1967.

Welch, Richard E. *Theodore Sedgwick, Federalist.* New York, 1965.

Welsh, Sister Mary Michael. *Catharine Sedgwick.* Washington, D.C., 1937.

Wightman, Orrin Sage. *Early Days of Coastal Georgia.* St. Simons Island, 1955.

Williams, Eric. *Capitalism and Slavery.* New York, 1961.

Williamson, Jane. *Charles Kemble, Man of the Theatre.* Lincoln: University of Nebraska, 1970.

Woodward and Hopkins. *The Views of Judge Woodward and Bishop*

Hopkins on Negro Slavery in the South, Illustrated from the Journal of a Residence on a Georgian Plantation. Philadelphia, 1863.

Van Story, Burnette. *Georgia's Land of the Golden Isles.* Athens, Ga., 1956.

ARTICLES

Cate, Margaret Davis. "Mistakes in Fanny Kemble's Georgia Journal," in *Georgia Historical Quarterly.* March, 1960.

Conrad, Georgia Bryan. "Reminiscences of a Southern Woman," in *Southern Workman.* February and July, 1901.

Dickins, Bruce. "The Story of Washington Square," in *London Times Literary Supplement.* October 13, 1961.

Geffen, Elizabeth M. "William Henry Furness, Philadelphia Anti-Slavery Preacher," in *The Pennsylvania Magazine of History and Biography.* July, 1959.

Heard, George Alexander. "St. Simon's Island During the War Between the States," in *Georgia Historical Quarterly.* Vol. 22, p. 249.

King, Roswell, Jr., "On the Management of the Butler Estate and the Cultivation of the Sugar Cane," in *The Southern Agriculturist.* December, 1828.

Anonymous, "The Law of Divorce—the Butler Case," in *Littell's Living Age,* Vol. XX, February 4, 1849.

Lombard, Mildred E. "Contemporary Opinions of Mrs. Kemble's *Journal of a Residence on a Georgian Plantation,*" in *Georgia Historical Quarterly,* December, 1950.

McDuffie, George. "Governor McDuffie's Message on the Slavery Question, 1835," in *American Historical Leaflets, No. 10.* New York, 1893.

Meyers, Andrew B. "Miss Kemble's Keys," in *Columbia Library Columns,* November, 1961.

Oliver, Egbert S. "Melville's Goneril and Fanny Kemble," in *New England Quarterly,* Vol. 18. 1945.

Scott, John A. "On the Authenticity of Fanny Kemble's *Journal of a Residence on a Georgia Plantation,*" in *Journal of Negro History.* October, 1961.

Sedgwick, Catharine. "Our Burial Ground," in *The Knickerbocker.* November, 1835.

Sedgwick, Henry Dwight. "The Sedgwicks of Berkshire," in *Collections of the Berkshire Historical and Scientific Society.* 1900.

Stearns, Bertha Monica. "Miss Sedgwick Observes Harriet Martineau," in *The New England Quarterly.* September, 1934.

Thorp, Margaret Farrand. "Harriet Hosmer, Leader of the White Marmorean Flock," in *Smith College Alumnae Quarterly.* Spring, 1965.

Wister, Frances Anne. "Fanny Kemble at Butler Place," in *The Germantown Crier.* May, 1959.

Zilversmit, Arthur, "Mumbet: Folklore and Fact," in *Berkshire History,* Vol. I, No. I, Spring, 1971.

UNPUBLISHED LETTERS, DIARIES AND REPORTS IN:

The Historical Society of Pennsylvania, The Massachusetts Historical Society, The Libraries of Harvard University (Weidener, Houghton, Dramatic Collections), The Library of Congress, The Folger Library of Wahington, D. C., The Library of Columbia University, The Berg Collection, The New York Historical Society, The Stockbridge Library and Historical Society of Stockbridge, Massachusetts, The Lenox Library of Lenox, Massachusetts.

INDEX